# Tradition and Invention in Architecture

# Tradition and Invention in Architecture

## Conversations and Essays

## Robert A.M. Stern

Edited by Cynthia Davidson

Yale University Press

New Haven and London

yalebooks.com/art

Designed by Pentagram Design
Set in ITC Galliard Pro by Yve Ludwig
Printed in China by Regent Publishing Services Limited

Stern, Robert A. M.
Tradition and invention in architecture : conversations and essays
/ Robert A. M. Stern ; edited by Cynthia Davidson.
      p. cm.
Includes bibliographical references and index.
ISBN 978-0-300-18115-9 (cloth : alk. paper)
1. Stern, Robert A. M. 2. Architectural design.
3. Influence (Literary, artistic, etc.) I. Davidson, Cynthia C. II. Title.
NA737.S64A35 2011
724'.6—dc23                                                    2011038096
A catalogue record for this book is available from the British Library.

This paper meets the requirements of ANSI/NISO Z 39.48–1992
(Permanence of Paper).
10 9 8 7 6 5 4 3 2 1

# Contents

————————

# Acknowledgments

---

This is the second volume of writings collected from previous publications and my archives. I am particularly grateful to Cynthia Davidson, who has thoughtfully selected and arranged these pieces to give new form to thoughts that span decades. Sarah Acheson compiled the source material and assisted in the research and preparation of the essays and their illustrations for publication as a collection. Michelle Komie, Senior Editor for Art & Architecture, Yale University Press, has been a most collegial partner in seeing the book through, and Peter Dixon kept the project on track and moving forward. It is always a pleasure to work with Michael Bierut and Yve Ludwig at Pentagram.

I thank Deborah Nevins, Inderbir Riar, and Alessandra Latour for allowing me to publish their interviews, and also Anna Kenoff and Reinhold Martin, who eased the way through archival material related to the Modern Architecture Symposia.

I am greatly indebted to the individuals and institutions who helped to find photographs and gave permission to use them, including Nancy Sparrow, Alexander Archive; Judith Johnson, Lincoln Center Archives; Anne Cassidy, New York State Archives; Christina Benson, NYC Department of Parks and Recreation; Kimberly Jacobs, Riverside Historical Commission; Gayle Mault, Foster + Partners; and Erica Stoller and Christine Cordazzo, Esto. I would also like to thank the photographers whose work is represented here, and who are credited at the back of this book.

# Preface
## *An Architect Should Recall and Invent*

———————

Architecture is an art of imagination and memory: it lives in the present and depends on the past for its meanings and ideals. How an architect approaches his or her work can vary as widely as the full array of styles that constitutes the history of architecture, but the intrinsic struggle is shared by all, whether self-proclaimed classicist, modernist, postmodernist, deconstructivist, parametricist, or whatever the latest "ist" to loom on the scene.

I believe that an architect must both recall and invent, participate in a continuum yet contribute to its evolution, strive to be fresh and inventive without casting aside the time-honored values and the fundamental discourse that make it all intelligible. For me, architectural history is not only inescapable, it is indispensable. Ironically, the past provides us with the last best hope for the future. We cannot imitate the past, but we can immerse ourselves in its traditions and canons, if we are to recapture the act of building as a reconciliation of individuality and community. Architectural culture is fluid.

The question today is, do our architects have the skill and scholarship, the art and wisdom, to discover and be nourished by a usable past, or do they take the easy way out, fetishizing the "new" as if it would ever thus be?

Styles may change, but the principles and values inherent in the history of our discipline are the core of architecture's meaning and success. Those principles and values also underlie the essays collected here. For an architect, writing is one way of reconsidering history while working in the present—always in search of the best from the past and the present, which allows us to invent for the future.

Robert A.M. Stern
New York City, January 2011

# I

---

# Regionalism and the Continuity of Tradition
## 1987

To speak of regionalism is to speak of tradition, adaptation, innovation—and invention. Regionalism is both an interesting and a troublesome concept when applied to architecture, for each of us has a personal definition of architecture, which we should reevaluate every time we design a building. For me, architecture is the art of building beautifully and of building appropriately—thus, regionalism is a key factor because it is about the task of designing appropriately.

But regionalism does not completely encompass the tasks we perform as architects. Opposite regionalism as a concept is universalism—the idea that, as my Columbia colleague, Kenneth Frampton, points out, we are all participants in a world culture. I believe that as architects we must recognize both universal world culture and regional culture, for we are undeniably tied to both, whether we like it or not.

An appropriate architecture is one that seems to grow out of a sense of place: a physical and a cultural matrix. To succeed, a regional architecture must encompass geography, culture, and, ultimately, tradition. But for the latter, two essential questions confront us: Is it possible to have a traditional architecture in the late twentieth century? And is it possible to have a traditional architecture again, given the history of this century?

For an artist to function within a tradition, he or she must be interested not only in the differences between things, but also in the similarities between things across time and from place to place. Meaningful art is the product of that by-now-classical intersection between tradition and individual talent that T.S. Eliot articulated so well over half a century ago. We have had a long period in which we talked about innovation and individual talent, which led us down some very strange byways in architecture, not to mention the other arts. The fundamental issue, from my view, is tradition and individual talent.

Tradition in culture consists of a society's enduring body of beliefs, deeply rooted in time and place. In a so-called primitive culture, tradition is often synonymous with day-to-day reality. But in a modern society such as America, tradition is the standard against which everyday things are measured.

What, then, is the place of innovation? I believe it is essentially a technical impulse and not an artistic one. Innovation belongs in the realm of science or technology, of economics or some quantifiable things, and not so much the realm of art, which is so inexorably wrapped up in culture and, therefore, in tradition.

In a formal art such as architecture, the design process is a critical synthesis over time and not the series of lurching leaps forward that innovation implies. I would even argue that science is not so much about innovation; technology is where innovation really works. In the middle of the nineteenth century, Joseph Paxton employed the relatively innovative technology of cast iron and glass to make the Crystal Palace (1850–51). But the Crystal Palace is interesting not only because it is innovative; it is also a wonderful synthesis between a new way of building and the culturally based forms of classicism. Paxton lifts the innovation of technology to the level of meaningful architecture. He shows us the past and the present in a new way. In this way tradition, adaptation, and invention—rather than innovation—are the relevant issues.

We must realize that America is not a traditional culture. It is a colonial place that invented itself at a certain moment in the late eighteenth century by declaring itself politically independent—a nation and a culture created by signing a piece of paper. As a result of these artificial origins and our subsequent evolution as a heterogeneous nation of immigrants, we have no real native traditions. Virtually all American traditions are, in a sense, artificial and therefore all the more valuable and more to be treasured.

We have often argued against our best traditions, saying, "Oh, they weren't ours. Spanish Colonial—that's just Spanish misunderstood; New England saltboxes—those were just Elizabethan Tudor buildings misunderstood." But we have brought these things here as part of our cultural baggage, and we have adapted them to our present circumstances throughout the history of this country. And we have made them ours and added to the ongoing tradition that they represent.

No nation's tradition is discrete unto itself. In discussing Spanish architecture we begin with Spain, but we must also go behind its traditions to the ancient world on both sides of the Mediterranean. We don't stop with Spanish architecture on the Iberian Peninsula. We must talk about it in the Americas, about what happened to Spanish architecture as it intersected with Native American traditions in the eighteenth century. We also must consider how Spanish architecture continues to be meaningful in the twentieth century, whether in Spain or California or Texas. Similarly, we must avoid thinking that a tradition in this country is not genuinely American because it does not look different from everything else that has happened in the world. Although none of our architectural traditions are native, except possibly the adobe architecture of the Southwest, we must see that we are fundamentally a culture that is *other*, and that our traditions are *other*. We bring them to bear here by using our inventiveness to make them our own. Thus, American architecture and distinctly American building types properly come about at the intersection of architectural traditions, innovative technology, and individual talent.

Thomas Jefferson understood this concept perfectly at the dawn of the republic. Described by the Marquis de Chastellux as "the first American who has consulted the fine arts on how to shelter himself from the weather,"[1] Jefferson knew that we could never make a purely organic, natural, American architecture. Instead, we would have to merge traditions from elsewhere with American circumstances. Seeking to bypass the confusions of eighteenth-century court life in Europe, Jefferson turned back the clock to seek traditions in the ancient world. He created not a regional but a world architecture for America by introducing the classical language of ancient Greece and Rome as a great tradition that would unite the country in an architectural language. Jefferson's achievement is something we periodically resist, believing that it demeans our culture. But it is naive to deny the role that classical architecture has played in the American scene. It is the great binder of our institutions, and although classical architecture is infinitely variable in relationship to place, it nonetheless distinguishes our institutions from the fray of local cultures to create a national culture.

*Fig. 1.* Louis Sullivan, Bayard Building, New York, New York, 1898–99

Similarly, we tend to look at the skyscraper as a uniquely American building type—perhaps *the* uniquely American building type. But the skyscraper, with its great poetry of height and its inhabited belfries, is frequently made more meaningful, more beloved, and more integral to our daily lives through familiar iconography. The tall buildings that look like Gothic towers or ancient lighthouses are the ones that seem to get under our skin and become part of our tradition. Even Louis Sullivan, who strongly pushed the design of the tall building toward a nonhistoricizing mode, was very much involved in the traditional expression of the tall building and the traditional manipulation of form that characterize the New York skyscraper at its best. Indeed—and this may be a parochial New Yorker's point of view—the greatest of his skyscrapers, the Bayard Building (1898–99), is in New York, not Chicago. In the Bayard Building (fig. 1), Sullivan uses natural forms as a replacement for traditional architectural language, but when those columns leap up, they rise to representations of angels, just as on a Gothic cathedral. Sullivan is referring to traditional, recognizable forms and at the same time using them very inventively.

That is our task—to use traditional, recognizable forms. It may seem the wrong moment to make this point, a time when everyone seems to be throwing a column—or maybe a Palladian motif—on a building with little concern for scale or context. But we cannot reject traditional forms just because particular buildings using them are silly, or poor architecture. Whether used brilliantly or banally, these familiar motifs satisfy the profound need for something time-honored and lasting, the yearning of a society sated on the impersonality and belligerent discontinuity of the International Style. As for regionalism, we must be very careful not to imagine any place as an isolated place, nor even, perhaps, to think in terms of region. Architecture does have traditions, and in certain areas of the country certain traditions thrive. But there are no "exclusives" in the representation of tradition. Spanish Colonial may prevail in Southern California (fig. 2), but it also exists in Texas, and even in the East. In Florida, a case can be made for Spanish Colonial on the basis of history and climate, but the style is also found in certain lovely New York areas—communities that one day decided to be Spanish Colonial

for the flimsiest of reasons, but that did so with conviction and thus created convincing architecture. Who are we to say that their decisions were not appropriate or at least sincere?

Lewis Mumford once observed that the "last way to achieve a good regional style is by practicing cultural isolation."[2] The best traditional architecture has always depended on the interplay of international styles of architecture—whether classicism or modernism—and local building traditions. There is nothing more and less American than the amalgamation of colonial motifs into the Shingle Style, the resuscitation of the Churrigueresque at the San Diego Fair by Bertram Goodhue (fig. 3), or Paul Philippe Cret's Mediterranean classicism at the University of Texas at Austin (fig. 4).

All art survives if it is a sincere assertion of belief. Traditional architecture is not convincing when it is just so many Mickey Mouse classical columns thrown up on a developer's whim or because the architect is reading the magazines. Traditional architecture is convincing when it comes out of a passionate feeling for the craft and the art of architecture—for what it means and where it is appropriate. We cannot deny the sincerity of Santa Barbara's Spanish Colonial architecture; but when it appears on the highway strip as a Taco Bell, that is a very different story. In short, quality is every bit as important as context.

Enduring art can never be built on a negative statement. We have tried to build an architectural culture for the past fifty or sixty years on a fundamentally negative concept—that everything that went before is no longer appropriate. The idea that we can start again sounds, on the one hand, rather optimistic because it implies a faith in our ability to innovate. On the other hand, it is a pessimistic idea because it asserts that innovation is all there is. Divorced from the past and waiting to be rendered meaningless by the future, the architect is alienated from everything but the present moment.

The age of architectural ideologies is over. There are no rules; there are only traditions and inventions. To be an architect is to possess an individual voice speaking a generally understood language. To be really articulate as an architect is to raise that voice to heights of lyricism, to make each element, each word, resonate with meaning. The pleasure of architecture lies in both fulfilled memory and what Le Corbusier called the "play of forms under the light"—not one or the other.

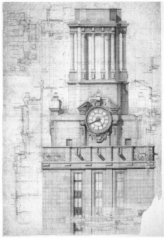

Architecture is a narrative art, and architectural style is analogous to poetic diction. Simple writing may communicate on a basic level but it does not give much pleasure. Since the time of ancient Greece, storytellers have embroidered their tales with references to and quotations from works of the past, thereby linking with tradition and perpetuating age-old tales. The complexity of narrative—its allusiveness, its resonance, its aggrandizement of the reader's own experience—raises the statement of a simple theme, whether literary or architectural, to the realm of art.

*Fig. 3.* Bertram Grosvenor Goodhue, California Building, Panama-California Exposition, San Diego, 1914–15

*Fig. 4.* Paul Cret, Detail of Main Building Tower, University of Texas, Austin, Texas, 1933

Believing as I do in the continuity of tradition, I work to create order out of the chaotic present by entering into a dialogue with the past, with tradition. The depth of that dialogue is the essence of architecture, as it is of all culture. Architecture is a dialogue with the past carried on in the present, with an eye cast toward the future. Rather than breaking with the past, we must try to root ourselves more deeply in it, for a knowledge of the past can nourish us, and a familiarity with its lexical subtleties can help reestablish a sense of decorum in our stridently individualistic present.

The idea that material progress is its own reward fits nicely with the idea that modern technology dictated the overthrow of traditional architecture. We now know that the benefits of material progress are mixed, bringing almost as many problems as possibilities.

In 1923 Le Corbusier offered the challenge, "architecture or revolution." For our moment, I would propose a different challenge in a more conciliatory tone: tradition and modernity. The public is entitled to buildings that do not threaten, by their very being, the aesthetic and cultural values of the buildings around them. Architecture is a public act, not a private celebration of what the architect had for breakfast that morning or the abstract pattern into which the napkin is folded; architecture is a commemorative celebration of place and culture. Yet architecture is not merely the constructed evidence of the culture's innovations, or a dance to the music of cultural time. Architecture has its own inner clock.

The architecture we innovated to express the brave new world of material progress is a mixed blessing, and we must examine it with care. We must face the role of tradition in a serious way, reclaiming what we once so naively threw away from our own education, knowledge, and sensibility. Every new building is an opportunity to reaffirm and reestablish the inherent order of things. Architects must stop worrying about self-expression and zeitgeist and start worrying about communicating clearly with their buildings.

Art is, and therefore art evolves. Stop worrying about whether you're doing something new and whether anybody cares. Nobody does. It is more important to do it well. It is necessary to go backward sometimes in order to go forward. Of course, each architect dreams of making a contribution, but we should not be obsessed with our individuality. We must dream, but then we must wake up and go on.

I agree with Lewis Mumford, one of the most important twentieth-century critics of American architecture, and one who continually rises in my esteem as I read and reread his work:

> The future of our civilization depends on our ability to select and control our heritage from the past, to alter our present attitudes and habits, and to project fresh forms into which our energies may be freely poured. On our ability to reintroduce old elements, as the humanists of the late Middle Ages brought back the classic literature and uncovered the Roman monuments, or to introduce new elements, as the inventors and engineers of the last century brought in physical science and the machine-tool technology, our position as creators depends.[3]

So let us talk less of innovation than invention, less of region than of place, less of what is different and more of what is the same, less of what is new and more of what is good.

# 2

---

# What the Classical Can
# Do for the Modern

## 1990

No doubt the artist is the child of his time; but woe to him if he is also its disciple,
or even its favorite. . . . He will indeed take his subject matter from the present
age, but his form he will borrow from a nobler time—nay, from beyond all time,
from the absolute unchangeable unity of his being. . . . But how does
the artist secure himself against the corruptions of his time, which everywhere
encircle him? By disdaining his opinion. Let him look upwards to his own
dignity and to Law, not downwards to fortune and to everyday needs.
—Friedrich Schiller[1]

Live with your century, but do not be its creature; render to your contemporaries
what they need, not what they praise.
—Friedrich Schiller[2]

I am a modern architect, a product of the continually evolving Western humanist
tradition. As such I do not believe that the present moment is necessarily the best
moment or even a particularly important one. Rather, I cast an eye backward to
help establish a vantage point, a critical distance to help me define my role in the
present and find my way toward the future.

As a modern, I am convinced of the continuing viability of the classical language of architecture.[3] It is not the only language possible, nor one that should
always be used in its pure form. But it is the basic language—the measure, the
root, the datum, which gives order not only to the lingua franca of the traditional

vernaculars of the preindustrial past, but also to the machine-age vernaculars of mass production. Of all the architectural methodologies yet evolved, I believe classicism best reconciles the idiosyncrasies of the local, the immediate, and the expedient with the grand, ennobling, and enduring values that draw people together in their diversity.

Though possibly once a fixed set of rules, classicism has been seen as an evolving grammar and vocabulary since the time of its revival in fifteenth-century Italy. As both a language and a point of view, it represents deep-seated cultural values without sacrificing versatility. The five Orders may be considered by some to have been divinely inspired, but it remains to the individual architect to work out their exact proportional and decorative attributes, to put them to work in the grander, more complex ensemble of buildings and cities. By these individual decisions the architect propels us into a dialogue between an idealized past and an evolving present. The depth of that dialogue is the essence of our Western culture: it not only inspires and guides us but also reminds us who we are, especially as we confront new challenges of building in the context of non-Western cultures.

While in and of itself classicism embodies no specific political or moral agenda, it is the public language of Western institutions. It reifies the shared experiences that to this day give the wider public a common voice, a common gesture, and a sense of collective identity. It brings the republican spirit of Washington to the county courthouses of the South and Midwest. If, as some have suggested, the memory of slaves mars the classicism of Jefferson's Monticello, what of Henry Bacon's Lincoln Memorial, whose testament to emancipation draws strength from a particular but nonetheless compelling interpretation of Greek democracy, and is further sanctified by memories of Marian Anderson and Martin Luther King Jr., each of whom chose it as a forum? Classicism is not particular to any one moment or region, or personal to any one architect. Great works of architecture, as surely as those of literature, painting, and music, operate on many levels; while they are a product of their social or political situations, they express transcending ideals. To have it otherwise would be to dismiss all art of the past, and indeed the present moment, and idly wait for social conditions to improve.

The perennial vitality of classical grammar, syntax, and vocabulary reveals the most basic meaning of architecture as ordered, intelligible, shared public space. Classicism presents the designer with a codified system of symphonic complexity for relating the smallest detail to the overall structure, for balancing geometry with human measure, and abstract shapes with literal depictions of nature or with verbal ideas. Its synthesis of rational composition, representational details, and empathetic form challenges the intellect of the initiate and delights the senses of the layman, as they pause for second and third moments to contemplate the play of light on carved surfaces, to delight in the representation of acanthus leaves, wreathes, and garlands, or to read the texts of inscriptions. To talk of a forest of columns, indeed to walk among one, is to experience nature in metaphor. The language of classicism not only embraces such metaphors, it embodies them: it has them built in.

Contrary to the antitraditional premises of stylistic modernism, the exploration of classical themes has never thwarted architecture's ability to come to terms with either new processes of production or the new types of building required by new programs. In fact, the opposite is true: by using known models and classical grammar and vocabulary, architects of mass-production technology's first great era were not only able to conceptualize some of the most complex public works ever built, but also able to make those works comprehensible to the public whom they were to benefit. Joseph Paxton's Crystal Palace (1850–51), Henri Labrouste's Bibliothèque Sainte-Geneviève (1843–50) and Bibliothèque Nationale (1862–68), Otto Wagner's Postal Savings Bank (1904–06), McKim, Mead & White's Pennsylvania Station (1906–10; demolished 1963), and various works of Auguste Perret are but some of the classical buildings of the mid to late nineteenth and early twentieth centuries that brilliantly and explicitly incorporate advanced building technology.

Many of us have come to value classicism anew because of ahistorical modernism's failure to provide satisfactory built responses to the very critical social, environmental, and cultural demands from which its proponents claimed to derive their theories. Modernism emphasized innovation over invention, disruption over continuity, interior monologue over public discourse. In arbitrarily rejecting the time-honored forms that resonate with a culture we have taken such pains over time to create, it introduced a kind of tyranny of the present (the "eternal present" was Sigfried Giedion's chilling phrase) that stripped away the rich historic complexities of street ensembles, neighborhoods, and sometimes entire cities, as it reveled in the very personal and self-important thrill of isolated invention. As we turn away from a reductive modernism and search for more culturally inclusive and more physically satisfying ways to build, classicism again demonstrates its validity and vitality, enabling architects to carve as well as to extrude, to construct and not merely assemble forms that go beyond the mere exemplification of extra-architectural social or literary ideals.

This renewed invocation of classicism, and beyond it of traditional building as a whole, is not intended to substitute one form of cultural absolutism—the imposition of the new—with another, the oppression of the old. Rather, it is intended to affirm the architect's role as a conservator of values; to call for invention rather than the too-easy innovation of "me too" shape-making; to plea for a "present-and-future-oriented" materialism infused with the ideal of cultural memory. It is precisely classicism's timeless otherness that makes it so germane to a culture that simultaneously and contradictorily celebrates explorations in outer space while it searches for its roots in the ethnic cultures of the preindustrial past.

How an architect approaches classicism today varies as much as the tradition itself, but the intrinsic struggle to protect and project its values is shared by all who recognize artistic creativity as a process of recollection and invention. Why an architect proposes classicism today is also worth asking: for so long the target of modernist contempt, classicism was made to serve as a symbol of social and political dysfunction and of a troubled status quo. Is not an adherence to the classical canon—to the discipline of its methods and the richness of its vocabulary—an optimistic undertaking for architects who operate in a culture that in other aspects equally values measure and bravura, computers and rock 'n' roll? Classicism offers the architect a canon, but what a liberal and tolerant canon it is. It proposes models of excellence in composition and detail. It does not set out on a singular route but points out various ways to participate in a continuum yet contribute to its evolution, to be fresh without resorting to self-indulgent iconoclasm, to celebrate the ideals and the fundamental discourse that bind people together rather than search for the cultural rifts that pull us apart, to reaffirm the commonalities amidst the chaos, which everywhere all too easily makes its own way without our help. With its deep cultural ties, its innate hierarchy of form and detail, and its capacity for purity and hybridization, classicism still seems, after nearly a century-long struggle to overthrow it, perhaps not inevitable and certainly not God-given, but surely much more than merely viable: taken in its broad sense, a classical approach to architecture seems to offer a fresh stimulus to modern architects seeking to recapture the act of building as a reconciliation of individuality and community, to reaffirm enduring, even timeless values in a dynamic culture continuously challenged by bold and often disturbing political and technological innovations. Classicism has flexibility and built-in tolerance, but do our architects have the skill and scholarship, the art and wisdom to work within its great canon? Isn't it easier to hide behind the headlines and profess the hopelessness of a world in disarray? Or to claim that nothing humanly noble can be done in a world dominated by machines? Isn't it just easier to fling a pot of paint in the public's face?

# 3

## Designing the American Dream

### 1986

American architecture is the stuff of dreams. Almost from the first, we have built not so much according to strict canons of taste as out of individual urge, and less to house our descendants for generations to come, like the Europeans, than to leave behind a symbolic story of ourselves in wood and brick and stone. Rather than join our architecture to the tradition of a place, we have had to create a style out of dreams on a continent that was virtually without architecture when our forebears arrived.

Even the very first American structures, in the deserts of the Southwest and on the shores of Virginia and Massachusetts, had a dreaminess to them. The settlers' houses in New Spain and New England were evocations of the ones they had left behind. In the raw landscapes, these transplanted structures must have seemed like welcome ghosts to the early Americans.

Thomas Jefferson was the first real American dreamer, and as builders of homes we have been dreaming in his footsteps ever since. Monticello, the house he built and rebuilt and poured himself into for fifty years, was a Roman temple, a borrowed pantheon. The god who lived in it, however, was not a religious figure but the new American family man, the individual democrat. The fundamental notion of Monticello is that a man's home is his temple. As such, Monticello is a portrait of Jefferson himself: comfortably formal, ingenious, forward-looking, original.

Jefferson established the direction that other bold men and women have followed during the past two centuries, as have the millions of people who build or buy their own places and fashion them into temples to their needs and tastes. We Americans invest more of our dollars and psychic energy into our homes

*Fig. 1.* Julia Morgan, Hearst Castle, San Simeon, California, 1919–47

*Fig. 2.* Henry Davis Sleeper, Beauport, Gloucester, Massachusetts, 1907–34

than any society has before. In doing this, we realize our dreams of the good life through architecture.

Variations of the dream house stretch from coast to coast, but after Jefferson's none is more famous—or certainly more extravagant—than William Randolph Hearst's California castle, San Simeon (fig. 1). Hearst was fifty-six when he started San Simeon in 1919, and like Jefferson he built his dream compulsively, until illness required him to move out of the castle in 1947. Hearst retained as his architect Julia Morgan, arguably America's first woman architect. In Hearst's mind, San Simeon was a ranch—a ranch for a king. The ranch was one-third the size of Rhode Island, with an airstrip and a dock for oceangoing yachts. The castle looked like a cathedral, with guesthouses clustered around it to provide more than a hundred rooms surrounded by terraced gardens. In the end what Hearst built was not a dream house at all, but a dream village, a veritable Spanish hill town. It is a real place with all the magic of the movies, which Hearst loved.

Henry Davis Sleeper, another great dreamer, could not have been more different from Hearst, or from Jefferson for that matter. Over a period of twenty-seven years, beginning in 1907, he added rooms haphazardly to what began as a twenty-five-room summer house in Gloucester, Massachusetts (fig. 2). Sleeper crammed his house with Americana, devoting many of the rooms to his visions of American history, so that the house is the story of America—or rather, *his* story of America and his family's place in it, going back to before the Revolution. Today visitors to Beauport, as the house is called, enjoy its eccentricity, as I do. But do they ever imagine how much it has in common with Jefferson's great home in Virginia? The similarity obviously does not lie in style. Beauport is utterly and chaotically romantic; Monticello is all neo-Roman order. But as self-portraits and autobiographies of their owner-builders, these two examples represent extremes of a fundamental truth about American houses.

The dream houses of two remarkable women, one in Connecticut and the other in Los Angeles, also bear witness to the power Americans invest in architecture as an expression of their ideals. Effie Pope, a strong-willed rich girl from

Cleveland, was sent to Miss Porter's School in Farmington, Connecticut, where she changed her name at the age of fourteen to Theodate—"gift of god"—after a grandmother, and "found" herself as a born-again New Englander. Theodate Pope was in other ways a woman far ahead of her time, and often frustrated by her situation. She set her sights on the then all-male Princeton University, but was refused admittance, not unexpectedly, because of her gender. So instead she made herself into a woman of property.

But Pope's high-mindedness required a bigger outlet, so she went to New York. Hoping to consolidate and fulfill her talents, she got permission to audit architecture classes, and hired private tutors. Soon she persuaded her parents to leave Cleveland and build a house in Farmington. What she had in mind was their retirement home, and her dream house. For it, she enlisted McKim, Mead & White to draw plans based on her drawings and ideas, and between 1898 and 1901 they together created Hill-Stead (fig. 3), a proud interpretation of George Washington's Mount Vernon.

But Hill-Stead is no slavish copy. The apprentice architect and her collaborators adapted Washington's form to her family's needs, taking only the two-story porch facade and planning the rest according to her view of a fine New England farmhouse, with generous rooms and flowing spaces. The architect Philip Johnson (fig. 4), Theodate Pope's younger cousin, sees in Hill-Stead the power of its builder's lifelong dream. The morning room, dominated by a massive secretary with a richly curved split pediment, is the room, he says, of a woman in executive control. Here, one feels, lived a formidable presence, one tough enough to twice survive the sinking of ships—the Lusitania in 1915, and later, in 1916, a steamer bound for South America, where she was to join her husband, John Wallace Riddle, a diplomat whom she married when she was forty-eight. Theodate Pope Riddle had by then become a registered architect in Connecticut.

At about the same time, an oil heiress from Pennsylvania was buying thirty-six acres on a Hollywood hill. Aline Barnsdall's passion was drama; she had studied it in Europe, and in Chicago she had commissioned Frank Lloyd Wright to build

a theater. For her Hollywood site, she thought Wright the only architect with a talent big enough to help her harness the "great force" of the American theater. Together they planned an "art community," with a theater, a house from which Barnsdall would preside, and apartments, studios, cottages, and shops. In the end, only Hollyhock House and two guest residences went up, but even so, Hollyhock House is one of the most theatrically successful works we have (fig. 5).

On the outside the house evokes Mayan architecture, presenting long, heavy lintels looming over wide doorways and topped with a frieze of abstract hollyhocks, Barnsdall's favorite flower. Within, the design brings together the elements—air, fire, and water—in a hearth with a shallow pool that reflects the sky through windows overhead. The living room opens to a garden court, which was later used as an outdoor stage, with a fountain for a curtain. Unlike Theodate Pope Riddle, who managed to dominate her architect (Stanford White offered her half-credit for Hill-Stead's design), Barnsdall succumbed to hers, but not without a struggle. She and Wright fought over the details of the design, sometimes by telegram across the world, when she traveled to Europe and he to Japan. But in the end the house is his California "Romanza," as he dubbed it. He strove to evoke in it both the architecture of the ancient Americans and the impositions of their Spanish conquistadors. Wright's description of his client—"neither neo, quasi, nor pseudo . . . as near American as any Indian, as developed and traveled in appreciation of the beautiful as any European [and] as domestic as a shooting star"[1]—stands, too, for the house he built for her.

It is Wright's conception of an archetypal American place that prevails, even though it is more illusion than substance. In its materials (the main structure is hollow tile, wood frame, and stucco), Hollyhock House is as much Hollywood as pre-Columbian, so, in a way, theater has the last word. Hollyhock House is an enduring stage set as much as a great architect's dream come true.

Today dream houses are still being built for people with money and the urge to express themselves in architecture. But those of us without a lot of money do the same. Inventive homeowners transform cookie-cutter houses amid endless tract developments into highly individual statements about themselves and the national culture. Even the most ordinary of suburban houses is redolent with symbolism. As Denise Scott Brown, the architect and urban planner, has written, "Houses with pitched roofs, colonial doorways and shutters tell us, without need of further signs, that here is a community that values tradition, pride of ownership and the rural life."[2]

It seems that we can't help but look for our symbols and build them. To me, this is the enduring truth about architecture. Thomas Jefferson speaks clearly to me through his singular vision of a house temple dedicated to an individual and an ideal. Theodate Pope Riddle commands my respect with her bold imagination. Hearst awes me with the force of his fantasies. As an architect myself, I look to buildings of the past not only for their forms and spaces, but also for their spirit. From them I have learned that to give my clients houses that will really be their own, I must satisfy not only their obvious needs, but also the demands of their dreams.

# 4

## Housing America

### *1920–1929*

#### 1991

Decades are false. While time can be neatly divided into ten-year intervals, trends of thought and action are rarely as amenable to simple categorization. Though the 1920s immediately conjure up brilliant images of a prosperous and playful era that ended with a decisive bang when the stock market crashed on October 29, 1929, in architectural and urbanistic terms the period's parameters are not quite so clear. In fact, it can more accurately be said to have begun with the cessation of the "war to end all wars" and ended with the election of Franklin D. Roosevelt in 1932.

The period got going in the wake of the nation's rise as a major player on the international stage, was characterized by an intense focus on the virtues of commerce and convenience as applied to the daily life of Everyman, and ended with financial collapse accompanied by massive self-doubt. Though its conclusion is best symbolized by the stock market's crash in 1929, the winds of self-confidence began to go out of its sails in 1927. (In so many ways the era reminds us of the 1980s, which began to misfire with the crash of 1987, only to conclude with the second crash of 1989.) The manifestations of a new spirit, defined in large measure by the modernist aesthetic, which would flower in the 1930s, were first felt in 1927.

*Architectural Record* began the period as a stylistically conservative magazine, but in the early 1930s came to feature some of the most important works of the avant-garde in both Europe and the United States. Like the rest of the profession, *Record* participated in the profound revolution of taste that marked the late 1920s and early 1930s, when "the battle of styles" between traditionalism and modernism was at its zenith.

While American architecture in the 1920s was dominated by the commercial skyscraper (as was that of the 1980s), this essay concentrates on an often

overlooked building type—housing. Then as now, housing was an important but
sublimated socioeconomic issue with profound architectural implications. But
more serious thought and work was done on the subject in the 1920s than is now
generally assumed. While the bulk of the architectural profession stood aloof from
the hard realities that the post–World War I housing shortages posed for the aver-
age American, there was a cadre of committed architects, planners, "do-gooders,"
and journalists who did care about the subject.

## New Models of Suburban Development

Though the federal government's effort in 1917 and 1918 to provide good, affordable housing for war workers was curtailed by Congress as part of peacetime
demobilization, that program, which included the construction of model towns,
continued to have a positive impact on the architectural profession and even
on market-driven housing throughout the 1920s. In a two-part series, "Garden
Apartments in Cities," published in *Record* in July and August 1920, John Taylor
Boyd, Jr. featured the work of Clarence Stein and Andrew Thomas, two architects
with very different backgrounds and intellectual orientations who made valuable
contributions to the housing movement in the 1920s.[1] It was Stein and Thomas,
working independently, who created the most compelling paradigms for middle-
class, suburban-style living close to the city's core.

A graduate of the École des Beaux-Arts, Stein was an intellectual who preferred theory to the day-to-day struggles of professional architectural practice. As
an apprentice in the office of Bertram Goodhue, Stein was in charge of designing
in 1916 the new copper-mining town of Tyrone, New Mexico. Tyrone was in many
ways the model for the government-sponsored war-housing effort, a new town
built by the Emergency Fleet Corporation and bearing many similarities to French
architect Tony Garnier's theoretical project, Cité Industrielle. After World War I,
Stein emerged as a socially committed professional who effectively absorbed ideas
from leading planning theorists, including Ebenezer Howard, Patrick Geddes,
Raymond Unwin, and Henry Wright, his sometime collaborator. Stein's first major
work, designed in collaboration with Wright, Frederick L. Ackerman, and Marjorie
Sewell Cautley, was the Sunnyside Gardens development in Queens, New York
(1924–28), sponsored by the City Housing Corporation (fig. 1). Sunnyside looked

*Fig. 2.* Clarence Stein and
Henry Wright, Radburn,
New Jersey, 1927–29

*Fig. 3.* Clarence Stein and
Henry Wright, Radburn,
New Jersey, 1927–29

back to prewar residential subdivisions such as Prospect Park South in Brooklyn, a suburban enclave where the gridiron street plan had been accepted with only modest alterations (such as landscaped malls, perimeter gateposts, and stringent land-use controls).

Going a few steps further, Sunnyside contained the germ of an intricate, hierarchically structured circulation system that was to reach its fullest expression in 1927 at Radburn, New Jersey, Stein and Wright's most innovative town design. Lewis Mumford praised Sunnyside as "an enclave in the midst of an industrial desert—using rows of attached houses and garden apartments to wrap the perimeter of the typical city block and define mid-block mews, which increases the overall density while fostering an atmosphere of suburban greenery."[2] Journalist Bruce Bliven saw Sunnyside as a collection of "seventeenth-century New England villages, each grouped around its common."[3]

On balance, many of Sunnyside's strengths have also been its weaknesses. The stripped-down traditionalism of Sunnyside's architecture paved the way all too smoothly for the detail-free barrackslike housing of the Depression and post–World War II era, and the developer's fervent emphasis on community was sometimes misinterpreted by the public as being antiprivate and anti-individual. Sunnyside marked the Indian summer of the suburban enclave within the urban milieu. The expanded geographic scope of development made possible by the automobile focused the eyes of the middle class on the relatively open land beyond the fringes of urbanism, an area that came to be labeled "exurbia."

### Separating Traffic by Type

Located ten miles from New York City, Radburn, New Jersey, was conceived of by Stein and Wright as a "town for the motor age" (figs. 2–3). The relationship between the car and the suburb at Radburn was akin to that between cat and mouse, with the car subverted and community life reoriented to pedestrians and bicyclists. Borrowing ideas from Frederick Law Olmsted and Calvert Vaux's Central Park, Stein and Wright separated Radburn's traffic by type: a system of walkways allowed children to go to school without ever having to cross a street. Grouped around cul-de-sacs that were intended to function as little more than

service alleys, the houses faced away from the street and toward continuous green-swards containing the town's walkways and bicycle paths.

At first, Radburn was viewed as a high point in town planning but a disappointment architecturally. Lewis Mumford considered its layout "admirable," but found the house designs not "particularly triumphant examples of modern architecture."[4]

But even the town's plan failed to function as Stein and Wright had hoped it would. For both children and adults, the automotive cul-de-sacs proved more compelling as foci of community life than the greenswards. Except for rare occasions of neighborly ceremony, the back doors of houses at Radburn functioned as the front doors might, with dinner guests arriving in their cars at the same place that deliveries were made, trash picked up, cups of sugar exchanged, and bicycles stored.

When the Depression hit, construction at Radburn was stopped with only one-fourth of the project completed. Although the notion pioneered at Radburn—that a town could be designed to provide both automotive convenience and country serenity—was never fully tested, it did form the basis for a number of idealized urban visions formulated at the close of the interwar period.

Another important figure in housing design in the 1920s was a self-taught architect named Andrew J. Thomas, who combined proselytizing and organizational skills with an entrepreneurial talent. Having developed techniques for decreasing costs, partly as a result of his experiences as supervising architect for the federal government's Emergency Fleet Corporation, Thomas set out to perfect, or at least rationalize, the tenement type. Thomas was so successful that, in the eyes of some observers, his designs afforded more light and air than was provided in the typical Park Avenue apartment. Because Thomas was content to pursue his reformist goals within the prevailing economic system, his work was consistently undervalued by his contemporaries and is still overlooked today.

Thomas's greatest achievement was Jackson Heights, Queens, a sprawling residential enclave developed by the Queensboro Corporation (fig. 4). Taking the city block as the unit of development, Thomas evolved at Jackson Heights a new housing type, the "garden apartment," a term that he probably invented. According to John Taylor Boyd, Jr., "the use of the block as the unit . . . reached

*Fig. 4.* Andrew J. Thomas, The Chateau, 1922, and The Towers, 1923–25, Jackson Heights, Queens, New York

its full development" at Jackson Heights.[5] Providing community amenities as well as housing accommodation, this development is a sub-city within the city.

The garden apartment adapted the compositional and aesthetic unity typical of palatial upper-class Manhattan apartment houses to the economic and social realities of middle-class tenants, a location in an outer borough, and the increasingly important role of the automobile. Thomas was influenced not only by prewar New York examples but also by work he saw in Berlin and Vienna, and by quadrangular dormitories being built by leading American colleges such as Princeton and Yale. Thomas also drew from his personal experience: unlike most architects of the time, who were born into wealth, Thomas had been born and reared in a tenement and began his architectural career building tenements. More than had any previous designer, Thomas imbued the multiple dwelling with a sense of "home," jettisoning high-style, academic classicism in favor of an eclectic mix of essentially vernacular ornamental details, many of them based on those used in Italian villas and Spanish farmhouses.

As in all of Thomas's work involving groups of buildings, the structures at Jackson Heights were massed to reflect the status of the block as the development unit and at the same time to preserve the character, individuality, and domestic scale of the components.

### Setting Standards

By 1924 Thomas's work at Jackson Heights had made clear that high land coverage and high density were not necessarily incompatible. Thomas also made the idea of neighborhood planning more glamorous than it had been before, and established humane and practical standards for housing in the city—standards that would prove influential in the reworking of prevailing legislation and the passage of the Multiple Dwelling Law of 1929.

In 1926, the architect and historian A. Lawrence Kocher introduced *Architectural Record*'s annual country house issue with an essay titled, "The Country House: Are We Developing an American Style?" Kocher responded to his own question by stating that American architects were arguably no closer to that end "than our novelists to the 'great American novel.' But if such a style is to be achieved it will be, not by the general adoption of any group of historic shapes and details, but by a free selection and development of styles to meet the newer and more diverse needs of modern life."[6]

With Kocher's arrival as editor in 1927, *Record* took on a new mission, the introduction of European modernism to American readers. However, European modernism had not been completely undiscussed or unseen in the pages of *Record* before the late '20s, and many of the formal experiments of the Modern Movement were known to a handful of American architects.

*Record* had given its readers an early jolt of stylistic modernism in February 1923, with Edith Elmer Wood's "Recent Housing Work in Western Europe," illustrated with examples encountered during a ten-month tour of England, France, Belgium, and Holland. Wood concluded that "architectural styles are conservative except in Holland, where an ultra-modern school has arisen, especially at Amsterdam, which is stirring the imagination of the younger men and women to great enthusiasm."[7]

Frank Chouteau Brown also noted the relevance to American practice of modernist Dutch housing in his four-part series "Low Rental Housing," in 1924.[8] Brown discussed the American "suburban type" and then examined examples from the Amsterdam School of Expressionism—including housing projects by U. Gratama, J.C. van Epen, and Michel de Klerk. Despite these articles, European models failed to affect mainstream American residential architecture, which tended to maintain traditional historical forms.

## Introducing the European Prophets to America

In 1928 Henry-Russell Hitchcock wrote a two-part series of seminal articles titled "Modern Architecture,"[9] characterizing two approaches: the New Tradition and the New Pioneers. The articles introduced a variety of European designs, ranging from a vernacular-inspired housing group by the English firm of Pakington, Enthoven and Grey, in Byfleet, to ardently ahistorical examples of modernism such as André Lurçat's house for his father-in-law Auguste Michel, near Paris, and Le Corbusier and Pierre Jeanneret's Lipchitz-Miestchaninoff residences in Boulogne-sur-Seine (figs. 5–6). Egged on by the zealotry of Philip Johnson and Alfred Barr, Hitchcock would eventually place himself squarely in the revolutionary camp of the so-called New Pioneers and help to establish the International Style as the right and true modernism. But in these two articles for *Record* he was more reserved in his judgment. "Despite their considerable achievement the New Pioneers are," he stated, "best considered as prophets whom the future will find false or true." As for their theory, Hitchcock concluded, it still "is largely a promise" since "for its full achievement it requires mass production."[10]

As the period drew to a close, *Record* kept its eye on modern European housing design but also sought out as many American experiments as it could find. For example, the magazine featured Rudolph Schindler's vigorously sculpted Lovell Beach House in Newport Beach, California[11] (fig. 7), and Richard Neutra's office-building project for his ideal city, Rush City Reformed.[12]

The late 1920s were a crucial time for modernism, not only in terms of its flowering in Europe, but also its dissemination in the U.S. At the decade's close, just as Walter Gropius, Le Corbusier, and other European modernists were

*Fig. 7.* Rudolph Schindler, Lovell Beach House, Newport Beach, California, 1926

transforming their polemics into actual construction, the economic tide turned and the opportunity to build diminished greatly. By the time the American architectural profession had begun to catch up with the pioneering efforts of the early modernists, the stock-market crash and resulting Depression shut down almost all building activity. As a result, the American chapter on the development of canonic modernism virtually closed after having been barely opened.

# 5

## Architecture and Place
### 1989

We are in the midst of a revival of American cities, yet the era when it was taken for granted that the development process automatically served the public interest is past. Just as faith in the redemptive values of new technology was badly shaken by the onset of modernist architecture, so too is our belief that any new building is by definition a good thing. Modernism was based on a kind of technological positivism in which the processes and products of industrialization and sophisticated technology were confused with the aesthetics of architecture. During modernism's hegemony we moved from pride of place to pride of placelessness, from the rich images of a Chrysler Building to the bland boxes of New York's Sixth Avenue, as architects and their clients alike began to conceive of buildings as industrial objects and not as representations of culture.

The days when urban development was welcomed for its own sake are gone. Less and less does the architect have just one client to satisfy: the developer; less and less does the developer merely have to get the money and building permits and build. The developer and the architect no longer share the traditional pleasures of the love-hate relationship. Now they are caught in a not so smooth love triangle with a new, often difficult, and always vocal love-object, the community they must court for the privilege to build.

For even a small project the community review process can be grueling, frustrating, downright obstructive, and sometimes comes to the sad end of satisfying no one. Yet as citizens first, and architects and developers second, we have to admit that if we are to succeed in remaking our cities, making them *places* once again, we owe much to the awareness and involvement of the community in the building process.

My own experience with community review boards and other public entities has not always been easy, but it has always been instructive and, frankly, reassuring. I divide the world into experts and real people. Architects are experts but I find that real people representing their communities often have ideas about the kind of development appropriate to their neighborhood, town, or city that are as good if not better than those of the experts. In fact, given the dubious quality of much recent building and the very telling criticisms offered by the public of that work, I put my money with the real people.

After all is said and done, the principal concern of community groups is context. Most people fear development because they fear that new buildings will not enhance their environment but do just the opposite. We have come to a sorry state of affairs totally unlike the one that prevailed throughout the nineteenth century, when new buildings were almost invariably greeted as improvements. Today development is frequently seen as a regression. An understanding of context can overcome this. Issues of context are quantifiable in terms of residential and commercial density and traffic flow, on- and off-street parking, and so forth, but often the less tangible issues are the most critical—issues that I would sum up as issues of "character." Community groups have become very sophisticated in defining what is and isn't in character, which is another way of saying what is and isn't contextual. The wish list, or demand list, depending on the community, of contextual qualities is long. One of the first is that a building respect the prevailing style of architecture, whether in materials, historical details, or overall profile. The problem here is that even the most coherent American villages and cities do not have one single style. Cities, like people, grow and evolve over time. Yet there is no reason to lose touch with what went before. So I would say that scale is one of the most critical hallmarks in contextual design, one which is best resolved, perhaps, by focusing on whether the street can survive the imposition of a larger building. Often it can, yet this depends on another series of contextual issues, centering on what kind of street-level amenities a new project offers. Whether in a suburban village or a bustling downtown, the street is the public space in American urbanism: the street is an outdoor room and as such requires that it be bounded by lively walls permitting people to come in and go out, just as in a room in any house, and that the walls be decorated with elements engaging the eye's attention. The street of a village or city center needs shops along its edge and boldly defined building entrances leading to lobbies where the public is welcome. In the language of development, mixed-use projects are essential to a lively urban scene: a street demands a high variety of activities along its edge.

Let me share with you two experiences that help illuminate the present and what I believe to be the future relationship of architects, developers, and the community. In 1983, I was invited by a young firm of architects, Martinez and Wong, to design a small office building for one of the most prominent corners in La Jolla village, a fashionable seaside neighborhood in San Diego where seventy years earlier the distinguished California architect Irving Gill had built some of his best work. Thirteen thousand people had signed a petition against this project, even before pencil had been put to paper, so outraged and frustrated was the community about architects' unwillingness or inability to design new buildings that would suit the texture and character of the place. The community's frustration was not at all unfounded. The character of recent development was brutal and banal.

Unable to elicit more distinguished architecture from developers and architects, the community had retaliated over the years by continually cutting back on the permitted building height. But size was not the real problem; character of use and character of form were. The thirty-foot height limitation imposed in coastal areas had preserved some natural views to be sure, but it had also failed to stimulate better architecture. Nevertheless, the community still believed size was the issue, and was now proposing to limit development to 10,000 square feet or less; our building was to be more than four times that amount.

To make a long story short, I was able to put the community's fears to rest by uniting the form of the new building with the traditions of building in the area. What I proposed was simple enough, to design a building that would fit in by speaking the prevalent traditional architectural language of Southern California, the Spanish Colonial style. In so doing I would pick up a thread of architectural history that had been broken with the introduction of abstract modernism in the 1940s. My design would interpret the Spanish Colonial as it was previously revived in the 1920s and in the more abstract, essentialized version, which Irving Gill had raised to the level of high art in such buildings as his La Jolla Woman's Club of 1913. In both its colors and its use of materials, the Prospect Point building responds to the local and regional tradition. The exterior walls are of cream-colored stucco while pitched roofs are of clay tile. On the second floor, generously sized wood-framed French doors open onto narrow, wrought-iron balconies. And in a very specific response to the place, the principal pavilion of the new office building is capped by a flattened semi-dome that recalls the dome at the nearby, much loved La Valencia Hotel.

Community pressure was also the principal circumstance that led to my work in Boston's Back Bay. The 222 Berkeley Street project had been originally conceived as the eastern component of a twin-tower scheme, developed by The New England/Gerald D. Hines Interests and designed by Philip Johnson and John Burgee. After loud complaints and legal actions from the community regarding the twin towers, a compromise was reached between the developers and the city of Boston, in which the eastern component of the block-long project would be somewhat reduced in size and would be given a distinctly different character. The complex mandate, presented to me as the new architect, was for a design with a distinctly Bostonian and Back Bay character. There was a strong community feeling that the new design should include the most highly regarded feature of the Colton Building now on the site, but to be demolished to make way for the new building, which has an appealing pattern of multifaceted bay windows. Reflecting the Colton Building, our design includes three-story bays on floors three through five and also includes bays at street level in reference to the typical late nineteenth-century townhouses of the Back Bay and the small-scale retailers of nearby Newbury Street. In response to the call for a Bostonian character, 222 Berkeley is clad in red brick and trimmed in granite. In order to make its contextual intentions more explicit, the design uses the Georgian vocabulary of late eighteenth- and early nineteenth-century Boston architecture, as well as the highly regarded twentieth-century revivals such as the locally admired Ritz-Carlton Hotel (Strickland, Blodget, and Law, 1927). The elaborate classical details for the Boylston Street entrance, which is flanked by paired columns carrying urns and entered through a revolving door housed in a tempietto, signal the public importance of the top-lit, publicly accessible winter garden inside. A variation on eighteenth-century orangeries, and on Boston's widely admired Horticultural Hall (Wheelwright & Haven, 1901), crowns the office tower, offering a distinct skyline silhouette that places it firmly within the American tradition of classical skyscrapers.

From my experiences in San Diego and Boston, I have come to the conclusion that the future of architects and developers depends not so much on our understanding of each other, but on our ability to work with the ultimate client, the public. I believe that this is a positive development. In the 1920s, developers and architects didn't have to be goaded into mixed-use developments of architectural and urbanistic distinction. Developers wanted a certain quality of urbanity and the public expected the same. The buildings of Rockefeller Center are huge and rather neutral in their design, but the center is full of life. It is proof positive that mere size is not the issue. Today, and in the future, we should do better. I'm certainly tired of anonymous buildings. As citizens, we have the right to demand an end to the anonymous nonplaces that characterize much of our built environment. As architects and developers, we have the responsibility to provide something better. Building is not a right, but a privilege.

# 6

---

# The Suburban Alternative
# for the "Middle City"
## 1978

In spite of a substantial body of opinion to the contrary, the Anglo-American sub-urb is a remarkable urbanistic achievement, not just a degraded species of town planning. A new and long overdue look at the suburb can revitalize the design of the seemingly inevitable suburban developments that ring our metropolitan regions. But, even more importantly, it can also supply much-needed models for the redevelopment of the vast, virtually empty urban wastelands that lie between the inner cores of our cities and the suburbs beyond in what, for the sake of argu-ment, we can call the "middle city." President Carter's recent trip to the South Bronx focused the nation's attention on our most devastated middle city. But other large sections of New York and whole neighborhoods in Cleveland, Detroit, and St. Louis also lie fallow, virtually empty of people and buildings, and with no discernible assets except those called the "urban infrastructure"—the network of streets and the utility systems buried in their rights-of-way. The development of these urban fringe areas was a debased or incompletely realized version of the high-density inner-city model, and they were never more than speculatively con-ceived way stations for an upwardly mobile immigrant population moving toward cultural assimilation. The tenements were knockoffs of the inner-city apartment house, just as the row houses were knockoffs of inner-city brownstones, in which two or three families inhabited the space occupied by one family in the original.

For the past thirty years or so, architects and planners, in their efforts to stem the flight of businesses to the rapidly suburbanizing countryside, have been almost exclusively concerned with the commercial revitalization of the inner city. And until very recently the generally accepted residential redevelopment model of our cities was the high-rise tower or slab built in a parklike setting. It is now clear

that this model does not provide an adequate response to the diverse aspirations
of large numbers of our citizens, no matter what their economic status. It is also
clear that we can no longer ignore the problems of the middle city, the vast land
areas between the inner city and the suburbs. In most cases, the high-rise apartment has been a developer's dream and little else. On the other hand, the one-,
two-, or three-family house on its own lot can, under the proper circumstances,
be as economically and technologically viable as the high-rise apartment—and it
has proven an overwhelmingly popular success as well.

I would suggest this to architects, planners, sociologists, economists, and
political strategists beginning to consider the burnt-out wastelands of our middle
cities: look to the suburb, especially to the pre-automobile suburb, for a work-
able redevelopment strategy. This model, with its tradition of freestanding houses
within walking distance of village centers (and usually of rapid transit stations),
has proven a viable format for development that can support a variety of people of
different age groups, lifestyles, and even economic and social levels.

New suburbs should be built where they are really needed—not in the remote
reaches of the outer city, but near the inner cities where the existing network of
roads, rapid transit, and utilities and the sudden availability of land with no evi-
dent higher use combine to make it possible to introduce this remarkable urban
format to a new consumer market.

In proposing the suburban model for the South Bronxes of our cities, I realize that I am taking on two sacred cows. The first is the notion that the history
of cities is and has always been one of increasing population and therefore population density. The second is that the suburb is the particular fief of the middle
classes, leaving the other forms of housing to those less well off economically and
to the rich, who not only can choose what they want but who are also able to
spend enough money to make their choices work. In challenging the former view,

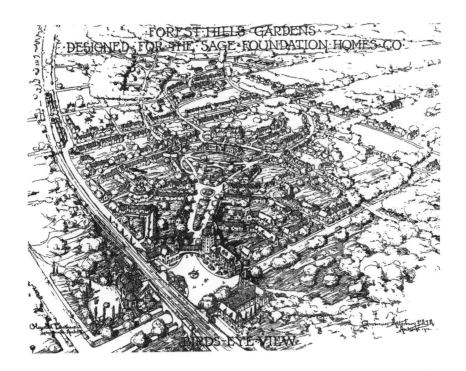

*Fig. 2.* Frederick Law Olmsted, Jr. and Grosvenor Atterbury, Bird's eye view, Forest Hills Gardens, Queens, New York, 1909

one merely contradicts dearly held theories of some physical and economic planners. But in challenging the latter, one strikes at the jugular of our national value system. Still, it is important to point out that, though home ownership is a sine qua non among the badges honoring individual success, in reality such ownership for the past thirty or more years has in effect been subsidized by the government as a result of the Federal Housing Administration, the GI Bill, and many other similar programs.

Suburbs are an important and unique part of industrial and postindustrial era culture. They are as much a product of our traditions and aspirations as they are of rapid industrialization and excessive land speculation. And, just as a history of the suburb needs to be written, so too must a new generation of architects begin to examine without prejudice the varieties of suburban types that have existed. For the truth is that the suburbs we are building now, based as they are on the automobile, are not the ones we idealize. It is the earlier suburb that represents the desirable paradigm, not only from the point of view of the design of the individual buildings, but also from the standpoints of convenience and of economic value. That is why Garden City and not Levittown, Shaker Heights and not Columbia, continue to ring the bell of status.

Many suburbs—like Hampstead Garden Suburb in London (fig. 1) and Forest Hills Gardens in New York (fig. 2)—are within the political boundaries of large cities, and this fact raises an important question about what a suburb really is. It is clearly a planning type. But is it also a political entity? A place? A state of mind? It can be any of these, but perhaps most important, the suburb is a dream, a dream of arcadia that can take two basic forms: that of the pre-industrial village set in an open landscape, and that of houses scattered across the landscape itself, whether prairie or forest. It is the relationship between the image of the village and the image of the open country that gives each suburb its particular character.

The Suburban Alternative for the "Middle City"

*Fig. 3.* Frederick Law Olmsted and Calvert Vaux, Riverside, Illinois, 1869

*Fig. 4.* Frank Lloyd Wright, Broadacre City Project Model, 1934–35

At Riverside, Illinois, for example, the two are nearly balanced (fig. 3). At Forest Hills Gardens, the village dominates, while at Wright's Broadacre City (fig. 4) and at Levittown, Long Island, it almost completely gives way to a continuous rural landscape. At its most basic level, this balance is expressed in the plan: the choice of curved or straight streets is an obvious clue to the designer's attitude toward nature on the one hand and the village on the other.

### The Beginnings of the Suburb

The American suburb has its origins in English housing developments of the early nineteenth century—in particular two villages included as part of John Nash's Regent's development in London (fig. 5). But it was with the establishment of Llewellyn Park in New Jersey (1850), Riverside, Illinois (1869), and Bedford Park, London (1875) that effective models of the suburb as we know it began to emerge (fig. 6). By the time of the American centennial, the suburban model was firmly established on both sides of the Atlantic.

The Anglo-American suburb succeeded because, among the affluent, it was an effective response to a growing dissatisfaction with life in the inner cities (environmental pollution, crime, and swelling immigrant populations were all serious urban problems a hundred years ago). Still, the suburban model was applied with equal success to the needs of the working and middle classes. In England, Bourneville, Saltaire, and Port Sunlight were all successful, model, working-class suburbs. American examples include Echota, near Niagara Falls and designed by McKim, Mead & White; Pullman, Illinois, designed by S.S. Beman; Torrance, California, by the Olmsted Brothers with Irving Gill, and a host of so-called "industrial villages" begun during World War I under federal sponsorship—including Kohler, Wisconsin, and Yorkship Village at Camden, New Jersey (fig. 7).

The modest single-family house, freestanding on its own plot, is the glory of the suburban tradition and the focus of the lifestyle that grew up with it and which we can call "suburbanism." From the time of A.J. Downing and A.J. Davis through the late work of Frank Lloyd Wright, America's best architects have been to some extent concerned with the overall design of the suburb. But it has been the attention paid to the design of the suburban house itself by our best architects

PARK VILLAGE EAST, REGENT'S PARK

*Fig. 5.* John Nash, Park Village East, Regent's Park, London, 1823–24

*Fig. 6.* Richard Norman Shaw and others, Bedford Park, London, 1875

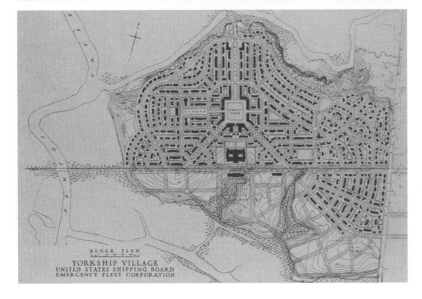

BLOCK PLAN
YORKSHIP VILLAGE
UNITED STATES SHIPPING BOARD
EMERGENCY FLEET CORPORATION

*Fig. 7.* Electus D. Litchfield, Block Plan of Yorkship Village, Camden, New Jersey, ca. 1915

The Suburban Alternative for the "Middle City"

*Fig. 8.* Frank Lloyd Wright, presentation drawing, watercolor, ink, graphite on paper, 15 x 25 in., Prairie House for *Ladies Home Journal*, 1900

*Fig. 9.* Frank Lloyd Wright, House for Edwin H. Cheney, Oak Park, Illinois, 1903

that has made this building type so richly and uniquely our own. Lewis Mumford has written in *The City in History* that "from H.H. Richardson to Frank Lloyd Wright the most graciously original expressions of modern form were achieved in the suburban house."[1] The standard urban and architectural histories, though, have usually relied on the most elaborate examples of suburban design, because, no doubt, these provide the fullest expression of an architect's ideas. It should nonetheless be pointed out that many remarkable designs for very modest suburban houses abound in the work of our leading architects—in the work of Davis and Downing, for example, or of Frank Lloyd Wright.

No architect, in fact, has had more influence on the suburb—or took it more seriously as a design problem—than Wright, but his impact was not nearly so great in the area of the individual house as it was in the area of landscape and townscape. The image of Wright's Prairie House (fig. 8) as a house in a small town, and on a small lot, has no precedent in the farm or ranch buildings of the American West, nor, of course, does it relate to any continental European precedent; it can

The Suburban Alternative for the "Middle City"

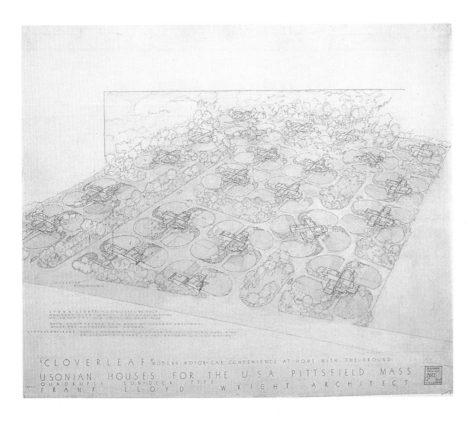

"CLOVERLEAF" MODERN MOTOR-CAR CONVENIENCE AT HOME WITH THE GROUND
USONIAN HOUSES FOR THE USA PITTSFIELD MASS
QUADRUPLE SUN-DECK TYPE
FRANK LLOYD WRIGHT ARCHITECT

be understood in terms of the small towns of the East Coast. With the introduction of the fully developed cross-axial plan in the Ward Willetts house in 1902, and in subsequent work like his Heurtley and Cheney houses (fig. 9), Wright began the gradual transformation of the traditional suburban streetscape. The narrow but relatively deep lot characteristic of nineteenth-century suburbs was not suitable for Wright's new house type. This de-emphasized the traditional, static relationship of front, back, and sides in favor of something new, based on the simultaneous inward and outward focus of the interior spaces and the composition of volume according to the principle of centrality and rotation. To accommodate Wright's Prairie Houses, lots had to become square in plan, and the centralized massing of his most resolved works led also to the abandonment of the traditional gable-fronted building in favor of a very low hip roof, or to the kind of gable roof characteristic of pre-Georgian houses in New England, with their roof ridges running parallel to the street. In his Usonian Houses of the 1940s and 1950s, Wright abandoned the cross-axial plan and at the same time adopted single-story plan types to establish the model of the sprawling ranch house, which often characterizes suburban development today.

Wright's impact was felt at the scale of suburban development but not of suburban house design. His 1942 site plans for unrealized government housing at Pittsfield, Massachusetts (fig. 10), for instance, have had a great impact on suburban land planning in the last thirty years, and though his proposal for Broadacre City can be dismissed as an extreme vision of the Arcadian ideal such as only Detroit might dream of but never have the genius to propose, it did articulate principles for a new kind of land planning based on the automobile that have come to govern suburban development since 1945. Wright, almost uniquely among architects, understood

*Fig. 10.* Frank Lloyd Wright, Cloverleaf War Industry Housing Project, Pittsfield, Massachusetts, 1942

The Suburban Alternative for the "Middle City"

[Fig. 125. Small Classical Villa.]

*Fig. 11.* A.J. Downing, Small Classical Villa, 1850

*Fig. 12.* Charles Rennie Mackintosh, The Hill House, Helensburgh, Scotland, 1902–04

both the magic of the automobile and its potentially destructive impact. Thus if the suburb is to be thought of as a legitimate urban form—and I think it must be—then Wright must be acknowledged as a twentieth-century urbanist equal to if not greater than Le Corbusier, a greatness to be measured not only in terms of theoretical insight, but also in terms of real impact on built form.

The suburban house is a specific type in its own right: neither a manor house nor a farm house, both of which involve lives economically connected to the land, it is a direct response to the requirement for efficient, servantless domesticity and to the need for reconciling the scale of the house with that of the personal transportation vehicle, be it the horse-drawn or, later, the horseless carriage. Most important, it offers its inhabitants a comprehensible image of independence and privacy while also accepting the responsibilities of community. The most successful suburban houses have addressed these issues within recognizable cultural contexts. In developing the suburban house, American and English architects have drawn on examples from the past in order to establish a continuity and sense of place in the open countryside where new suburbs have traditionally been built. Mid-nineteenth-century suburban architects tended to design in an "associational" manner; virtually each of A.J. Downing's or Samuel Sloan's villas was intended to evoke a specific earlier architectural style (fig. 11). And there was always the implication that the style carried with it a mood or characteristic that the prospective occupant could seize on as emblematic of his own nature.

Later in the century, the suburban house was seen as a principal mechanism for the establishment or reestablishment of appropriate national styles. In England, C.F.A. Voysey's beautifully crafted suburban houses, typified by his own house, The Orchards, abstracted typical village architectural imagery. Charles Rennie Mackintosh's Hill House (fig. 12) was a commentary on vernacular Scottish form, and Edwin Lutyens' Salutation was a true revival of the Queen Anne style. In America, the Shingle Style was in large part an interpretation of the saltbox architecture of pre-Georgian New England, and the Colonial Revival was a reinterpretation of the Adamesque Georgian of the late Colonial and early Republican period. In each of these cases, the styles invoked were those of the pre-industrial age. And in virtually all cases, it should be emphasized, the process was one of eclectic vocation and not one of archaeological reproduction.

The Suburban Alternative for the "Middle City"

In the twentieth century in England, two vernacular styles dominated—the Tudoresque free-cottage style and the "true" Queen Anne or Georgian. But in America the Shingle and Colonial styles were quickly rejected in many parts of the country as too closely related to the East to meet the imagistic need of the Midwest, South, and West. To discover a regional style where none had before existed was an exciting prospect. Under the influence of Wright an attempt was made to forge a Prairie Style that would at once connect back to New England and evoke the rude houses of the pioneers and the endless landscape on which they had found themselves. And in the years leading up to World War I, Southern California, under the influence of Bertram Goodhue, adopted a loosely Hispanic language of form, borrowed in part from mission architecture but more evidently from the buildings of Mexico and Spain.

*Fig. 13.* Robert Rodes McGoodwin, French Village, Chestnut Hill, Pennsylvania, 1927

*Fig. 14.* Irving Gill, Woman's Club, under construction, La Jolla, California, 1913–14

This kind of regionalism took root not only in the design of single-family houses but also in suburban developments. Often, references to a local vernacular style were combined with references to a European prototype, as, for example, in the suburb of Chestnut Hill, which is located within the city limits of Philadelphia (fig. 13). Chestnut Hill was largely developed by one man, George Woodward, Jr., in the late 1910s and 1920s. A number of very good architects built houses there, including Robert Rodes McGoodwin and the firm of Mellor, Meigs & Howe. Architects working there acknowledged a common style based loosely on the French farmhouses of Normandy and on the local vernacular stone architecture that could be seen in abundance in the adjacent village of Germantown. Thus Chestnut Hill today seems not only romantically evocative but contextually responsive, a grouping of new buildings that continues a regional tradition. Later architects building in Chestnut Hill, like Kenneth Day, Oscar Stonorov, Louis Kahn, Romaldo Giurgola, and Robert Venturi, have chosen not to acknowledge the Chestnut Hill style that was once so firmly established.

It is important to note that regional association has not in the past thwarted technological invention, nor has it confounded the move toward abstraction that characterized much of the best work of the 1910s and 1920s in America and Europe. For example, the work of Irving Gill in San Diego exhibits many characteristics that we consider modernist, although it also participates in the Spanish Colonial tradition. It is also technologically innovative: Gill's famous concrete tilt-up wall was executed for a building designed in a distinctly Spanish Colonial mode (fig.14).

### The Contemporary Suburb

Only with the coming of the continental European modernist styles—conceptual and self-referential (process oriented) as opposed to perceptual (pictorial) and representational (content oriented)—did an abrupt shift in the relationship between American architects and the suburb develop. Under the impact of European modernism, with its continuing polemic on behalf of collectivization and machine technology, the tradition of serious suburban design was abandoned in the late 1930s and 1940s by our best architectural talents just as our suburbs burgeoned to unprecedented size. At a time when our very best talents should have been thinking about the suburb and the suburban house, they were pursuing issues like architectural mass production or the joys of building "one-off" houses as monuments that would establish reputations that led to careers designing museums or office buildings.

Today our best architects have abandoned the suburb to the ordinary practitioner and to the speculative builder. And the discipline of town planning at the suburban scale has been allowed to die. For the past thirty years, very few efforts have been made to understand the suburb and suburban architecture. No wonder the level of prevailing speculative residential development is so low. Even the comparatively enlightened "cluster" and "townhouse village" developments, where the quality of the site planning is reasonably acceptable, usually lack the architectural elements that would help establish that sense of place so necessary for the images of community and continuity.

The English and Americans are uncomfortable in large, densely built cities. Our urbanism is shaped by the prejudices and preferences of this shared cultural heritage. London is a city of vast land area and low population density—a collection of loosely connected villages that set the stage for the kinds of urbanism that the automobile has made possible in Los Angeles and Houston. For fifty years or more, communications systems have enabled businesses to move away from the centers, and even our densest cities, like New York and Chicago, have experienced a diffusion toward the expanding suburbs. In fact, the actual density of a city like New York—once one goes beyond the two dense cores of Lower and Midtown Manhattan—is far lower than the city's image in literature and film would begin to suggest. Outside Manhattan, much of New York is a city of attached one-, two-, and three-family houses, interspersed with apartment houses usually no more than six stories high. For this reason, it can be argued that New York and most other American cities are, like London, collections of small towns united not by a uniform street grid or superhighway system, but by a system of roads that generally preceded urbanization and by underground and elevated rail systems that even now can make the suburbanization of our cities feasible.

The pattern of low-density residential centers focused on transportation and shopping hubs persisted until the end of World War II. Only with the development of the vast parkway and interstate highway system of the post–World War II era did it become possible for a new sprawling kind of suburb to develop. Dependent only on good roads, the new automobile suburb can be established just about anywhere, and with the recent emigration of industry and commerce from the inner city, even the road connection back to the city has become less important.

One need only to look at the growth of cities like Phoenix to realize that suburban pressure is a factor that cannot be ignored. Yet it is too easy, too glib, to say that Americans are so anti-urban that Phoenix—a city virtually without a center—is the future. Phoenix does nonetheless suggest that the suburbs of the thirty years just past are of a very different kind from the ones we saw earlier—perhaps they are a subspecies, but they are suited to the nature of our cultural heritage, to our vast geography, and to our lifestyles, which we must recognize as shockingly profligate.

Our suburbanism, then, has been of two kinds. The first is based on the image and, to a considerable extent, reality of the small town and its life, connected back to the city by rail and local roads. The second is based on the new mobility provided by the automobile. It is a diffuse landscape, without the sense of town, interspersed with low-density development and occasionally interrupted by linear shopping "centers."

What is missing in the second, newer category of suburb is an architecture rich enough to record the struggle between the image of Arcadia and the reality of life in the twentieth century. Also missing is any sense of collective space, the focusing qualities of a village and its green, a market square, or a civic plaza. But unquestionably the most important problem with the new suburbs is their love affair with the automobile. The car not only killed Main Street, it has killed the traditional suburban town as well.


## The Future of the Suburb

Some optimistic notes can still be struck. The old suburbs continue to function and continue to be desirable places to live. Though the wonderful heterogeneity and the strong sense of place established, for instance, at Forest Hills Gardens does not seem to be recognized or even remembered by most historians, the development itself continues to function admirably. And, prodded by the example set by sociologists like Herbert Gans, some of our architects are trying to get the profession to face up to the reality of the post–World War II suburb—if not to love Levittown, as Venturi and Scott Brown have put it, then at least to recognize that it exists, that it will not go away, and that people live in it. At the same time, we should not lose sight of the fact that Levittown is at best a dim reflection of the really inventive prototypes it emulates. In rediscovering the suburb, architects should not lose their critical judgment, but should cast aside their prejudices and do a little serious research. They must also recover from the failure of nerve that has crippled them over the past thirty years and get to work in an area where symbolic image and economics are valued as much and probably even more than the play of light on volumes set in space.

There will be no new ideas about suburbs until our thinking frees itself from the biases and orthodoxies of our recent architectural and urban theories, especially those peculiar cultural biases and cultural prejudices that have encouraged us to see old cities and old buildings—traditions and recognizable forms—as worthless and wrong. Nor will we be able to deal confidently with the suburb until we free ourselves from the belief that new suburban ideas (or, in fact, new suburbs) can only grow on virgin land beyond the edges of existing development. Suburbs will not go away, nor should they. In fact, they may well hold the key to the solution of urban problems that were hitherto deemed insoluble.

# 7

## In Praise of
## Invented Towns

### 1999

Thank you to the members of the Seaside Institute for the honor of the Seaside Prize, which is made more special because it commemorates not a person, or even an ideal, but an ideal rendered into an ever-evolving reality—a town and community. I love Seaside and I learn from Seaside. It is a place of great beauty and superb intelligence, sympathetically set in nature yet distinctly man-made, a place that confronts the junk of so much American urbanism with a splendid alternative (fig. 1).

What is it that makes Seaside so compelling? On the one hand, it is a resort—a good-time place, enjoying a wonderful beachfront site, where one can escape from all the stresses, rigors, and obsessions of big-city life. On the other hand, it is a town, as urban as any. Perhaps what strikes me most about Seaside is how these two aspects are related: a "resort town" replete with the rich measure of contradiction the phrase implies. Resorts are places of escape, yet they are often idealized versions of what we left behind at home, or what we would like to have at home but don't. So we have city life and its seeming opposite, escape into nature, in one place.

For architects and their clients, resorts are design laboratories where new ideas can be tried out without the fear of failure we might suffer from in the so-called real world of everyday life. At Seaside the laboratory experiment can be judged a great success. In this town a cure for many, but not all of the diseases of modern urbanism has been identified. This cure, developed by Robert Davis and planned by Andres Duany, Elizabeth Plater-Zyberk, and Léon Krier, is not only a resounding success, it also opens up fertile fields for further experimentation. Seaside is not the last or the first word on town-making, but it projects an optimistic view of the future of conurbation.

Although it is new, Seaside is a place enriched by the past. I refer not only to the broad tradition of architectural form-making that informs its houses and buildings, designed by so many talented architects, or even to the time-honored principles that underpin its brilliant plan, though these are very important. I refer principally to the specific, distinctly, if not quite uniquely, American tradition of capitalist-sponsored town development, a tradition that existed for almost 100 years before World War II when the public was served by a development community that worked with architects and planners to create new towns. These invented towns—I would say planned towns, but *planning* has become a dirty word—are among the most humane and interesting works of art we Americans have ever made. Our invented towns are a principal glory of our culture. Invented towns—planned towns—have shown, as Seaside does again, that developers and architects working together can meet the material and spiritual needs of people coming together as a community. I stress this point because between the 1930s and the 1960s—the years when planning got its nasty reputation—architects, planners, developers, and government officials conspired to impose on us and on the landscape an abstract ideal for how people should live together, promoting that ideal as a better way to live—better, because in a blinkered conception of modernity it rejected the slowly evolving patterns of urban settlement in favor of the ethos of the factory assembly line. In actual practice, the reality of the assembly line is now pretty much a thing of the past, giving way to teamwork. Would that such were the case of "assembly line" planning; instead, we are still saddled with a debilitating and deteriorating townscape so unwelcome that by association the very idea of planning, of inventing towns, was repudiated by the citizenry, who came not only to distrust planners and their architects but also to believe that planning was a form of totalitarianism. Seaside restores our faith in urban planning and urban design as ways to achieve viable works of art.

What I mean by invented towns is this: towns planned from scratch, willed into existence by land developers and surveyors who occasionally were inspired to do great things. Invented towns are as much part of the bedrock of our physical culture as the landscape itself. The tradition of the invented town in America often combines high idealism with bottom-line pragmatism: it is the tradition of private enterprise seeking to respond to a perceived social need. In other words,

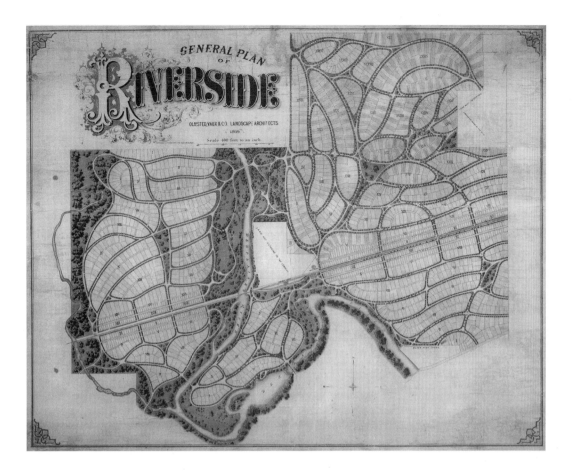

the idea is to invest in the development of land, not merely to subdivide it and sell it off. By its singular quality Seaside reminds us how the idea of town development had virtually disappeared in postwar America; it shows us just how low we have allowed our expectations to sink. Seaside has reawakened us to the grand American tradition of planned developments as the legacy of developers with a genius for synthesizing artistic and practical considerations.

In the few remaining moments I would like to put Seaside in a historical perspective—that of the invented American town. I would like to address three such towns built between the Civil War and the Great Depression and then conclude with some recent projects that show how the example of Seaside is helping to transform today's patterns of urban development. The first town is Riverside, Illinois, the brainchild of the developer E.E. Childs. Located nine miles west of Chicago's business district, Riverside was begun in 1869 and has since served as the base-case model for inventive American suburban town design. Childs lifted his strictly for-profit real estate enterprise to the level of environmental art by hiring the planner and landscape architect Frederick Law Olmsted, as well as Olmsted's architect-collaborator Calvert Vaux, to transform a flat, flood-prone, 1,600-acre agricultural site into an elegant suburban town. Olmsted thought that a gridiron plan was "too stiff and formal," but he recognized its value as a logical way of subdividing land for resale. In a brilliant move—one that soon became a planning standard—Olmsted modified the typical right-angle street grid by gently curving it, thereby providing both easily divisible real estate and the illusion

*Fig. 2.* Frederick Law Olmsted and Calvert Vaux, General Plan of Riverside, Illinois, 1869

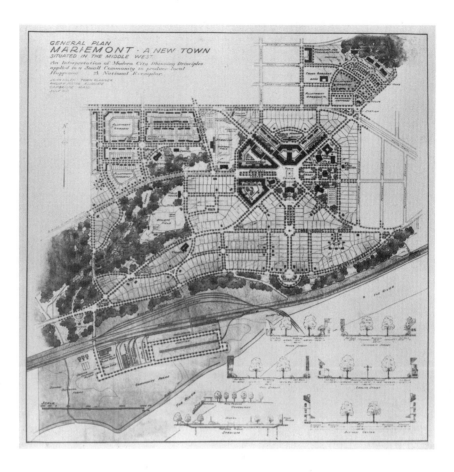

of a town at peace with nature (fig. 2). Childs began Riverside by building a
commercial block and a resort hotel close to the railroad station, signaling his
intention that his town be distinct, lively, and urbane. The hotel, designed by
William LeBaron Jenney in a Swiss chalet style, not only offered a social focus
for the fledgling community, but also introduced visiting urbanites to suburban
town living.

Riverside was a pure expression of the expansion made possible by the railroad age. Fifty years later, Mariemont, outside Cincinnati, Ohio, expressed the
impact of the automobile. Conceived before World War I but only begun in 1921,
Mariemont was developed by Marie Emery, who recognized that the car would
soon become a principal feature of American life. Consequently, Emery and her
town planner, John Nolen, made no effort to integrate the nearby main line of
the Pennsylvania Railroad into the new town. Instead, the plan for Mariemont
called for a formal central square, complete with a city hall, as a culmination to
the axis of the main road leading east from Cincinnati (fig. 3). Nolen established
a careful hierarchy of streets. Diagonal roads leading from the square were to be
lined by shops and apartments, with the more naturalistically planned neighborhoods set beyond. In so many ways, Seaside has learned from Mariemont and
other plans of John Nolen, who in the 1910s and 1920s also gave form to about a
dozen Florida cities.

At the same time that Mariemont was begun, George E. Merrick, who had
made his fortune in Florida by supplying citrus fruit to Miami's expanding hotel

industry, set out to build "a suburb where castles in Spain are made real." Merrick deemed it essential that a dreamlike environment, evoking another time and place, be established. Coral Gables was planned by Merrick's uncle, Denman Fink, and the architect Phineas Paist. Outstanding features included a series of canals and imposing entrance gates and plazas that gave spatial definition to an otherwise monotonous, flat site. Merrick founded the University of Miami to provide a cultural focus for his new town. Most of the town's houses were built in a Spanish Mediterranean style, according to a mandated design code, but Merrick also built individual enclaves based on exotic architectural cultures, including those of China, Dutch South Africa, and France. These villages were not just stylistic whims: each created a neighborhood focus and, more importantly, adapted suburban house planning to higher densities.

Perhaps the most ingenious element of Coral Gables' town design was the transformation of an abandoned pit, from which much of the oolitic limestone used to build the suburb's early houses had been quarried, into the Venetian Pool (fig. 4). A swim club for residents, the pool was equipped with caves, a waterfall, an island, diving boards suspended from towering rock formations, and a miniature sandy beach. Even the pool reflected the mixed values of American urban invention: it functioned not only as a recreational center, but was also a setting for spectacular promotional stunts, in which members of Merrick's army of 3,000 salesmen would hawk his development.

The great tradition of invented towns masterminded by individual entrepreneurs of vision and fortitude virtually disappeared after World War II with the ubiquitous spread of suburban nonplaces that lacked nearly all of the identifying features of the best of their predecessors. Shockingly, until recently, the city planning profession has on the whole supported and even encouraged this uniform pattern of suburban sprawl. Though it remains the dominant pattern of land development, the classic subdivision is at last being challenged, largely as a result of Seaside, by another model—traditional, pre–World War II town design. Though the public has embraced Seaside, those who advocate a return to traditional town planning are frequently dismissed as naive, out-of-touch, socially irresponsible romantics longing for the good old days. We are not. Rather, we are hardheaded professionals who, mixing pragmatism with idealism, recognize

SUBWAY SUBURB

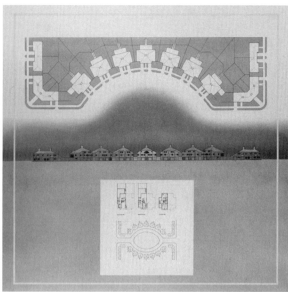

Fig. 5. Robert A.M. Stern
Architects, Subway Suburb
Scheme, 1976–80

Fig. 6. Robert A.M. Stern
Architects, Subway Suburb
Scheme, 1976–80

that the true nature of postindustrial life, experienced so much on the road—both along the strip and on the information highway—makes traditional community living more important than ever.

As an architect, it has been my privilege to participate in, and to some extent, help revive, the tradition of the invented town. I have learned from Andres Duany and Elizabeth Plater-Zyberk, who, while students of Vincent Scully at Yale's School of Architecture, discovered for themselves the rich tradition of American town planning. When Andres worked in my office he helped kindle my interest in our lost urbanism, so that in 1976 I offered a theoretical project titled Subway Suburb as my contribution to the Venice Biennale (figs. 5–6). Immodestly, I believe that Subway Suburb marked the beginning of the effort to turn the tide away from the destructive planning patterns of the postwar era. It put the idea of town-making back inside the town, showing how what had been a suburban phenomenon could be put to work rebuilding the devastated wastelands of inner cities. Subway Suburb proposed to return to the tradition of enclavelike suburbs built within the confines of the city, not as in the nineteenth century, on undeveloped land, but on abandoned land in blighted, marginal areas. In the manner of Coral Gables, the Subway Suburb mixed high-style formal elements such as regency crescents with the vernacular of working-class cottages.

Recently, in collaborating with Jaquelin Robertson and learning so much from Duany and Plater-Zyberk's work, especially here at Seaside, as well as working with so many others, including Ray Gindroz, we have been lucky enough not only to plan a whole town, but also to help see it through to reality. Celebration, Florida, promises to be the largest American planned suburban town ever (fig. 7). We had a great client, The Walt Disney Company, whose head, Michael Eisner, and chief development officer, Peter Rummell, saw an opportunity to do something significant and set an example for development. Celebration draws on some of the most successful American towns—both those that evolved naturally, like East Hampton, Long Island, and Charleston, South Carolina, and those that were invented, like Savannah, Georgia, and Forest Hills Gardens, New York. These

*Fig. 7.* Robert A.M. Stern Architects and Cooper, Robertson & Partners, Celebration, Florida, 1987–97

models were carefully studied and then adapted to the realities of current residential requirements. Rather than a collection of houses sprawled across former farm fields, Celebration, which in its full build-out will have about 20,000 residents and encompass 4,900 acres, is a town with its own compact center, allowing residents to carry out many of the requirements of their daily lives within a short distance of their houses. The downtown incorporates many of the amenities typical of towns, such as a town hall and post office, a comprehensive K-through-twelve school, a bank, a movie theater, and restaurants and stores, above which there are apartments so that there is a twenty-four-hour population.

In addition to master planning the town center and providing detailed architectural design for "background" buildings, our team provided guidelines for special civic buildings that were designed by others to enhance the town's architectural and stylistic variety. Neighborhoods radiate out from the town center in a warped grid plan that allows for easy visitor orientation while creating picturesque views down curved streets. Most streets provide public parallel parking, which in the town center is supplemented by parking lots located at the center of the blocks. Our design extended to the smallest details, including the town's signage. Houses were designed according to a carefully planned "pattern book," which ensured an appropriately southern character to the architecture. And the large backyards endemic to recent housing developments were traded in for small building sites and expansive common spaces that foster a sense of sharing and community (fig. 8).

While Seaside is an invented town powerfully realized as an isolated vacation spot, visitors are now demanding Seaside-like quality back home. So far most of the Seasides and Celebrations have been built on new ground. But I believe that the real challenge is not beyond the edges of cities, but back in the cities themselves. While at first glance the suburb may seem to have hastened the demise of our older cities, I believe it may well help reinvent them. Not every part of every city is Manhattan or the Loop in Chicago or Peachtree Center. The neglected expanses of what was until the 1950s downtown Detroit and St. Louis, and the

In Praise of Invented Towns

*Fig. 8.* Robert A.M. Stern Architects and Cooper, Robertson & Partners, Celebration, Florida, 1987–97

abandoned open lands of New York's fringe areas, such as Brownsville or East New York, or areas of the vast empty wasteland that is so much of Atlanta just beyond its downtown—those are the places where the action must begin. Maybe, just maybe, a few strong-willed entrepreneurs with bold vision will transform the still unexplored wilderness of our urban decay into thriving communities based on the great tradition of the invented town.

# 8

## Landscape and Gardens
### *A Conversation*
#### 1987

*Landscape designer and architectural historian Deborah Nevins and the architect Robert A.M. Stern, who have collaborated on the book* The Architect's Eye *and on various gardens, discuss gardens, education, and collaboration.*

ROBERT A.M. STERN: The broader issue of landscape in the 1950s and '60s was one of ecology, which diminished the traditional role of the garden and the inter-relationship between individual buildings and specific sites. While I think ecology is important and appropriate, the art of garden design—the very special realm of a disciplined and idealized nature that is one of the great privileges of civilized life—had faltered. It could just as well be argued that the art of architecture as a problem of composition and form had faltered during the same period. Architects and landscape architects got overly involved with social planning and entrapped themselves in something called "brutalism," a name all too accurately reflecting the ideas behind it. We have brutalism in the landscape as well as brutalism in the architectural realm, and both deliberately arrived at. Now we are in reaction—at least, I think you and I are in reaction—to that, and that's the jumping-off point of our work.

DEBORAH NEVINS: Contextualism in recent architecture has naturally led to a larger look at the connections between house and garden, building and land-scape. The interest in history and traditional forms has brought a parallel interest in looking anew at landscape, and in so doing rediscovering people who actually started to create a modern landscape in the late nineteenth century.

And in doing that, people have begun to discover the possibilities for garden design, which had been neglected. Until the Depression the garden in America was a focus of interest for the very rich and the middle class. There's a whole literature of garden design books, influenced by people like Gertrude Jekyll, written for the middle class. It was with the Depression that large-scale landscape gardening—and small-scale as well—was rejected, probably because people didn't have the time and money to make those gardens. Now gardens are again becoming the concern of the middle class and not just the very rich.

RAMS: I think the relationship of the building to the landscape is very, very important and was not emphasized enough by the previous generation of architects. In the heyday of the International Style the building was seen as an object in a continuous green space, and the connections were made principally through the building's glass wall. The view to the outdoors was not framed as through a window or door; rather, it was a kind of wallpaper, or fourth wall, to an interior space. That's very different from the notion I think we're interested in today, in which the outside space has the same solid-and-void, room-upon-room quality as the indoor. A person experiences the building and the garden as separate-but-comparable entities.

DN: The idea of closure applies to the house as well. The beauty and definition of the room is sought again, as compared to the open plan. Similarly, why garden rooms are so popular has to do with the twin ideas of containment and separateness from the larger world. We are really creating a kind of Eden of privacy where you foster a community of family and friends. It's also a horticultural Eden with possibilities of great beauty. We need the same thing in the larger public landscape: spatial definition and plants used in extremely beautiful ways.

One person I admire a lot is Dan Kiley. Some of his work—like the Miller residence or the Danby, Vermont, farm—uses very formal arrangements of trees and shrubs and pathways in a nonquotational sense. He defines spaces in a very formal way using appropriate plant material.

RAMS: Well, Kiley uses architectural devices, such as axes. But the problem is that after you've got everything to line up on axes, and you've made a few square cuts in the landscape, just like in architecture, you need more. Composition per se isn't satisfying enough. There is the absence of secondary experiences that syncopate against the main experience or just reinforce it, or sometimes give a little bit of each. Finally, you need to ornament the composition.

Through Kiley's influence, as much as that of anybody else, we have rediscovered the elements of landscape composition. Trees, for example, are wonderful when planted in regular groves, but much more wonderful is the way trees are handled by Le Nôtre, who punctuated his compositions with urns and balustrades, with topiary that emulated shapes out of architecture or nature or both. These devices give you much more to see and to experience.

The problem is that the eye can absorb a tremendous amount of information very quickly, and if you don't give people enough detail to concentrate on they start to put in their own detail. In the case of blank-wall buildings they write graffiti or put posters on them. In the case of gardens, they race through or don't even go into them because they can figure it out from a distance. So it is a matter of recapturing details, decorations, ornament. And I think all of those things are essential to both architectural and landscape design.

DN: Well, I like the use of ornament but it's not all so black and white. Groves of trees, clearings in groves, and hedges can be modulated in a spatial way to articulate the landscape. They are the basic grammar. They can punctuate the landscape as much as ornament, and they can create magical places. For example, you enter the garden at Hidcote and find a single tree on a hedged lawn. The incredible subtlety is that the tree is on a mound with steps leading up to it. The tree is given tremendous monumentality. It's a combination of formalism and archetypal landscape forms. For me, such forms as a clearing, the lone majestic tree, the grove, and the orchard are historical forms. They carry the weight of centuries of man's revering the natural landscape and of his making art of this inspiration.

RAMS: Oh, no question, but then you go from Hidcote's lone tree to the next room, and it has something else with much more detail, and the third and the fourth. It's a whole succession of gardening experiences. But, without those richer, embellished experiences, Hidcote's lone tree in the clearing would not have the magic it does. It's like taking a meal in which you might have a sherbet between two rich courses—it clears the palate or reminds you of primordial things or whatever. But I think you can't build an architecture only on primordial trees in clearings.

DN: No, we need a combination, a resonance of what the most powerful landscapes have. And that's what is interesting about Hidcote. It was designed by a very artistic hand in a very formal way in the twentieth century. Yet there are passages like the one I've described that embody a synthesis of those artistic and formal, man-made and civilized things, as well as a memory of something else. Even with Le Nôtre at Vaux-le-Vicomte there are formally planted woods on the edge of parterres. That's the kind of synthesis I'm looking for.

RAMS: It's all well and good to talk of groves and archaic forms and so forth. I think those *are* the fundamental elements of landscape architecture, just as earth, fire, air, and water could be said to be the fundamental elements of our cosmic being. Finally, it's what you *do* with earth, fire, air, and water. You need more. You need beautiful urns, lovely benches, and stairs.

DN: I agree. But ornament alone, without the fundamental things we've just talked about, creates finicky gardens, which don't give long-term satisfaction.

RAMS: Of course, the great gardens—with a few exceptions—have been ones where the architectural structure has been quite elaborate and the planting has reinforced that.

But I think what I'm saying and what you're saying is the same. The inherent nature of plant materials is one of the challenges. If you want to have flowers at all you can't just scatter all the annuals and perennials that we love, and that nature provides, in the field. They won't grow, they won't survive, and they can't be maintained. So you're forced back into certain conventions, of which the herbaceous border is one. Bedding-out in a kind of square Victorian box is another. The "cultivated" wildflower meadow is a more recent idea. Inevitably one needs some kind of artificial, formalistic convention, unless you want to grow flowers in the greenhouse or the cutting garden.

DN: That's true. Gardening conventions are quite important. At a recent conference of landscape professionals, I showed a big herbaceous border I designed in New England. There was great distress that we would all go back and do "grandmother's gardens"—a style of the past. Well, that's ridiculous. Flowers and plants are never a thing of the past. They are a continuum. They're always there.

But the issue here is bigger than a question of style. It really comes down to formal versus naturalistic. Now naturalistic, of course, is never really like nature—it's all man-made.

RAMS: It's interesting that Le Corbusier, the most articulate spokesman for nonhistoricizing architecture, placed his buildings, and indeed the whole organization of his great city plan of the 1920s, in a formal garden plan. He used known paradigms of garden design as a way to give his buildings setting and context. He arranged those great towers as in a Le Nôtre garden, as though they were great obelisks of privet. The spaces between were filled with what he called English, free, or naturalistic gardens. We use the two major Western types—the classical and the naturalistic.

DN: And you don't have to be a designer who does only one or the other. The issue is expansiveness, in taking the right approach in the right situation and not being afraid to do the grandmother's garden if it's appropriate. It depends on the possibilities, the problem, and the economic resources at hand.

RAMS: I've come to the point in my life where if a client says "I want Georgian," and I can see no real reason why not, I would do it. Georgian is more than a single movement in history; it is, by now, a tradition, a language of architectural expression, part classical, part vernacular. It is an architectural equivalent of a melding of classical landscape with the naturalistic.

DN: In terms of style, too, you see a parallel to what's been happening in architecture, though there are fewer styles in landscape actually, and there isn't so much a battle of the styles. Historical quotation in landscape architecture is very different by the nature of the problem, I think, from that in architecture, where you can see the possibilities of doing a house derived quite closely from a model in the past. For example, to copy exactly a specific garden such as Versailles makes for very bad garden design because every site is so essentially different. It's not a question of *not* using historical models. It's a question of direct quotation making bad landscape design.

RAMS: I think that landscape design seems as much about the use of historical models as architecture. Though it's possible that someone will evolve a new stylistic synthesis in landscape equivalent to the modernist style in architecture, it doesn't seem likely given that such a synthesis in fact didn't come to pass in the modernist era. Garden designers *tried* to effect a new style but really carried on only the naturalistic tradition. Russell Page, at the Festival Gardens in London, came as close as any to a synthesis. Basically, he used plants on the pavement as though making abstract geometric paintings, which is fairly valid, though not very different from classic French parterres or from Victorian bedding-out. But, whereas modernism in architecture had a missionary moralism to it, it's hard to see the same in gardens.

You see, I'm not interested in copying the past but in building upon it, in working as part of a tradition, rather than in ignoring or overthrowing it. The styles exist. None of them make better people. Le Corbusier said if we have more glass and the windows are set horizontally we'll all be better people. Well, that's poppycock. Nobody's any better now, and we may be a certain amount worse. I don't think we should mix the art of architecture with the philosophy of ethics. For me, the styles, including the modernist ones, are modes of *expression*.

Now, discussing styles this way sounds cavalier and trivial to a moralistic modernist, but the real triviality is to think that if you hone in on one stylistic mode for moral reasons that that's going to make more appropriate buildings or make you a responsible, ethical architect—that ideology will carry the day. What will carry the day, finally, is the quality of the work, the intensity with which it's felt, elaborated, and executed.

DN: Exactly. The lesson of the past decade is that one can use both the formalistic and the naturalistic. The previous generation's focus on only the latter would account for the unstructured parks and suburbs we encounter all over.

On the large scale the problem is also maintenance. The place where landscape gardening surely could come back is at the corporate scale in the suburbs. Pepsico, of course, has done that with Russell Page, but there could be a lot more. Corporations could put more attention—and more money—into better landscape design.

RAMS: Well, that realm was fairly well covered, even in the '50s. No, I was thinking of Copley Square in Boston, which, after two competitions, has yet to find what I would describe as a distinguished expression for its possibilities. And I was thinking about what's about to be done to Bryant Park in New York City. It has some functional problems that a few policemen could solve more quickly than anything, yet they're going to mess it up in the name of social planning.

DN: The only problem there is that the trees weren't maintained as they should have been, but the park's old design is wonderful.

RAMS: Last year I worked on a scheme for Pershing Square in Los Angeles (fig. 1). John Wong of SWA made a proposal that, along with four others, was selected in the first stage of an open competition. His plan used very solid classical planning principles. For the second stage he asked us to help elaborate some of the scheme's architectural elements. We worked together in refining and adjusting the plan, and our proposal was extremely popular in public presentation. Finally, an argument was made that all this old stuff of finite spaces and fixed axes was

inappropriate for Los Angeles, which as a place is open and endless. Well, Los
Angeles may be open and endless, but Pershing Square has four gigantic walls
of buildings bounding it. Really, the argument was the same traditional-versus-
modern one that we discussed earlier.

DN: That's exactly the point. I did a competition last year in Houston for the
Sesquicentennial Park (fig. 2). My entry had seventeen small interconnected gardens. There were actually seven prototypes, which were then repeated as very
simple rectangular gardens. It provided small spaces within a large parking lot.
It got to the exhibition stage, but some of the jurists didn't feel it could be
maintained, and that's another popular misconception. I think you certainly can
maintain public gardenlike rooms if the plant material is well considered and not
too elaborate.

RAMS: The maintenance argument is a red herring. Is the cost of maintenance
really the fundamental issue? In our affluent society shouldn't we both conceive
and maintain our landscapes as we do our buildings? Shouldn't landscape architects demand better maintenance?

DN: Absolutely. Landscape architects should also provide the public realm with
more formal and closed spaces, a better range of plant material, and even plant
labels to teach the public about the possibilities of horticulture. Corporations
could use their large landscapes to create arboreta, not as teaching arboreta in a
formal or academic sense, but in a casual way to inform the public more about the
natural palette that gives so much pleasure.

RAMS: Well, I'm nervous about educating people in that sense. I think the real
question is what happens in the schools. Many landscape architecture programs
are involved with only a few parts of the story. There's an awful lot of horticulture and there's an awful lot of ecology and, of course, you can't be a landscape

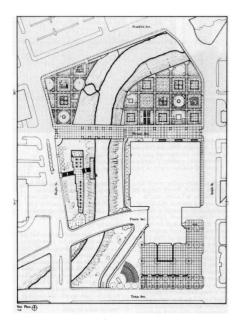

*Fig. 2.* Deborah Nevins, Site plan, Entry for the Sesquicentennial Park Competition, Houston, Texas, 1985

designer without a command of your materials. But where is the part about design, real detail design? How does one put steps and walls and all the small elements together to make a garden or a park? Architecture schools are by no means faultless. How, in fact, *does* the building adjust to the site? Architects are suddenly interested in gardens but only in a kind of abstract pattern-making way, and there's too little knowledge of the elements.

DN: Recently I went to a symposium on botanical gardens, and a professor of landscape architecture from an Ivy League university talked about a garden designed by a former student. It was very expensive—the client spent perhaps $100,000 for a small suburban house. There were paths in the garden but they didn't go anywhere. Upon asking why, the professor was told, "There wasn't enough money."

The point is that the first concern should be spatial organization. Students have got to be taught that lesson in better ways than they are at the moment. I think also the problem with landscape architecture has been that the schools not only haven't emphasized the attitude that we're talking about, but there's very little emphasis on history other than a sort of large-scale history. I think most landscape architects don't know who Ellen Shipman and Warren Manning were. They're just learning who Beatrix Farrand and Gertrude Jekyll were. Students are incredibly uninformed about their own profession. For the landscape architecture student to be taught more about the history and principles of architecture will make landscapes better structured than we've often seen. I think—I hope—that's changing. Certainly architects are getting more interested in landscape, which will help foster collaboration.

RAMS: In the old days, when the Beaux-Arts philosophy held sway over American schools, there were joint projects between architects and sculptors and painters. Of course, the sculptors and painters were expected to be decorative, and this is once again becoming possible. There are now artists—even those working in modernist modes—who are willing to sublimate their art to a larger scheme of things. There were also joint projects between architects and landscape architects, and this collaboration was intended as a model for future professional work. Such a collaboration continues to be fruitful. In our office, building and setting are conceived of as complementary.

DN: I know some big design firms have landscape departments, but I wonder if they really try to serve some kind of collaboration between disciplines. Or is it just a landscape architect putting down enough trees to satisfy local authorities?

RAMS: I think the nature of their architectural work is such that the kind of landscape we're talking about and the kind of attitude toward public space we're talking about is very alien. I worry much more that people don't have any *ideas* about gardens. Also, I'm not sure architects and landscape architects know how to work together anymore, because often I've found that potential collaborators from landscape architecture wished to impose certain a priori ideas about how the garden would relate to our buildings. Frequently this was a result of my having moved toward a more classicizing and historicizing mode and their being in some kind of modernist twilight zone. Somehow the landscape architect believes the landscape should have its own life outside the building. Now, maybe that's also from the twilight zone in which the building was the objectlike "figure" and the landscape was the "ground." These things are very complicated.

The great model of collaboration between architect and landscape designer in our century was that of Sir Edwin Lutyens and Gertrude Jekyll. There is the example of Beatrix Farrand as well, who could work at Princeton under Ralph Adams Cram and at Yale under James Gamble Rogers and manage to produce gardens that always seemed to be almost inevitable and absolutely of the place.

DN: That's exactly Farrand's brilliance. There are two reasons why she was forgotten. One is that she never wrote anything except at the outset of her career—an article published in *Scribner's* in 1906. The other is that her brilliance was understatement: the magic of her spatial planning, her knowledge of horticulture, and her ability to make spaces that seemed so right that one doesn't sense immediately "the great artistic hand."

RAMS: Well, the amazing thing about a place like Gothic Yale is not only that the buildings look like they were there for hundreds of years, but the landscape also looks like it's been around for hundreds of years. And it looks sort of totally undone. Just there. That's what the whole thing is about, isn't it?

DN: Well, she wasn't a humble person, I tell you.

RAMS: Oh, I'm sure she wasn't. Only arrogant people can have the confidence to do something modestly, because they know who they are. They don't have to impose their self-justification on others.

DN: There are passages in her letters about using certain vines and methods to accent the architecture and not obscure or cover it. In other words, she built with the architect.

RAMS: Of course there were architects who provided the armature, which invited the best collaboration with the landscape architect. As in all things, it's a two-edged sword. Any genuine collaboration has to begin with a clear understanding of who does what and then a sense that whoever does one thing is not more important than the other person.

DN: I think landscape architects know what landscape architects do, but in terms of collaboration there could be a problematic situation. For instance, who designs the steps down from the terrace?

RAMS: The architect.

DN: No, it could also be the landscape architect. There at least has to be a meshing of sensibilities between the collaborators for the thing to work. That is where the role of spatial planning comes in. Both have to tie together and work together. Part of the fear of landscape architects, in response to what you've just said, is being put in the role of only providing trees and bushes.

RAMS: If the designer is insecure then he thinks that. You have enough time in your life either to be insecure or to be a designer. You can't be both. You have to know that you're part of the whole thing, the final product. You want to get credit for your efforts, of course, both for your ego and for financial survival, but if the thing is successful—and successful in all its parts—everybody shares in the glory because they shared in the conception. Only a fool goes around saying I did those steps and Dick or Jane did those plants.

Another problem occurs when people don't collaborate regularly. Then each time it's a totally new educational process. It's easier to collaborate on a regular basis. Obviously it's quite nice to have people in your home base who have different areas of expertise. We've long had our own interior design section, for instance.

DN: And now you have landscape architecture.

RAMS: Yes. With larger planning projects—suburban developments—we work with SWA. Their attitude is very good, but we still have interesting conversations when we get to the more specific elements of the design of these larger projects. The two people I've worked with most, Rick Lamb and John Wong, have been at the American Academy in Rome. Both have a richness of vocabulary and a sense of the historical possibilities of landscape design, which is not typical of many other landscape architects we know.

DN: In terms of the whole profession, though, I think a synthesis is evolving in landscape architecture that tries to bring some of these ideas, formulas and spatial organizations into a usable vocabulary for today. Still, there is the reaction to people doing herbaceous borders, traditional gardens, and so forth. It is a familiar mind-set. What we need is the courage to draw upon all the available modes of expression.

# 9

## The Fall and Rise of New York
### *Trends and Travesties in the Service of Community Pride*
#### 1987

"Ford to New York: Drop Dead." So ran the *Daily News* headline reporting the federal government's refusal to bail the city out of its fiscal crisis in 1975—arguably marking the city's psychological as well as economic nadir in its 350-year history. With New York teetering on the brink of default, the rest of the nation seemed unmoved, perhaps even gleeful.

In this tale of economic collapse, New York was hardly blameless. During the three decades following World War II, the city, self-importantly intoxicated by its role as a world capital and confident in its limitless ability to meet, and pay for, every public want, from the most basic—education—to the most absurd—comfort stations for dogs—squandered its capital, blindly ignoring the realities of its transformed demographics. For almost a hundred years it had prospered as a clearly defined and unified metropolis, a virtual city-state. Now, in an era of urban decentralization, it was but one focus among many in a megalopolis that sprawled from Washington, D.C.'s Virginia suburbs to the borders of New Hampshire. Decentralization, nurtured in the economically depressed 1930s as a way to rationalize and humanize the hyper-urbanism of the industrial era, transformed the tri-state area of the New York region into a vast sprawling suburbia that had very nearly drained the lifeblood of the central city. New York need not drop dead; it was already semicomatose and seriously in danger of gradually, if not necessarily peacefully, slipping away.

But just when the nation seemed content to watch the city expire, not so much with a bang as with a whimper, New York rallied. Typically, ballyhoo preceded real growth. Capitalizing on the city's greatest asset, its rich cultural bank account, New York State waged an advertising campaign mostly on the city's behalf, calling upon the professional men and women who sang, danced, wrote, painted, and fielded fly balls to boost morale and tourism by singing a syncopated, wacky, memorable musical one-liner: "I love New York."

The summer of 1976, with its elaborate Bicentennial celebrations, marked a turning point in New York's ability to convince the rest of the country that not only was it not dead, it was also not hopelessly corrupt or cynical—that in fact, New York was as American as the stars and stripes. In that long summer of regeneration, New York welcomed the world's tall ships into its harbor with weather and setting conspiring to create the single most memorable event of all the nation's Bicentennial celebrations. Then the city hosted the National Democratic Convention, placing itself on the center stage of the presidential political arena at the critical moment when politicians for the first time felt themselves free of the divisive, tragic events of the Vietnam War era. Buoyed by the summer of 1976, a "new New York" began to emerge. Concurrent with an upswing of the city's mood was an inspired critical assessment of the architecture and urbanism of its most famous borough. In his book, *Delirious New York: A Retroactive Manifesto for Manhattan*, the Dutch architect Rem Koolhaas celebrated Manhattan not merely as a prized piece of real estate or a triumph of commerce over convenience, but as a "laboratory: a mythical island where the invention and testing of a metropolitan lifestyle and its attendant architecture could be pursued as a collective experiment in which the entire city became a factory of man-made experience."[1] *Delirious New York* was a European's imaginative, passionate tribute to the city, which would, as its author stated, "inevitably . . . be read against the torrent of negative analyses that emanates from Manhattan about Manhattan."[2] For jaded New Yorkers, Koolhaas's book was a real shot in the arm and proof that at least in the eyes of some observers, the Big Apple was not rotten to its core.

New York's optimism was not, however, merely a matter of hype or imagination. A new city government, under the leadership of Mayor Edward I. Koch, elected in the fall of 1977, drastically cut back services in order to balance the books. This was not a task that was likely to win the mayor friends, but Koch executed it effectively and even with a measure of wit, continually asking his constituency, "How am I doing?" Koch was not only ideologically but also temperamentally well-suited for the job, almost reveling in the role of municipal Scrooge.

Real economic changes stimulated a turnaround of the city's fortunes. Serious efforts were made to hold on to what the city had: corporations, including AT&T, were offered tax abatements on new construction as motivation to maintain operations in New York; renovated housing was also encouraged by the J-51 program, which granted tax exemptions from increases in assessed valuation. But most importantly, New York benefited from circumstances outside its control: the world political situation grew increasingly unstable and as never before investment of capital from foreign sources flowed into the United States, and into New York in particular, because for most foreigners New York exemplified the United States and because foreigners felt comfortable in its cosmopolitan atmosphere. While a large share of investment was from Western Europe, New York was also attractive to the third world; it was particularly favored by the Marcos family of the Philippines, who gobbled up and improved some of the city's choicest real estate.

The Fall and Rise of New York

New York, which had suffered the loss of 600,000 manufacturing jobs between 1946 and 1976, also capitalized on the nationwide economic shift away from manufacturing and toward such areas as publishing, advertising, merchandising and marketing, the arts, and education. When Herbert Bienstock, the regional commissioner in the Federal Bureau of Labor Statistics, asserted in 1976 that New York was a "mighty lively corpse," uniquely prepared to utilize massive corporate investments as it was already the "undisputed center of the nation's knowledge-oriented industries,"[3] a lot of people sat up and took notice. Furthermore, New York's relatively compact size and its superb public transportation system made it particularly attractive to corporations and commuters who had become painfully aware of fuel costs during the "energy crisis" following the Arab oil embargo of 1973–74.

For New York's revival to be complete, it had to renew itself, not only as a productive and stimulating place to work, but as a compelling place to live. Though the city's economic future was far from certain, demographers observed a trend toward the reverse migration of affluent suburbanites back into the inner city. All at once, it seemed, residential neighborhoods throughout the city, particularly in Manhattan and Brooklyn, began to take on new luster: rundown Columbus Avenue transformed itself into the Rue de la Quiche; what had been Gowanus or South Brooklyn became Cobble Hill; and a new word was coined: *gentrification.*

The housing supply fell so far short of demand, however, that at least in Manhattan it was possible to sell practically anything in the way of shelter at virtually any price; this situation showed no relief until the mid-1980s when the curtailment of an abatement program designed to stimulate new residential construction resulted in a glut of apartment buildings in Manhattan that were hastily undertaken to slip in under the gun. For the most part these new apartment towers were nondescript. The pretensions of their names—L'Isola, The Corinthian, The Monarch—belied the grim banalities of their undifferentiated massing, the unornamented bleakness of their facades, and barren, inhospitable plazas grudgingly provided in order to cash in on development bonuses. A few of the new buildings rose above the mass of dreary designs, but the aesthetic heights they achieved were not very lofty. One positive trend was the provision of apartments in Manhattan suitable for family living, with a few buildings actually trying to reproduce, albeit at a reduced scale, the rational planning and elegant proportions of typical pre–World War II apartment houses. Beyer Blinder Belle's 60 East Eighty-eighth Street (1987) and Kohn Pedersen Fox's 188 East Seventieth Street (1986) are probably the most successful, combining sound planning with a massing and facades that convincingly pick up on the vernacular classicism of the pre–World War II glory days of inventive traditionalism. Two apartment buildings, The Gruzen Partnership's Memphis Uptown at 303 East Sixtieth Street (1987) and Rothzeid, Kaiserman, Thomson & Bee's Memphis Downtown at 140 Charles Street (1986), exploit the "avant-garde" Italian design trend of the early 1980s with awkward rather than provocative designs.

The most positive news to be found in the housing field was the transformation of many rental buildings into cooperatives and condominiums, stabilizing neighborhoods and encouraging the kind of continuing reinvestment hitherto reserved only for single-family houses in the outer boroughs and the suburbs. Sometimes the upgrading of existing housing had mixed results. This was particularly true in the case of single-room occupancy buildings that were remodeled into attractive apartments, providing housing for the affluent but displacing, and often leaving homeless, the poor, elderly, and mentally ill.

At the same time that the city's housing stock was improved, whole new categories of buildings were adapted to residential use. Outmoded manufacturing and warehousing loft districts in Lower Manhattan became the fashionable residential neighborhoods of SoHo and Tribeca. A case could be made for the loft buildings as incubators of new business and as centers for low-skilled employment, particularly on the edge of Chinatown, where new garment factories run by recent Hispanic and Asian immigrants recalled the long-departed but not necessarily regretted "sweat shop" operations run by Eastern European Jews and Italians once housed in the same buildings. It is clear, however, that lofts have proven far more productive for the city's new role as a service and culture center, providing places for artists, who pioneered them in the late 1960s, and then by the mid-1970s, as residences for young professionals and business people, better known as yuppies. The success of the loft conversion trend opened up other architecturally significant, outmoded building types for residential use. Older office buildings containing small floors, such as 55 Liberty Tower (Henry Ives Cobb, 1910; restoration and apartment conversion by Joseph Pell Lombardi, 1981), downtown on Liberty Street, make dandy apartment houses, helping to transform the financial district into a round-the-clock neighborhood for the first time in over a hundred years.

Most of the new housing stock is pricey. Middle- and low-income New Yorkers do not fare well, even in the outer boroughs, where very little is being done to stop the decay of older residential neighborhoods. A notable exception to this is the redevelopment of Charlotte Street in the middle of the burned-out South Bronx. An international symbol of the nation's failure to come to grips with its urban problems, the Charlotte Street neighborhood, like others in the outer boroughs, was abandoned and left to ruin by a lower-middle class fleeing to the suburbs. For almost two decades, American politicians visited Charlotte Street with promises to rebuild, but nothing was done. This was probably all right, because the prevailing model for urban redevelopment in the 1950s and 1960s, the tower-in-the-park, was a proven failure sustained only by an unspoken conspiracy between intractably idealistic architect-planners who clung to the theories of the 1920s and 1930s and elected officials who were unwilling to surrender to the urban poor the sacred symbol of white middle-class status, the single-family house on a green suburban lot. Edward Logue changed all this when, in 1983, as president of the South Bronx Development Organization, he trucked in prefabricated, Levittown-style ranch houses to create a suburban enclave called Charlotte Gardens (fig. 1). Though the architecture was banal at best, and the failure to recognize the fundamental misfit between a metropolitan street grid and a typically stretched out ranch house was ludicrous, Charlotte Gardens nonetheless represented a sincere effort to rebuild the outer boroughs of the city, not as an extension of Manhattan, but as a collection of distinct residential neighborhood enclaves comparable to those near ideal developments of the pre-Depression era such as Prospect Park South in Brooklyn, and Sunnyside or Forest Hills Gardens, both in Queens.

Landmark designation helped stabilize neighborhoods in the outer boroughs, including parts of Bedford-Stuyvesant in Brooklyn, which had suffered great

devastation in the 1950s and 1960s. Landmarking also fostered some interesting, new, and very expensive suburban housing. In Riverdale, thirty-three new houses, constituting Delafield Estates (1980–88), were designed by James Stewart Polshek and Partners to surround Edward Delafield's mansion, Fieldston Hill. On Staten Island, the Ernest Flagg House, landmarked in 1967, stimulated the development of a new residential enclave, Copperflagg (1983–89), which was designed by Robert A.M. Stern Architects.

In Manhattan landmarking similarly proved itself to be not only a stabilizing factor but an economic stimulant. On the Upper East Side, which was designated a historic district in 1981, a new type of apartment house, the sliver tower, was born in response to a market that would pay almost anything to live amidst the district's charms. But the sliver, which developed a single building lot to its maximum FAR, was challenged as a disruption to the neighborhood scale and eventually outlawed. One proposed sliver tower, designed by Diana Agrest and Mario Gandelsonas for 20–22 East Seventy-first Street, was a distinguished design, but it was blocked as an imposition on its landmark neighborhood. Most of the sliver towers that were built were dull or mindless or both.

While the city was developed and redeveloped as a place to live, it was as a place to work that a "new New York" was most fully realized. After decades in which bland, glass and metal curtain-walled high-rises dominated the skyline, turning the mountain range of soaring towers from the 1920s and 1930s into a mesa of flat-topped mediocrity, the skyscraper reasserted itself as the preeminent architectural symbol of municipal pride. Hugh Stubbins' Citicorp Building marks the critical turning point (fig. 2). The first major corporate skyscraper to be built since the recession of the early 1970s had abruptly ended the building boom of the 1960s, its construction between 1976 and 1978 began as an act of faith in the city's capacity to rise from its own ashes. As built, however, Citicorp's attitude to the city was, at best, wary; the building's obsessive internalization of services was a frankly anti-urban gesture. Ground-level stores turned their backs on the street and faced an interior court that, although a lively gathering place, functioned

more like a suburban mall than an active participant in the urban drama. St. Peter's Church had sold its site to the bank and was promised a new building as a part of the new complex. The new St. Peter's Church, however, was overwhelmed by the swaggering sixty-story, aluminum-clad tower that rose above it on four, 127-foot-high legs, a reiteration of an old story of New York real estate, wherein Mammon, not God, triumphs (fig. 3). Citicorp's unornamented, contextually undifferenti-ated, slick, thin-skinned, strip-windowed facades reflected what was by the late 1970s a traditional modernist approach. Even the building's great ski jump-like, diagonally pitched roof, conceived of as part of a solar heating system that was ultimately scrapped because of technical problems, and then for a while intended to house apartments, succeeded as a bold, skyline-enhancing, corporate advertise-ment, a symbol for Citicorp and for New York's rebirth.

The AT&T Building (1978–84), though smaller, went much further toward exhibiting the major tendencies of architecture that began to emerge in the late 1960s—the tendencies that are popularly described as "postmodernist"—tenden-cies that at the basic level mandated an architecture that resumes its traditional responsibility to represent ideas beyond those of functional accommodation and constructional reality (fig. 2). Whereas the designer of Citicorp seems to have cre-ated a skyscraper icon almost inadvertently, Philip Johnson and John Burgee set out deliberately to create a symbolically charged corporate monument that would pick up where the skyscrapers of the golden age of the 1920s left off. Restoring a sense of narrative to the architecture of the city, AT&T pointed the way toward a renewed vision of New York as a man-made mountain range of symbolic tow-ers. A modernist slab cloaked in overtly historicist forms, the AT&T Building was ordered as a column with a base, shaft, and capital. With its pedimented top, punc-tuated by a vapor-filled oculus, AT&T recalled the aspirational quality that had characterized an earlier generation's swaggering skyscraper designs. And while the management of AT&T eschewed as undignified the life-giving commercialism of Citicorp's shopping mall, its grandly scaled street-level loggia nonetheless provided a sheltered space for brown-bagging New Yorkers to enjoy their lunch breaks.

*Fig. 2.* Midtown looking east: Der Scutt, Trump Tower, 1983; Philip Johnson & John Burgee, AT&T Building (now Sony Tower), 1978–84; Hugh Stubbins & Associates, Citicorp Center (now Citigroup Center), 1976–78

*Fig. 3.* Hugh Stubbins & Associates, St. Peter's Church at Citicorp Center, 1978

The Fall and Rise of New York

*Fig. 4.* Edward Larrabee
Barnes, 535 Madison
Avenue, 1982

*Fig. 5.* Philip Johnson
& John Burgee, 33 Maiden
Lane, 1984–86

*Fig. 6.* Murphy/Jahn,
Park Avenue Tower, 1987

*Fig. 7.* Philip Johnson
& John Burgee, 53rd and
Third (Lipstick Building),
1986–87

Suddenly, "designer architecture" was big news in a way it had not been since the glory days of the late 1920s. Philip Johnson glowered from *Time* magazine's January 8, 1979, cover, clutching a model of AT&T, and the developer Donald Trump propelled himself into the media limelight with a tower of such stupendous vulgarity that only hard-core puritans could not but secretly love it (fig. 2). The developer George Klein was the first in New York to bring a regular line of "designer buildings" to the speculative market, carving out a special niche for his Park Tower Realty Corporation by erecting a series of relatively small office buildings that, by virtue of their individuality—personality, one is tempted to say— contribute a measure of richness and variety to the streetscape virtually absent in the postwar modernist era, which preferred to wrap its typical buildings in the architectural equivalent of plain vanilla. The art gallery of Manhattan's streets is immeasurably enriched by Klein's almost seasonal collection, consisting of I.M. Pei and Partners' 499 Park Avenue (1981), Edward Larrabee Barnes Associates' 535 Madison Avenue (1982) (fig. 4), Johnson and Burgee's Federal Reserve Building at 33 Maiden Lane (1984–86) (fig. 5), Murphy/Jahn's Park Avenue Tower at 65 East Fifty-fifth Street (1987) (fig. 6), and Kevin Roche John Dinkeloo and Associates' Morgan Bank at 60 Wall Street. It is said that Klein was inspired by the Texas developer Gerald Hines, who has been credited with inventing the so-called "signature building" in Houston and who has brought his talents to New York, where his firm is responsible for two buildings completed in 1987, Johnson and Burgee's oval tower at Fifty-third Street and Third Avenue, popularly known as the Lipstick Building (fig. 7), and Kevin Roche John Dinkeloo and Associates' E.F. Hutton Building on Fifty-third Street between Fifth and Sixth avenues.

Now, a decade after the design of the AT&T Building began, skyscrapers are being built or proposed all over town that attempt to recapture the romantic, dizzying, skyward trend of the 1920s: Fox and Fowle's proposed office complex, South Ferry Plaza, is capped by a domed tower intended to serve as a symbolic lighthouse for the harbor at Manhattan's tip; if realized, Kohn Pedersen Fox's proposed building at 383 Madison Avenue will bring to Midtown a soaring Egyptoid tower taller than the Chrysler Building; Helmut Jahn's vaguely Moorish CitySpire, rising adjacent to the City Center theater, rekindles the city's romance with skyscraper living as it creates a memorably modeled silhouette (fig. 8).

While most people welcome the alternatives the best new buildings offer to the blandness of the postwar era, the price for that variety of shape, richness of surface, and amenity has, as often as not, been bonuses offered by the city to developers, bonuses that permit additional height or mass or both, bonuses that have raised questions about density and the city's capacity to absorb the crowds these buildings bring with them. As welcome as the current building boom may be in both artistic and economic terms, the overriding concern has become density: is New York simply overbuilding itself? While this question will, and no doubt should, be rigorously investigated and debated, it raises another question: is congestion itself a problem? In the 1920s, architects such as Harvey Wiley Corbett celebrated what has come to be known as the "cult of congestion," arguing that it was a principal ingredient in New York's vital urbanism. The challenge, Corbett argued, was not to limit high-density development but to find effective methods of adapting traditional urbanism to the new scale. In his book about New York, Rem Koolhaas exulted in that tradition, stating, "Manhattanism is the one urbanistic ideology that has fed, from its conception, on the splendors and miseries of the metropolitan condition—hyper-density—without once losing faith in it as the basis for a desirable modern culture. *Manhattan's architecture is a paradigm for the exploitation of congestion.*"[4] Perhaps the question to ask is not how much should we build, but how well can we build, for isn't the propensity to pack as much as possible into a small space the quintessence of New York? As debate over the issue of density continues, the seemingly insatiable hunger for developable land in Manhattan has focused attention on the potential of existing buildings' air rights. Particularly controversial have been attempts to build high-rise projects above low-rise landmark buildings or, through the transfer of air rights, on an adjacent property; these projects necessitate the approval of the Landmarks Preservation Commission and often become issues hotly debated among both professionals and a general public increasingly protective of the city's architectural heritage. In 1975, the Landmarks Preservation Commission's approval paved the way for Emery Roth and Sons' fifty-one-story Helmsley Palace Hotel, which rose in 1980 as an uninspired, but not altogether malevolent, glass and metal behemothic backdrop for McKim, Mead & White's Villard Houses of 1882 (fig. 9). The remodeled townhouse grouping's schizophrenic

*Fig. 8.* Murphy/Jahn, CitySpire, 1987

*Fig. 9.* Emery Roth & Sons, Helmsley Palace Hotel (now New York Palace Hotel), 1980

*Fig. 10.* Attia & Perkins, Republic National Bank Tower (now HSBC Bank Tower), 1981–83

fate as a modest home for the Architectural League and other civic-minded groups, and as the garishly decorated lobby and public rooms of the Helmsley Palace Hotel, perfectly reflects the city's mixed priorities. Far less smilingly, the nearly incoherent architectural hodgepodge that constituted Attia and Perkins' expanded Republic National Bank headquarters of 1983 saved, but practically swallowed, the robustly classical Knox Building of 1902, which stands on the southwest corner of Fifth Avenue and Fortieth Street (fig. 10).

In some cases the transfer of air rights left the landmark building untouched and resulted in projects that enhanced the architectural context. The heavy masonry construction of Johnson and Burgee's twenty-six-story building at 33 Maiden Lane entered into a lively architectural dialogue with its distinguished neighbor, York & Sawyer's Federal Reserve Building of 1924. Similarly, Helmut Jahn's CitySpire picks up on themes established by the landmark City Center (1922–24). Cesar Pelli's Carnegie Hall Tower appears as an extension of the adjacent music hall, with similar massing, coloration, and exterior building materials. To the east of Pelli's tower, the situation is not so harmonious. The sheer black glass facade of Metropolitan Tower (1987), an inert minimalist mass built by the developer Harry Macklowe, forms half of a monolithic "Russian Tea Room sandwich," with the "hold out" townhouse owned by the famous restaurant in the middle.

The most controversial and widely documented air-rights case has been that of an office tower designed by Edward Durell Stone Associates proposed to replace the community house of the Byzantine-inspired St. Bartholomew's Church on Park Avenue between Fiftieth and Fifty-first streets. The proposal was denied approval by the Landmarks Preservation Commission in 1985. Following subsequent failed attempts, argued on the basis of economic hardship, to reverse the landmark ruling, the church filed a suit against the city challenging the landmark law's constitutionality; the suit is currently in litigation.[5] Other congregations face similar situations. The Church of St. Paul and St. Andrew, located on the northeast corner of West End Avenue and Eighty-sixth Street, was designated a landmark in 1981 after plans for its demolition were announced. The church, facing rising operating costs and dwindling attendance, was refused a hearing to consider reversal of its landmark status by the New York State Supreme Court and is currently considering renewed challenges.

One ineluctable fact of the day is that the ahistorical and anti-urbanistic modernism of the postwar era now seems very old hat. As popular and professional tastes change, the leading exemplars of the previous generation's taste—buildings of landmark quality that are not yet the requisite thirty years old to be designated landmarks—are threatened with destruction or stylistically inappropriate renovation. The indiscriminate and usually mindless renovation of modernist buildings is only beginning to have its effect. Often it is of no consequence—one banality is much the same as another. But occasionally work of real distinction, or at least historical significance, is altered. While it is difficult to decide whether the austere original lobbies of Walter Gropius, Pietro Belluschi, and Emery Roth and Sons' Pan Am Building of 1963 were significant, or significantly bad, surely the kitsch of the 1986–87 installation by Warren Platner is hardly a notable model of current taste.

More chillingly, in 1983 New Yorkers were caught up short by the news that Lever House, the landmark building of 1952 designed by Skidmore, Owings &

Merrill, with Gordon Bunshaft serving as chief designer, was slated for destruction. One of the first fully realized glass and metal curtain-wall structures, with significant urbanistic implications, Lever House was to be replaced by a forty-story tower that would more effectively exploit the economic potential of its block-long site on Park Avenue. The situation was complex: Fisher Brothers, who had commissioned Swanke Hayden Connell to design the replacement, owned the site; the developer George Klein owned the building itself; the Lever Brothers Company, which had originally owned the building and vigorously opposed its destruction, remained the principal occupant. Further complicating matters was the fact that the designation of Lever House as a landmark, which had been authorized by the Landmarks Preservation Commission the preceding year, when the building became thirty years old, was awaiting final approval by the Board of Estimate. Amidst pleas for the building's survival from architects of all stylistic bents, as well as from the general public, approval was ultimately granted, and a sympathetic building on the adjoining lot has been designed by Kevin Roche John Dinkeloo and Associates but not realized.

*Fig. 11.* Museum of Modern Art façade: Cesar Pelli & Associates, west wing, 1985; Philip L. Goodwin and Edward Durell Stone, original building, 1939; Philip Johnson, east wing, 1964

Recently, alterations to two key buildings have been proposed, raising hackles among die-hard modernists and preservationists alike. The trustees of the Guggenheim Museum, completed to designs by Frank Lloyd Wright in 1959, and the Whitney Museum, completed to designs by Marcel Breuer and Hamilton Smith in 1966, have both initiated plans for major expansions, spurred on, in part, by the 1976 decision of the trustees of the city's third major museum devoted to contemporary art, the Museum of Modern Art, to greatly expand its facilities. As initially designed by Cesar Pelli, the Museum of Modern Art intended to erase all external vestiges of its original Philip Goodwin and Edward Durell Stone museum building (1939) and of Philip Johnson's addition of 1964, clothing both of them in the same skin intended for the new wing and the residential tower rising above it. This act of historical vandalism was abandoned after it was widely criticized by preservationists and architects, and the gallery of the city's streets is much the richer for the juxtaposition of modes that now characterizes the complex's collective façade (fig. 11).

A more harmonious marriage of the recently modern with the historically modern was effected at 500 Park Avenue, Skidmore, Owings & Merrill's elegantly minimalist, twelve-story, glass and aluminum building, originally built in 1960 for the Pepsi-Cola Company and later owned by Olivetti. Threatened with destruction, it was saved by the transfer of air rights to an adjoining lot and the subsequent construction of James Stewart Polshek and Partners' contextually sensitive forty-story, granite- and metal-clad office and condominium tower (1986). A less distinguished but nonetheless notable building, Harrison and Abramovitz's C.I.T. Building of 1957, at 650 Madison Avenue, is not being treated so respectfully. Not only is the mid-rise building being surmounted by a towering addition by the firm of Fox and Fowle, but what was once a skillful, innovative essay in black glass is being resurfaced in fairly ordinary reflective green glass.

The loss of monuments from the recent past is not always a cause for concern. The proposed destruction of Charles Luckman's Madison Square Garden of 1968, which itself tragically replaced McKim, Mead & White's masterpiece, Pennsylvania Station, has elicited no cries of protest, only prayers that its replacement will be an improvement. While new buildings and recycled buildings

gave tangible form to New York's revitalization, the city's increased prosperity also brought to life old projects that had slumbered with the city during the 1970s. Conceived of in the 1960s, when such projects as South Street Seaport and the Marriott Marquis Hotel were finally completed in the mid-1980s they seemed caught in a time warp. As developed by the Rouse Corporation, Phase I and Phase II of the Seaport were completed in 1983 and 1985 respectively; by then the "Rouseification" of America was so complete that the Seaport's mix of urban architectural history and suburban shopping mall ambiance seemed formulaic and but a weak echo of developments in other cities (fig. 12). For the first time in a century, New York seemed a pale reflection of Boston, where the Rouseified Faneuil Hall Markets had been open since 1976. John Portman's Marriott Marquis in Times Square similarly seemed out of step with the rest of the city's growth (fig. 13). By the time the hotel was completed in 1985, Portman's unabashedly glitzy, soaring interior spaces, which he had pioneered in the Hyatt Regency Hotel in Atlanta in 1967, and had perfected to the point of parody in his Detroit Plaza Hotel of 1977, seemed passé and provincial. On the street, the hotel, envisioned as part of a massive renewal of Times Square, was a brutal fortress, an isolated bastion of maximum respectability defending Aunt Maude, if not necessarily Uncle Lem, from the naughty, bawdy, gaudy charms of the city's most democratic public place.

Super-scale projects currently promise to change the city still further. Skidmore, Owings & Merrill's not too modestly titled Worldwide Center will cover the entire square block of the old Madison Square Garden site, cleared in the 1960s and left vacant for two decades. Moshe Safdie's twin towers for Boston Properties on the site of the New York Coliseum facing Columbus Circle, proposed to rise fifty-eight and sixty-eight stories, are a curiously leaden version of Hollywood's vision of the Emerald City, awkwardly placed amidst the real-life Oz of Manhattan.

The ongoing development of Battery Park City, a 92-acre city-within-a-city built on landfill in the Hudson River alongside the World Trade Center, proves that large-scale projects need not transform New York into a Brobdingnagian urban nightmare. As planned by the urban design firm of Cooper/Eckstut Associates, Battery Park City stands in marked contrast to earlier schemes for the

landfill site that eschewed existing urban models in favor of towers-in-the-park, but ended up, more often than not, as towers randomly scattered like so much litter amidst treeless concrete plazas. As planned, Battery Park City builds upon New York's architectural and urban past to create a vital old-new place: lining an orderly arrangement of streets and small parklike squares, carefully articulated apartment buildings by leading New York practitioners, including James Stewart Polshek and Partners and Ulrich Franzen and Associates, as well as the internationally acclaimed architect Charles Moore, who worked in association with the firm of Rothzeid, Kaiserman, Thomson & Bee, attempt to rival, or at least to echo, the best residential architecture of the 1920s and 1930s (fig. 14). A grand riverside esplanade recalls earlier waterfront promenades such as that at Carl Schurz Park. Though the quality of the individual buildings is less than those they seek to emulate, the ensemble is a notable success, bringing to the new New York the scale, architecture, and ambiance of a genuine neighborhood that grew up over time, rather than of a sterile, forever-new development. To the north of the residential area, Cesar Pelli's World Financial Center provides offices for 30,000 employees while also giving essential public amenities to the city, including the nobly proportioned Winter Garden, a glass-enclosed, temperature-controlled town square realized at metropolitan scale (fig. 15).

Much further north, stretching from Fifty-ninth to Seventy-second Street along the Hudson River, the site of the former Penn Central rail yards stands empty, awaiting the development by Donald Trump of a vast project called Television City. An initial proposal by the architect Helmut Jahn calling for seven skyscrapers towering above acres of open space was abandoned following strong indications that it would not be granted city approval. Trump then replaced Jahn with Alexander Cooper who, as he had done at Battery Park City, adopted elements of the existing city, notably the canyonlike continuities of Park Avenue. But the sheer size and density of the project, though reduced from the original proposal, remains staggering: Television City will include 7,600 apartments, a vast shopping mall complete with suburban-scale parking facilities, and the world's tallest building. How ingeniously Cooper can translate the metropolitanism of an earlier era remains to be seen—can diversity within a supervening order be achieved at mega scale?

*Fig. 14.* Charles Moore and Rothzeid, Kaiserman, Thomson & Bee, One Rector Park, 1986; with, on left, James Stewart Polshek & Partners, Liberty House, 1986, and, in background, Jack Brown and Irving E. Gershon, Gateway Plaza Apartments, 1982–83

*Fig. 15.* Cesar Pelli, Winter Garden, World Financial Center, 1988

The Fall and Rise of New York

Fearful that the city will succumb to gigantism and render itself uninhabitable, many New Yorkers have adopted a strong antidevelopment sentiment, charging that zoning regulations are cleverly circumvented in the city's high-stakes real estate game and demanding that the construction of super-scale projects be stopped or their designs significantly modified. Neatly lumping together issues of postmodernism, size and density, and preservation, the critic Ada Louise Huxtable recently went so far as to state: "What is new and notable in New York City's unprecedented building boom is that all previous legal, moral and esthetic restraints have been thrown to the winds, or more accurately, to the developers, in grateful consideration of contributions to the tax base and the political purse. . . . Greed has never been so chic."[6] Holding the city itself largely responsible for its own undoing, Huxtable writes: "This is a city that thrives on its neuroses, and megalomania is the current style. One almost longs for good old days of paranoia, the time of fiscal crisis when the message from Washington was drop dead."[7] Regardless of one's critical assessment of the city's new buildings, or one's doubts regarding the city's ability to shape positively its own energy and growth, Huxtable's conclusion that one neurosis is preferable to another is at best dubious and at worst dangerous. What competent physician would encourage a patient to choose to live with limited options and low self-esteem, even if the risk of higher spirits were a measure of overambitiousness or conceit?

Sylvia Deutsch, chairperson of the City Planning Commission, has thoughtfully countered Huxtable's assertions, stating, "New York City cannot afford a simplistic approach. . . . Painting with a broad brush makes good headlines; it doesn't make for good planning."[8] Deutsch argues that historically New York has had an impressive record of dealing effectively with planning and density issues. Since the Comprehensive Amendment of 1961 was added to the pioneering New York City Building Zoning Resolution of 1916, the nation's first zoning ordinance, the city has established "contextual zones," which further restrict development. Additionally, ongoing revisions, subject to public review, have shown that the resolution "is neither frozen in time nor a malleable instrument to be bent each month to a different angle."[9] Whether or not the city's standards for judging appropriate development are stringent enough is a matter open to debate. What is clear is that an economically healthy city is better than a sick one, and that whatever the fate of projects currently on the boards, the continual, if not constant, rebuilding of New York, which has been an integral part of its history as a metropolitan center since the Civil War, seems unlikely to halt, no matter how loud the cries of preservationists and idealistic community groups. Although the preservation of architecturally significant buildings and districts and the introduction of strong regulations to guide future development are essential, efforts to block indiscriminately the basic processes of development that run counter to the larger economic and social trends shaping the form and texture of New York are destined to fail.

Volatile, anarchic, sometimes maddening energy defines New York; this is New York, the city that never sleeps, the city in perpetual motion, the city where, as Ellen Thatcher says in John Dos Passos' *Manhattan Transfer* (1925), "You can get away with anything if you do it quick enough."[10] Like booze pouring forth from a bottle, the city's energy is dynamic and intoxicating. "If a city may conceivably be compared to a liquid," Carl Van Vechten writes in *Parties: Scenes from*

*Contemporary New York Life* (1930), "it may be reasonably said that New York is a fluid: it flows."[11] In light of the growing concern regarding density, rather than fight New York's tempo, it might be fairly asked: Why not go with the flow? And right now the flow is going up—in the form of towering skyscrapers.

The city's new proud towers recall the heyday of the 1920s not only in their architecture but also in the curious combination of anxiety and optimism that they reflect. Major corporations—J.C. Penney, Mobil, and International Paper, to name a few—have left or are currently planning to leave New York for greener pastures elsewhere, yet the city's economy is booming. New York's unemployment and office vacancy rates are among the lowest in the country, and the city is once again the nation's preeminent manufacturing city—this time around, however, the city is not producing goods but rather ideas and ingenious, previously unimagined methods for borrowing and lending money, methods which help to fuel many of the offices and factories that have left town. The growth of financial institutions, which the *New York Times* recently labeled "the debt industry," is in large measure responsible for the resurrection of the city's economy and its current building boom.[12]

While the stock market continues its seemingly limitless, albeit vicissitudinous climb, how long the debt industry can continue to prosper is anyone's guess. But whatever turn the economy takes and whatever its effect on building activity, a few things are clear: the goods and services required for everyday life can be manufactured and performed, if they must, in anonymous glass and metal boxes located anywhere, but the task of making something out of nothing is reserved for only a few special places. Hollywood realizes our collective dreams on celluloid. In New York, the dreams are more tangibly captured, in glass and steel and stone. Now, as in the glory days of the 1920s and 1930s, the city is a real-life movie set. New York is a place where ordinary people elevate the mundane activities of daily life to the level of high drama, or at least to that of a screwball comedy; it is a place where architects transform apartments, factories, and office buildings into dreamlike works of art. New York knows that the city exuberant without the city livable is useless, but it also knows that the city cannot live by orderly plans alone.

Perhaps the explosive New York of the 1980s is more difficult to comprehend and cope with than the stagnant New York of the 1970s, but it is also truer to itself. Before World War II, most New Yorkers believed that a new building going up would be better, not merely bigger, than the one coming down; in the decades following the war much of the city was rebuilt in an arrogantly anti-historical, anti-urban manner, with countless bland, placeless, glass-and-metal boxes giving us good reason to lose the faith. The tragic loss of Pennsylvania Station in 1963 shocked us into recognizing the need to protect our architectural past. We must now find the courage to believe in our own ability to create a rich architectural future—once again creating monuments that both reflect and define the spirit of a continually emerging new New York.

# IO

The Buell Center
*An Interview with
Robert A.M. Stern*
1986

*It has been Robert A.M. Stern's month [February 1986] in the sun. It began with a Toast/Roast Dinner given by The Architectural League in celebration of the television series* Pride of Place, *which he conceived and moderated. Among the genial and very funny roasters were Vincent Scully, Jaquelin Robertson, Peter Eisenman, Stanley Tigerman, and Suzanne Stephens. Next came a two-day symposium, "The Building and The Book," sponsored by the Temple Hoyne Buell Center for the Study of American Architecture, of which Stern is the director. To find out more about the Buell Center,* Oculus *interviewed architect Stern in his office.*

OCULUS: How long have you been director of the Buell Center?

ROBERT A.M. STERN: I am the first director of the Buell Center, and have been so since 1984. The five-million-dollar gift to Columbia University was made in 1983, and Julia Bloomfield was the acting director, putting the process in motion while a search for a director took place. I was elected effective July 1984.

O: What is the center's purpose?

RAMS: It is the Temple Hoyne Buell Center for the Study of American Architecture, and while there is a formal statement of purpose, the essence is to effect greater communication of a serious and scholarly kind between architects and landscape architects, urbanists or city planners, and the general public as well as the professionals working within those fields. So we want to bring together, or to make the best use of, the research and the thought of the people who are historians, critics, theorists, men and women of practical nature in the field, and so forth. We want to be as broad-based as possible, but we don't want to lose sight of the fact that we are in a university and that we want to elevate the discourse on everyone's behalf.

O: What is the organizational arrangement of the center—its trustees or directors, and so on?

RAMS: We have a board of advisors, and we are part of the university though an independent agency. As such the dean of the School of Architecture is automatically a member of our governing structure. Phyllis Lambert is the chairman of our board of advisors, which has rotating members from the faculty of architecture, from the faculty of art history, and other members. The membership includes practicing architects, like Kevin Roche and Bruce Graham; scholars, like Adolf Placzek, who is our Avery librarian emeritus; people who combine scholarly and journalistic backgrounds, like Ada Louise Huxtable; and people like Ben Holloway, who are involved in the world of building, but who do not approach it from within the disciplines of history or practice.

O: What kind of faculty-student arrangement do you have?

RAMS: We do not have a teaching function. As part of my having moved from the active part of the faculty to the directorship of the center I am giving a large lecture course on American architecture from the centennial to the bicentennial—that is, from the Civil War to the present. That is not an official program of the center; it is a course that I give in the School of Architecture. Dean Polshek essentially said, "Since you are the official representative of American architecture on the campus, I think it's appropriate that you give a course that sets out some of the goals and preoccupations of the history of your subject." Fair enough. But the center does not have a teaching function. We would like to have programs that students would come to, and we have had seminars in which students have been invited to participate.

O: What are the physical facilities and location of the Buell Center?

RAMS: As part of the gift, a certain amount of money was set aside to renovate East Hall, which is adjacent to Avery Hall. East Hall is one of the buildings that predates the McKim, Mead & White campus plan. The campus was originally the Bloomingdale Insane Asylum—and some would say that we have changed name but not function. In any case, we will occupy the top, third floor of East Hall and will share the ground floor. We hope to start renovation in the 1986–87 academic year.

O: What else should we know about the organization of the center?

RAMS: Currently my assistant director is Ann ffolliott, and we have one other assistant, Liz Gerstein, who is a recent graduate of the University of Pennsylvania in art history. And we have two or three student assistants as needed. But because we are still in the formative stage we do not have the full use of all the funds that will ultimately come to us. So we are not yet moving along at full tilt. But we don't want to get top heavy in administration anyway; I don't like a lot of administration.

O: You have chapters of the Buell Center elsewhere, I understand.

RAMS: No. There was an early idea to have a network of study centers around the country. At the moment we have put that program into a kind of quietude while we better formulate our own programs. We do have an informal working relationship with the Southwest Center for the Study of American Architecture at the University of Texas at Austin. And the director of that center, Larry Speck, is on our board. But there is no contractual or other kind of relationship. We imagine that we can be of mutual assistance in structured and unstructured ways with other centers around the country from time to time.

O: What do you see as your major activities and accomplishments over the past two years?

RAMS: Well, I think all the accomplishments have been major, but they are different in scope. I am very proud of what we have done so far, and they have deliberately been efforts to address different audiences within our general mandate. At the most scholarly level, at the suggestion of Professor Gwendolyn Wright of Columbia's GSAPP, as it is now called (the Graduate School of Architecture, Planning, and Preservation), we have initiated a series of seminars. We had three the first year and are having three this year. So it seems to be a tradition. They are concerned with American scholarship in architecture. The way we attack the subject is to take two or three recent books and examine them with their authors present to see what light they might shed on how people approach certain subjects, sometimes familiar subjects like critical and historical monographs on architects. We compared at one session recent books on McKim, Mead & White and Bertram Grosvenor Goodhue. And at a recent and extremely lively session we looked at five guidebooks prepared by local chapters of the American Institute of Architects and invited the authors of some of those guidebooks to be here. We invite the publishers of the various books and we invite scholars and architects from our own faculty and from neighboring universities—within the scope of our financial ability to fly a few people in. We invite them here to discuss the books. These have been most stimulating and useful occasions. Books are frequently reviewed in the daily press or the scholarly journals, but the people who write them seldom have an opportunity to reply, except in an occasional hostile letter to the editor. Here there is a chance for people to share what went into making the books, and really to get a higher level, or a different level, of criticism than we are used to in the journals. And that has been a very good program.

O: Why has there been such a concentration by the Buell Center on publishing?

RAMS: Because we are all victims of the word. And also because it is the means by which we communicate. And because within a university setting publishing is the way ideas are communicated.

O: And the way art history is pursued too.

RAMS: It's the way theory is made, history is pursued, and, in fact, the way current architecture is often presented to the world at large. Most of us see buildings only in the magazines. So it is a principal means in the communication of architecture.

O: That sounds timely and current, but there have been those who have wondered why there is not more of a concentration on actual American architecture instead of on books and magazines about architecture.

RAMS: We will talk about actual architecture from time to time. The books are a way to get at architecture. The seminar on guidebooks was instantly brought to a head by comments by Robert Geddes—who is an architect, an educator, and a former dean—about the fact that architects assess their own buildings very differently from other architects who might write about them, and differently from architectural historians who prepare guidebooks. So I think these were very valuable experiences. In any case we are having a second program that is meant to bring a foreigner to our shores to comment on American architecture. Last year we had Andrew Saint, the English historian. This year Francesco Dal Co will come in April and deliver a lecture on Mies van der Rohe, which is apropos given the hundredth anniversary of Mies's birth. And in another seminar we will discuss the tall buildings of Kevin Roche. Kevin will be the guest then. This is occasioned by Dal Co's book on Kevin's architecture, which will be published shortly. And we will have a number of architects, all of whom have done tall buildings, present to discuss this architecture. Of course the book is the occasion for this discussion, but the presence of these many architects—ranging from Stanley Tigerman to Bruce Graham to Helmut Jahn—should provide a very stimulating occasion.

O: Who will be the invited audience on those occasions?

RAMS: The seminar will be made up of the people who will be there as our guests. A seminar does not have an audience. I don't think that our best service is to have public occasions in which everybody speaks for the history books and for the quick laugh from the audience. A seminar is something where everyone is equal around the table, where everyone talks for the mutual edification and enlightenment of all, and where people can be candid.

O: Perhaps this direction is responsible for questions about why the Buell Center is so quiet and local?

RAMS: We are a center and an institute. We are not there, as I see it, to replace the public discourse that is essential to architecture and should be the responsibilities, in New York City at least, of the AIA, the Architectural League, plus a variety of museums—like the Museum of Modern Art—that have public programs, particularly in relationship to their exhibits. We will have programs that are public. We are trying to fund, at the moment, a very large program on the Hispanic influence on the architecture of the Americas. That will bring architects and scholars from Spain and various Western Hemisphere countries to join together with their colleagues from the United States to discuss this critical subject. This will be a major public symposium, and will result in considerable discourse. And we hope it will stimulate further researches and increase knowledge. We just finished a public symposium, "The Building and The Book," in which we tried to share problems and possibilities of publication of both books and periodicals. We took the historical view but ended up with absolutely candid assessments of the present situations in those two fields. Interestingly, though we advertised the symposium quite extensively, and used the mailing lists of the AIA and the Architectural League, our audience was largely, but not exclusively, I am happy to say, made up of people who are historians and from the journals. Though I think that any architect would have been very interested by the discussions, both historical and, at the very end, when Tom Wolfe made a surprise appearance from the audience to comment on Tom Hines's very thoughtful analysis of how Wolfe's *From Bauhaus to Our House* was received by the press. We can make the occasions, but we can't force people into the room.

O: There seems to be a variation in your interpretation of the word *public*. In this case I was thinking as much about students at the university.

RAMS: When I divide the public up I include all of those groups. I am more interested in the categories of principal interests that people have, whether they think of themselves as historians or architects or interested laymen or critics. There are both students and practitioners in every one of those fields. It certainly was a public program—its success exceeded my expectation—and we are going to try to raise the money to publish the proceedings.

O: It has been suggested that during his sabbatical Dean Polshek might be preparing to retire from the deanship of the GSAPP at Columbia, and it has been further suggested that you might consider such a deanship if it were offered to you.

RAMS: [Laughter] Dean Polshek, who is a wonderful dean, and to whom I owe everything that is good that has happened to me at Columbia, is coming back in the fall and I have no reason to believe otherwise. And I am extremely happy and fully occupied, intellectually and in every other way, in my position as the head of the Buell Center, where I believe I can make a considerable contribution to the university.

O: It has been suggested that you are *too* occupied with too many projects—architecture, writing, television, lecturing—to give adequate time to directing the Buell Center.

RAMS: I spend a lot of my working hours in planning and working on the center. My job is not to be the day-to-day administrator of the center, which Ann ffolliott and her staff do very well. My job is to shepherd its intellectual life—its programs, publications, and so on. I do not play golf; I do not play tennis; I used to ride horseback, but I gave it up. And I find that there are a lot more hours in a day than many people think. I am happy to be able to use them to the benefit of directing the Buell Center.

O: You mentioned that the proceedings and papers from "The Building and The Book" symposium will be published.

RAMS: Even if we have to publish it in a more modest way than I would like, we can do it. But I would rather have it be a nice publication. I think people take things seriously in direct relationship to the care with which the document or the building or the meal is prepared. Our first symposium, by the way, which precedes my tenure as dean—or director, rather—but which was very much part of my work as a faculty member in getting the center going—and I shared that responsibility at the time with David DeLong and Helen Searing—was the symposium "American Architecture: Innovation and Tradition." It kicked off the center in '83. We are bringing the book documenting the proceedings out this spring, published by Rizzoli. That will be, I think, quite a beautiful book, quite thoughtfully put together, and really quite a major document.

O: You mentioned something earlier about the relationship between practicing architects, or practitioners, and scholars, or academia. I wonder if you would say something more about what you envision that to be.

RAMS: I think the schism between the two is somewhat of a false one. At Columbia we have many people who teach and practice, and who make serious contributions to the field of architecture both in their writings and in their work as architects. I like to number myself among them to be sure, but I think of Aldo Giurgola, who has taught at Columbia for more than twenty years, who has written, and whose many buildings—in the States and some of the schools he built in Italy after the recent earthquake—have offered historical insights. I don't think history is only offered in the pages of books. I also think of Klaus Herdeg, and junior faculty members like Mark Hewitt, who is an architect and is currently engaged in historical research.

O: At Columbia.

RAMS: Yes. And Susana Torre, who is in charge of the Spanish symposium, is another in our group. So I think that we have, just within our faculty, which the center must draw upon and nurture at the same time, we have that commitment. I think that other architects are interested in both subjects. We are all very busy, but we must take time. Architecture is a scholarly pursuit. Particularly now, if we are going to reintroduce traditional styles into our architectural vocabulary—traditional vocabularies into our architectural compositions—we must approach them with more than just a quick glance at a Kodachrome slide. I would say that traditional architecture of the nineteenth and early twentieth centuries—whether it was the highly academic work of McKim or the highly interpretive work of Goodhue or Eliel Saarinen—was fundamentally scholarly. Fundamental scholarship lay behind that work. And we need to restore that.

O: Does that answer the question why the focus of "The Building and The Book" symposium was the history of publishing rather than the history of criticism?

RAMS: The history of criticism, which is deeply favored by some, seems to me a secondary subject only to be arrived at after we deal with broader issues. Publishing is a medium that involves criticism as well as presentation of work on its own terms.

O: You may have some teaching to do in that regard. I don't think everyone automatically sees your vision of publishing as integrally bound up with architecture. Most people, it seems to me, feel that publishing is something peripheral, perhaps parasitic, in relation to architecture.

RAMS: In the modern world since the Renaissance, the building and the book have been intimately intertwined. There was this man named Vitruvius who left a little manuscript that seemed to get people pretty excited, and there was Alberti, who was, I am told, interested in books and buildings, and Palladio . . . and I believe Thomas Jefferson, who was no small potato in these things, had a very large architectural library and put considerable value on the establishment of a national library, to which he contributed his books. So the architect who is not interested in publishing is both ill informed historically and also quite naive about how his or her buildings will be understood by both his or her fellow architects and the interested public. Also, let's get right down to it, the client as well. We try to introduce all those themes in the Buell Center investigations. So the architects who did not attend missed an opportunity to gain a critical insight into their own relationship to the world at large and to their day-to-day functioning.

O: What do you see as your goal for the center in the future?

RAMS: You haven't even let me tell you all the programs now underway. I am looking forward to our program of bringing foreigners to talk about American architecture. We have, for a long time, thought it was our purview in America to study European architecture. . . . Now, it is wonderful that Europeans and Japanese are turning their attention to our architecture. I am very concerned that there is an absence of serious scholarship and a decline in the number of students studying architectural history, and therefore giving us a less critical dimension about ourselves. That is a function of the number of jobs out there and the fact that there was no forum for them to exchange ideas. So we have started a program called The Buell Talks in which graduate students in the midst of working on their doctoral dissertations come and give short presentations on an aspect of their work. Prominent teachers and scholars are in the audience. And that has been very stimulating, though that is definitely a closed-door situation, because of the proprietary nature of the students' research. We are in the early stages of working on a symposium for this fall in honor of Edgar Kaufmann, Jr., on the occasion of the fiftieth anniversary of Fallingwater. It will be a wonderful opportunity to focus on Edgar's contributions—he has taught architecture, having been a student of Wright, and having been a major client and curator of a great work of architecture. We will bring together scholars to talk about this most important building. That will be public, and will probably occur in early November. Probably it will be inaugurated with a lecture by Vincent Scully, followed by a day-long symposium. We are always thinking of the big picture—with symposia of various scales leading to publications. We hope to make a new space in Buell Hall for small exhibitions that will lead to scholarly catalogues. As a beginning, I have inaugurated, with my board's permission, a series of documents on American architecture, on which we are in the early stages of editorial work. Drawing on the resources of Avery Library and other collections of architectural drawings, letters, and documents, and also dipping into obscure or difficult-to-obtain periodicals, we are putting together affordable paperback books illustrated with scholarly introductions and careful annotations. To wit:

> Scully is putting together a new extensive selection of Shingle Style material from the pages of *The American Architect and Building News* with a new introduction. It will augment the material that is very inadequately illustrated but brilliantly discussed in his book, *The Shingle Style*.

> William Jordy is going to do a compilation of drawings of the work of Joseph Urban, which have been at Columbia for almost fifty years but unattended to by scholars.

> Leland Roth of the University of Oregon will write on *Ladies Home Journal* houses from 1896 to the First World War.

> Ellen Coxe is putting together a book called *The Vocabulary of Memory*, which will show how various architects from the 1870s to the 1950s frequently viewed the same building, but with very different eyes, and how those views informed their own architecture.

> Ken Frampton will do a book in that series on the Paul Nelson drawings, which have just arrived at the center.

Those publications, which we will bring out in conjunction with Rizzoli, will be extremely interesting. Eventually we hope to bring fellows to the university at both the senior and junior levels to pursue special projects at Columbia. Then, we are trying to do an exhibition in conjunction with the American Wing of the Metropolitan Museum on the drawings for the Cathedral of St. John the Divine, which the young scholar Janet Adams has researched under Professor Jordy at Brown. She has uncovered many drawings that were thought lost from the original competition. It should be an extremely beautiful show leading to a book. It should have many benefits—scholarly, cultural. . . . And then we are working on . . .

# II

The Modern
Architecture Symposia
*An Interview with
Robert A.M. Stern*
2006

*In December 2006, Inderbir Riar of the Buell Center at Columbia University sat
with Robert A.M. Stern to discuss his role in the university's Modern Architecture
Symposia, which were the focus of the Buell Center project, "Between History and
Historiography: A Critical Edition of the Proceedings of the Modern Architecture
Symposia at Columbia University, 1962, 1964, 1966."*

INDERBIR RIAR: Let me start by asking, very generally, about your involvement
in the three Modern Architecture Symposia. You attended the first conference as
a guest; you participated in the 1964 symposium as an assistant to Henry-Russell
Hitchcock; and in 1966 you joined Philip Johnson to present your respective "top
ten" buildings from 1907 to 1917. Perhaps you can discuss where you were in 1962
and how you became involved with 1964, and then we can turn to 1966 and the
"top ten" lists.

Let's start with your connection to the main players, like the organizers,
George Collins, Adolf Placzek, and Philip Johnson.

ROBERT A.M. STERN: Well, in the late 1950s I was an undergraduate at Columbia,
where I got to know George Collins and Adolf Placzek, whom I knew particularly well from working summers in Avery Library. And I met Russell and Philip
at Yale, when I was a graduate architecture student. Philip was around Yale quite
often in those days. He'd been teaching there before my time, but not that much
before. Russell was no longer teaching at Yale, but he came down from Smith very
often. He'd lecture and he was very much on the scene. He was bored at Smith,

you know. And he was doing research at the library at Yale and so forth, and I was interested in history.

In '64 I took a year off from the architecture school and enrolled in art history. I did all the course work for an MA in architectural history, but I never wrote a thesis, which you had to do in those days.

IR: This was at Yale?

RAMS: At Yale. So I was in my most high art-historical mode. And ultimately, the work I had started to do, which had got me interested in George Howe, began as a term paper for Vincent Scully. It ultimately led to a book, which wasn't published until 1975, because once I finished architecture school I got involved in practice and it was hard to concentrate on the book. But I did finally get it done. So that's really the long and the short of it.

IR: The other figure I was thinking about in the background is of, course, Vincent Scully, whom you just mentioned.

RAMS: Well, Vincent Scully hates things like the conferences we're here to talk about.

IR: Why is that?

RAMS: I think they make him nervous. But he also has a low tolerance for pedantry, which scholarly conferences typically have a high degree of. However, the 1964 conference is particularly memorable for me because of Scully, his wife—or soon to be wife, I can't remember exactly—Marian LaFollette Wohl, and Colin St. John—Sandy—Wilson. I remember the four of us driving down to the 1964 conference, the one in which Scully gave the talk on the "Doldrums in the Suburbs." Vince was railing against the idea of the conference. Sandy wasn't particularly looking forward to it either. But after the conference, on either Friday or Saturday night, Sandy dragged us down to Greenwich Village—I think it was to the Village Gate, where Miles Davis was playing. Or wasn't playing, because Miles Davis was famous for blowing one note. And of course at that moment—this is the period of the British invasion, of rock 'n' roll and all that—to me, Miles Davis was about as out of it and uninteresting as could be. Vince had no opinion about it one way or the other, as I recall. But to an Englishman like Sandy, Miles was "it." And in fact, that night Miles Davis lived up to his reputation for being so difficult. . . . "What are we doing here?" I wondered. But there we were.

I remember the 1966 symposium very well. I was at the Architectural League finishing up a year's residence as the first J. Clawson Mills Fellow. During that year I organized exhibits, which made the place quite lively. It was May or so, '66. I was putting the finishing touches on "40 under 40," the last of my projects as Mills Fellow. And I was working on getting married. I was very distracted. [Laughter] But Philip and I did put this list together for the symposium. I'm sure we had one or two lunches at The Four Seasons to develop it—each of us made a list. And you can see that over the years I've been pretty consistent about my choices.

IR: I want to ask you about your interests, because Philip Johnson has only one American building, and you list three. While you only share one building—Wright's Robie House—you both mention projects by Behrens, Loos, and Gropius. What were your overlapping and diverging interests in this proto-modernism, circa 1966? Did they perhaps signal a larger intent for both you and Johnson?

RAMS: Well, I don't remember Philip's exact motivations, but we did each deliver informal remarks.

IR: I'll give you an example. You each singled out one building, in particular. He said that Sant'Elia is "the best man today," and you said Wright's Robie House is "unquestionably the greatest and most significant building of the decade." There is a difference in terms of the tone, let's say, between you and Johnson. For instance, he said, "I chose the buildings that amused me completely off the top of my head," while you said, "All the buildings I've chosen are multiviewed and complex." I'm very struck by this description because of your suggestion of a kind of "complexity and contradiction" and perhaps a stab at the received imagery of modern architecture. Was this, indeed, your intention?

RAMS: Multiviewed or multivalent?

IR: Multiviewed. Although that might be a transcript error.

RAMS: I think it's an error. *Multivalent* was the hot term of that period.

IR: Why is that?

RAMS: Multivalent—meaning you can read it in different ways. Look at Charles Jencks, although the symposium was *avant* Jencks. I can't remember precisely why I picked the Robie House, but I can give you some idea of why I might have. . . . The Robie House is unquestionably, from that decade, an unbelievable tour de force of composition. Wright tackles an urban site in a quite suburban way.

But Grand Central Station, another of my choices, marked my already growing dissatisfaction with modernism in general and the arguments that the modernists put forward as though no other architect had ever responded to modern life. And Grand Central's complexity of section—the cutaway is the great section drawing—probably inspired Sant'Elia.

Grand Central was an internationally known building even before it was completed in 1913. Yet in 1966 it was not taken seriously as a canonical work of the early twentieth century—a successful marriage of architecture and infrastructure.

IR: What do you think that meant, that said this was a reintroduction of a kind of architecture?

RAMS: I really should have said "introduced," not "reintroduced," key figures and buildings that had literally been eliminated from the historical narrative. Take, for example, the case of Lutyens. We were introduced to Lutyens through Bob Venturi's *Complexity and Contradiction*, which I already had a draft manuscript for in about 1963 because I published it in *Perspecta* 9/10 (1965). Lutyens's work had also been the focus of a seminar I took with Scully at Yale at about the same time, I think in 1964. But other than that, Lutyens was unknown—except, of course, to Hitchcock, who gives his work a passing mention in his 1958 Pelican history.

IR: In the late '60s, Alison and Peter Smithson revisited Lutyens, as did Venturi and Scott Brown, but this was after the third symposium. The Smithsons trashed Lutyens as part of their polemical encounter with Venturi and Scott Brown. But I want to tie this return to Lutyens to something that Philip Johnson says in this transcript. He says, "The historians among us architects should get ready to respond to our choices"—"our" meaning you and Johnson. Do you think that, by '64 and '66, there was a tension between, say, "pure" history and practice? Did historians acknowledge this kind of intellectual labor of the architect-as-historian?

RAMS: Well, the difference between architectural history at Columbia and at Yale, which Columbia's historians tended to pooh-pooh, was that Yale's was an engaged history and Columbia's was often a kind of disengaged history. Architectural historians at Columbia didn't much like the student architects in the architecture school, and they didn't much respect the architecture faculty, either. They regarded them as yahoos. Probably they were right in some respects. It was not a distinguished moment at Columbia's architecture school.

As I saw it then, Columbia's historians, with the exception of George Collins, were disengaged from current practice, and if they had ideas about modern architecture, those ideas were tightly bound up with Pevsnerian notions from the 1930s. Hitchcock—Scully's mentor—and Scully were quite different. Hitchcock was an impeccable scholar, an obsessive scholar. But he always was writing about the contemporary scene as well. So his articles in *Zodiac* were very important and remain so today for those interested in the postwar period. And architectural students read those articles in those days. Scully, of course, was always criticized as being "not a scholar."

IR: Criticized by whom? By other historians or by . . .

RAMS: Well, yes, by the Wittkower school of thought that was based at Columbia. The practitioners, those who went to Yale, who to this day still set their sights by Scully's insights, revere him as an engaged intellectual, a public intellectual. You can't accuse Collins or Rudy Wittkower of being public intellectuals.

Sybil Moholy-Nagy was also important at Yale, although she was stuck at Pratt—she would always say she was *stuck* at Pratt—because she had no degree. She'd been a hootchie-cootchie dancer, I'm told, in Germany [Laughter].

But whatever, Sybil had an on-again, off-again friendship with Philip Johnson and Paul Rudolph. And ultimately she wrote the first book about Paul Rudolph. Sybil's relationship to Rudolph was very touchy. For one thing, she had come up to Yale to give a lecture, and the occasion took a disastrous turn. Sybil's slides were paper-mounted, and as the projectionist was trying to advance the carousel the slides were all crumpling. Yale, unlike Columbia in those days, prided itself on its sophisticated audio-visual equipment. When the student handling the slides in the booth was unable to perform, Betsy Chase, a docent of the Art Gallery, went into the booth to help. Then Scully went up. And then Paul Rudolph. Sybil, in full frustration and with her great sense of theater, looked up at the booth and said, "If those four monkeys in the booth can't get my slides to work, I'm leaving." Whereupon she threw her mink stole over her shoulder and walked out of the auditorium, leaving poor Rudolph—who had a lot of trouble with women in general—to drive her to the train station and thinking his whole future career had just been set back. Ultimately, she was his biographer. But it took years to heal that breach.

Columbia had Yale envy in a big way in those days. That is, the architecture students did. In fact, in the 1960–61 academic year, when a man named Charles Colbert had been dean at Columbia for one or two years, the entire first-year class applied to Yale, causing Rudolph to write a letter to the president of Columbia saying something like, "Look, we can't take on this responsibility. There must be something wrong." And Columbia students envied *Perspecta*. Over the years, they started their own student-edited publications, but they have never had, as they say in show business, any with "legs." Another way to understand the differences between Yale and Columbia in those years is to look in all the early issues of *Perspecta*. You find lots of architectural history by many of the people involved with the MAS. And *Perspecta* 7, which assesses the current scene—Saarinen, Rudolph, Kahn, Johnson, Johansen—with Sybil holding forth, will give you a fine idea of the different way the discourse was undertaken at Yale as opposed to Columbia.

IR: I was going to get to *Perspecta*, but I want to back up a bit. Because what we're generally discussing is essentially the reassessment of the Modern Movement, which starts in '62, hot on the heels of Reyner Banham's *Theory and Design in the First Machine Age*. Indeed, the organizers were desperately trying to get Banham for every conference, and he never came. And then they backtracked from him to people like Pevsner and so on.

RAMS: Banham came to the United States for the first time, I think, in 1962, and he came to Yale. As a result of his visit, he wrote the review about the Saarinen colleges, which were still under construction, in which he said Yale was a very sick place, meaning that Yale had already repudiated modernism through Saarinen. But Banham also debated Philip Johnson at the Metropolitan Museum of Art. The debate was organized by the Architectural League, as I recall, but held in the Grace Rainey Rogers Auditorium at the Met. And it was a complete dud. Banham didn't have a thing to say. He just stood there and said, "Oh, you know, it's nice to be here." Banham seemed completely overwhelmed by America, because in those days the difference between the U.S. and the U.K. was much greater than it is today, and transatlantic travel for academics was comparatively rare. And the British scene was still in a postwar mode. But Yale, which is traditionally Anglophilic, had quite a bit of contact with the U.K. Rudolph had brought James Stirling and Sandy Wilson over to teach, and in 1961–62 Richard Rogers and Norman Foster were advanced graduate students. At Columbia, Michael McKinnell and John Fowler and Peter Eisenman were sharing an apartment in 1960. Fowler ended up teaching at Yale, while Eisenman went to Cambridge to get a Ph.D.

IR: One of the remarkable things about the symposia—especially, I think, in 1962—was the decidedly *American* character. That is to say, they were a reconsideration of the Modern Movement by American scholars. On the one hand, there was the emergence of a decidedly American take on European modernism (a polemic perhaps indebted to, but also departing from, the International Style); on the other, there were American historians engaging specific instances of American architecture—for example, William Jordy and Scully.

RAMS: Jordy is not trained as an architectural historian. Jordy's Ph.D. was in American Studies at Yale, so his approach in this context can be said to be über-American, as it were. Scully's first interest was literature; then he went on to art history. Yale art history comes out of the French—Henri Focillon, *The Life of Forms in Art*. And if you want to understand the difference, you have to read Focillon. And you have to read George Kubler, *The Shape of Time* (1963). It's totally different from the German *Kunstgeschichte*, pseudo-scientific approach pursued at Columbia.

Now why all these Americans? Well, there were Americans like Jordy and Scully, who principally tackled American subjects. There were Americans like Collins, who did not tackle American subjects. And there were Americanized Europeans like Moholy-Nagy, who courageously, if rather brutally, tackled sensitive issues related to the diaspora of European modernist architects in the 1930s.

IR: I'm thinking about your role in this and projecting ahead to *New Directions in American Architecture*. Did you see yourself as a kind of Americanist?

RAMS: Oh, absolutely. It was them against us [Laughter]!

IR: Were the lines really that clear?

RAMS: Well, it was very clear. For example, Foster and Rogers were each awarded Fulbright scholarships to study in America. But Norman returned his Fulbright, choosing to come on a different scholarship, the Henry Scholarship. And the reason he did that was so he could work in America, absorb what was going on in American practice.

IR: Indeed. He goes to work at Anshen & Allen in San Francisco.

RAMS: He and Richard travel around the country, but Foster stays on and works in big offices. As to the American historians: Scully's Ph.D. was on an American topic but he never wanted to be called an Americanist, nor has he confined himself to topics in American, or even modern, architecture. Hitchcock supported—fostered—the study of American architecture, interpreted American architecture. Jordy, I mentioned, of course. Who else was in the mix?

IR: There was Allen Brooks, for instance.

RAMS: H. Allen Brooks, another Yale graduate.

IR: Oh, is that right? So it's a kind of cabal.

RAMS: [Laughs] Allen Brooks's books and papers are at Yale. Allen Brooks was Canadian and went to Dartmouth and then Yale. You have to check everybody's degrees. Carroll Meeks, of course, was Yale, but he was not well at the time of these symposia. He not much later died of emphysema.

IR: And then Leonard Eaton, who is looking to Europe and to American influences.

RAMS: Right. Well, Eaton doesn't belong to either the New York or New Haven set. He was brought in from the Midwest.

IR: And then David Gebhard, who brings the sort of western American perspective.

RAMS: Gebhard was new on the scene, but he would soon become quite respected among those tackling American topics, particularly overlooked topics like the Prairie School and Southern California Mediterranean Revivalism. He died rather young. Dead of a heart attack. Biking. That's what you get for exercising.

IR: [Laughs] I'm going to return specifically to your position. Again, I'm thinking of *Perspecta* 9/10. It might be interesting to read the conferences against that very specific issue. The reason I'm saying this is because there seems to be an entirely different kind of reevaluation of American architecture in this issue. It has "Doldrums in the Suburbs," which came out of the '64 conference. It has selections from Venturi's *Complexity and Contradiction in Architecture*, an article by Charles Moore, and projects by Venturi, Moore, Rudolph, and Kahn. Was an alternate case for history *and* design being made? The reason I'm asking this is, again, to return to your selection of the "top ten" list for the 1966 conference.

RAMS: *Perspecta* 9/10 is—I believed it then and I still believe it—a landmark publication. It was deliberately intended to break the hold that the diaspora architects and historians held over contemporary practice and discourse. It definitely reflects the Yale culture that opened up so many vistas for me; for example, the article by Hitchcock about youth and age among the early modernists in the very first *Perspecta,* which inspired me to commission Adolf Placzek, the Avery librarian at Columbia, to expand on that theme in *Perspecta* 9/10.

The *Perspecta* polemic in the magazine's early years was that the first generation of modernists, the high modernists, was basically either dead or dying. And really out of ideas, with the exception of Le Corbusier, who did surprise us with new work almost to the end; Gropius had become totally unpredictable and sometimes really embarrassing, while Mies had become all too predictable.

Second, there was this new generation that was already in its forties and early fifties, who almost to a man had mostly been trained by Gropius. But these men— there were also some women, but they were much less visible—many of whom are included in *Perspecta* 9/10, were a reaction to Gropius, even if they could never quite get over him. Edward L. Barnes is a perfect example of the Gropius acolyte. Rudolph was always saying, "Gropius is a great teacher, but I think he did things wrong." Philip Johnson had rejected Gropius ever since he studied at Harvard. I'm sure he was given a very rough time at Harvard when he was a student, being a Germanophile and crypto-fascist. But I'll leave that history to Joan Ockman

[Laughter]. But by the 1950s and 1960s Johnson was totally invested in Yale.

I have a theory that Yale, not Harvard, was the true inheritor of the Bauhaus idea. From 1949 on, Josef Albers was running the art program, and Paul Rand was in charge of graphic design. And the architecture school was under George Howe, who, though trained in the Beaux-Arts method, had become a modernist but was always skeptical about modernist ideology.

IR: In terms of pedagogy?

RAMS: He put his faith in a man named Eugene Nalle. Nalle was Yale's Johannes Itten.

So Yale was totally different from Columbia, which was a kind of last gasp Beaux-Arts place with no strong sense of direction. One year, when he was either on leave or not well enough to teach his course, Carroll Meeks assembled a series of lectures by historians. One of these was by George Collins, whose piece in *Perspecta* about Gaudi's structure was the talk he delivered at Yale in the architecture school. Not in the history of art department. Yale architecture students in the early '60s were exposed to some of the finest historians of the day.

The other thing to remember, the difference between Yale and Columbia, is the institutional relationship between art history and architecture. At Columbia they were two different entities with virtually no interaction. At Yale, Scully and Meeks at different times held joint appointments in architecture. There was real intimacy between the various programs.

IR: I want to go back to something you said about the perspective of modern architecture as either dead or dying. I'm wondering how you, in that sense, read these conferences. Because there certainly is a stab being made here to recuperate modernism, to not see it as a dead end or dying.

RAMS: Well, I don't think they were recuperating modernism. I think what was interesting was that the various participants were attempting to sort things out, separating the polemicizing and myth-making from the actual events. Sybil's talk about the diaspora, though filled with anger, had a powerful impact. Scully's talk on "Doldrums in the Suburbs"—trying to sort out what was going on and taking a realistic look at modernism in America—was also very important, stripping away many of American modernism's pretensions.

IR: They're not all worth reading [Laughs].

RAMS: What was interesting in the earlier conferences was just getting all this information out. Check and see what was available in English at that time and you'll be amazed at how little was there—the kind of glut of monographic publications we enjoy now didn't exist. Basically, people were still reading *Space, Time and Architecture* as if it were history rather than polemic. Scully would never let any of his students read it. He regarded it as a kind of tract and not history. And it isn't history, but it has become history.

Now Philip, of course, was the great fun person, if you will, in all this. Russell was just a little bit older, but seemed much older. In fact, he seemed old. And

Russell was boring—one of the most boring lecturers ever to come down the pike. [Laughter] Philip, on the other hand, was irreverent and a spellbinder. He knew his history. He knew many of the people being discussed firsthand. And he would talk about them as people and as architects. He was still in correspondence with a few of them, especially J.J.P. Oud—until Oud's death in 1963. That correspondence has been published somewhere or other.

IR: This raises a very interesting thing, because at some level one can do this by generation. The older guard, like Johnson and Hitchcock, knew the European modernists. And then there are guys like you who are students at the time, who very quickly get involved in polemical things.

RAMS: You should also think about Charles Jencks, who was at Harvard in its Sertian slumber. But Jencks is a smart guy, and when he finished architecture school he went to the University of London and got his Ph.D. under Reyner Banham. But Jencks's first serious book of history, *Modern Movements in Architecture*, is full of the same kind of discovery of the modern—if I could find my copy it would probably be filled with my hosannas: I probably was writing in the margins, "Yes! Yes! Yes! Right!"

IR: But what do you think you were responding to in terms of "yes"?

RAMS: Well, I was responding to the sheer mediocrity, the complete boredom of the late International Style. I was responding to the absence of intellectual content in architecture. By the way, at the same time, in 1964, Eisenman came back from the U.K. and started CASE. I wasn't invited to its meetings because I was just a student, but Scully, who went to the first meeting, said it was a horror—again, a reflection of his dislike of such gatherings. If I'd been there I could have gotten him through it. So there were some others—Jencks, who is my age, and Eisenman, who is seven years older than I am—who were in active rebellion against the recent past and who turned to the study of the history of modern architecture as a way to sort things out and clear the stage for a new generation.

IR: Returning to you writing in the margins of Jencks's book, against the kind of entrenchment of a certain level of "form". . .

RAMS: And the Gropius and the Giedion stuff. And the notion that architecture was some sort of trajectory based on "constituent facts." The phrase "constituent facts" is Giedion's, and was ridiculous. What are the constituent facts of modern architecture? Those are facts that Giedion decided would suit him. Another person in this story in this period is Christian Norberg-Schulz. He himself did not appear in New Haven that I remember, but Sandy Wilson had *Intentions in Architecture* literally under his arm. And we all had to read *Intentions in Architecture*. At that same time, by the way, Venturi came to Yale to give a course in history and theory that he'd been giving at Penn, which was, in effect, engaged in a distinct vision of practice. In those days there was something called a Yale-Penn axis. It was talked about, not made up retrospectively.

IR: The Yale-Penn axis is very interesting. Even from the cover of *Perspecta* 9/10 you get this image of half of Charles I's palace in Granada and Kahn's Unitarian Church in Rochester squashed together.

RAMS: That was put together by the graphic designer of the magazine. It was not a genius thing of the editor. I would love to take credit. The designer was Jerry Meyer, a student in the graphic arts program. As soon as I saw it, I said, "Yes, that's it."

IR: So tell me about this kind of reaction, the "Yes, that's it," or sort of "eureka!" moment . . .

RAMS: Well, the thing about Venturi, and even Charles Moore, was that not only were they interested in history, they were comfortable in it. They could talk about it and they wrote about it and they incorporated its lessons in their design work. In *Perspecta* 6 there's Charles Moore's article on Hadrian's Villa, still one of the best discussions of that amazing place. Moore and Venturi were comfortable talking about history, they were comfortable about incorporating its lessons in obvious ways in their work as architects.

And this was so amazing. Rudolph had brought us to the threshold of this kind of comfortable relationship to the past in his writings and in his teaching. He always referred to historical buildings when he sat at your desk and offered you a crit. He would say, "You could do it like Wright." If he thought it was appropriate, he'd show you how what you were doing related to Fallingwater or some other building, and he'd sketch it out. And his references could be buildings from the premodern past. His range was not narrow.

Now, of course, there's another thing to remember about this young generation, not mine, but the previous one, who were imbued by Gropius with an ahistorical approach to design. Most of them had not been to Europe until after studying architecture. Most Americans had been cut off from Europe by the Depression and then the Second World War. After the war, with traveling fellowships and other subsidies, Gropius's students did go to Europe and it was a revelation to them, which put Gropius's methods in a new and less favorable light. Kahn, who had been to Europe in '29, went back again to the American Academy in Rome in 1950, and that released him to become the Louis Kahn we know. His travels are well documented.

So the generation of American modernists were coming back with all these ideas about Europe and talking about Italian hill towns and so forth. So all of that was in the air. And students in my generation of architecture school at Yale were very history minded. There was a lot of history at Yale.

IR: One of the ways I've described this to myself is the idea of putting History— with a capital *H*—back on the drafting table.

RAMS: It was. It was a moment when, for the first time in a generation, architects dared to put history books on their drafting tables rather than hiding them in their lockers.

IR: The architecture students are not being formed to become historians. They're still becoming architects. But there is a renewed interest in form. I'm thinking of the fact that contemporaneous with the symposia were the publications of Venturi's *Complexity and Contradiction in Architecture* (which, as Venturi has admitted, may have been better served by being titled *Complexity and Contradiction in Architectural Form*) and Rowe and Slutzky's articles on transparency in, again, *Perspecta* 9/10.

RAMS: That wasn't in *Perspecta* 9/10, it was in *Perspecta* 8. Bob Slutzky had been a student under Albers at Yale, and Colin Rowe had spent a year at Yale in '48. I don't think he knew Scully then. They had a kind of standoffish relationship later because, I think, in some way they both had the same charismatic power among architects, although at different places. I know Colin hated being at Cornell—he was stuck up there in the arctic woods. And there was Vincent at Mother Yale, which is not Cornell.

IR: I want to project ahead a few more years to the Whites vs. Grays debates. I'm extrapolating willfully, but do you think there is a central relationship in terms of the "Whites" and the "Grays" to "history"—but, of course, in different camps—or do you think history is more appropriate to one group than the other?

RAMS: Oh, no. When I finished the Mills Fellowship at the Architecture League, I went to work for Richard Meier, and then, with Richard's permission, I invited Bob Venturi to the office and he looked at the few things that Richard had done. Richard had only been in independent practice for about three years. After the visit, Bob and I had a drink. I said, "Well, what did you think?" He said, "My god, Bob. The International Style revived." [Laughter] What's new about that? That's historical. Another example of the shared sense of history among the Whites and the Grays can be seen in Peter Eisenman's obsession with history.

Michael Graves knew the Corbusier books inside and out. That certainly wasn't typical of the young people at SOM. The Whites and Grays turned to history as a way out of the utilitarian banalities of what came to be called Late Modernism.

Graves and Eisenman went to teach at Princeton, where Jean Labatut was still on the scene, carrying forward, however vestigially, the Beaux-Arts approach to form making. Also, Princeton offered the Ph.D. in architecture, so historical research and design were even more closely connected than at Yale. Charles Moore got a Ph.D. at Princeton. And Venturi did his undergraduate work there. Donald Drew Egbert, the historian, who was not asked to participate in the symposia, was a powerful influence on Moore and Venturi, yet nobody seemed to know who he was, as far I know. One of his brightest students, Neil Levine, became Scully's brightest student.

**Modern Architecture Symposium 1966**
**1907–1917: Ten Significant Buildings**

As selected by Philip Johnson:

1. Adolf Loos, Kärntner Bar
2. Walter Gropius and Adolf Meyer, Fagus Shoe Factory
3. Le Corbusier, Dom-ino Project
4. Peter Behrens, German Embassy, St. Petersburg
5. Peter Behrens, AEG Turbine Factory
6. Frank Lloyd Wright, Robie House
7. Mies van der Rohe, Kröller House (project)
8. Antonio Gaudí, Crypt of Guëll Chapel
9. Josef Hoffmann, Stoclet House
10. Antonio Sant'Elia, Città Nuova

As selected by Robert Stern:

1. Adolf Loos, Steiner Villa
2. Walter Gropius and Adolf Mayer, Werkbund Model Factory
3. Frank Lloyd Wright, Coonley Playhouse
4. Hans Poelzig, Werdermühle, Breslau
5. Peter Behrens, High Tension Factory
6. Frank Lloyd Wright, Robie House
7. Michel de Klerk, Housing and post office block
8. Edwin Lutyens, Palace of the Viceroy, New Delhi
9. Warren and Wetmore, Reed and Stem, Grand Central Station
10. Charles Rennie Mackintosh, Glasgow School of Art

# 12

---

# The Relevance of a Decade
## *1929–1939*
### 1964

The years 1929–1939 constitute a chronological convenience for this Symposium on Modern Architecture and not a meaningful architectural era. The period we should be talking about extends from 1927 through World War II to about 1950 and, indeed, lingers on in certain recent works of Walter Gropius and some of his students. I should like to discuss the inadequacies of 1929 as a beginning date for this period. Later on today Vincent Scully will discuss the inadequacies of 1939 as a terminus—a point he has already suggested elsewhere.[1]

Nineteen hundred twenty-nine is less meaningful a beginning for this period than is 1927, niggling though such a distinction may seem to be. Although two significant monuments date from 1929 (the Villa Savoye and the Barcelona Pavilion), it was in 1927, especially at the Housing Exhibition in Stuttgart, that, as Reyner Banham has written, the "mainstream of modern architecture found its International Style."[2] So it was in 1927 that the leading "form givers" of the period to come produced their first significant works: Mies van der Rohe's Apartment Building at Stuttgart, a far cry from his apartments on the Afrikanische Strasse in Berlin (1926–27), was his first experiment with the steel cage; Le Corbusier's double house at Stuttgart culminates his development from the "Citrohan" projects of 1920–22, and his Villa Stein at Garches, also completed in 1927, is unquestionably his first masterpiece, though it can in turn be traced back to his work at La Chaux de Fonds and to the Maison La Roche; Alvar Aalto, a comparative newcomer, was already pointing to the future with his preliminary designs for the Viipuri Library in Vyborg, Russia.

Nineteen hundred twenty-seven was also the year when the League of Nations Competition brought the question of the monumental possibilities of the new architecture face to face with the established forces of the old guard. Ironically, it was Baron Victor Horta, the pioneering architect of art nouveau, who presided over the jury that would veto the scheme on a technicality.[3] Similarly, Gropius's Total Theatre project for Erwin Piscator and his Civic Center project for the town of Halle, both of 1927, mark the first of a series of projects for the kinds of mass-democratic programs that were to become a central preoccupation of the period to come. It was also in 1927, at Stuttgart, that Gropius began to experiment in earnest with prefabrication—another major interest in the following twenty years.

But it is to America that we must turn, for more than any other country this period was hers. Consider the impact the following events must have had on such conscience-stricken conservatives as George Howe, A. Lawrence Kocher, and Raymond Hood as they contemplated, with wavering commitment (and some confusion), the new architectural styles, ranging from Paris jazz-modern through the various international modes embodied in works by such men as Bernard Bijvoet and Johannes Duiker, Le Corbusier, Hans Scharoun, Hugo Häring, and Bruno Taut.

In America, 1927 was a year of tremendous technological progress: radio-telephone service was established between New York and London, San Francisco and Manila; the first national radio networks were established; television was given its first public demonstration; the movies began to "talk"; the Holland Tunnel—the first underwater vehicular tunnel in the world—was opened to carry automobiles under the Hudson River; Henry Ford, after producing his fifteen-millionth car, ceased production of the Model T and brought out the consumer-oriented, highly styled Model A.[4] It was the year in which the stage designer Norman Bel Geddes, having conceived the first "streamlined" train and the first "streamlined" automobile, established himself as an artistic consultant to industry.[5] Calling himself an industrial designer, Bel Geddes gave birth to a profession that was to challenge seriously the position of architects throughout the next twenty years and, in a number of key instances, to set the pace for design. From the point of view of technology, the most provocative challenge to architecture during this period was the work of Buckminster Fuller, who, in unveiling his Dymaxion House in 1927, hurled the first volley of his extended polemic against the International Style.[6]

Nineteen hundred twenty-seven was also a time when America began for the first time to sense her cultural independence from Europe—and, indeed, to feel that Europe, broken by World War I and the ensuing economic chaos, was no longer able to lead. America's new role was perceived first by a French writer, André Siegfried, who wrote in his book of 1927, *America Comes of Age*, that America had evolved an "entirely original social structure . . . [which] may even be a new age, an age in which . . . Europe is no longer the driving force of the world."[7] Our own writers, especially our critics and historians, reinforced this sense of cultural independence. Vernon L. Parrington's book of 1927, *Main Currents in American Thought*, was posited on a belief that American literature was not merely a provincial branch of English thought but a full-blooded literature in its own right, while Charles and Mary Beard's book of the same year, *The Rise of American Civilization*, was predicated on the belief that there was not only civilization in America but that there was an American civilization. At the same time that these events were bespeaking a kind of nationalism, Charles Lindbergh's solo flight across the Atlantic on the night of May 21, 1927, may be said to have announced a new international age.

Nineteen hundred twenty-seven saw the establishment of the first museum devoted to modern art, Albert Gallatin's Gallery of Living Art at New York University. It was also an important year for our painters. After ten years of wrestling with European cubism, many of them, in their insistence on the direct representation of recognizable objects, finally acknowledged their inability to accept either the analytic or synthetic approach. A new and thoroughly American kind of "modernism" emerged, which can be best described as precisionism, though many other terms have been employed.[8] Charles Demuth's enigmatic painting of 1927, *My Egypt*, reflects the American artistic temperament at this decisive moment. Aware of the inherent beauty of industrial structures, though not completely enchanted by them, Demuth's typically American concern for the recognizable image—in this case, two grain elevators—and for the material object prevents him from attempting a reorganization of the shapes into a new pictorial order similar to the attempts of the cubists and their more contemporaneous descendants, the purists. Instead, *My Egypt* is, as John McCoubrey has written, a depiction of "twin commercial colossi," an unmistakable expression of Demuth's "wry comment on the nonexistence of an American past."[9]

Stuart Davis's decisive *Eggbeater Series* of 1927–28 and Charles Sheeler's photographs of the Ford plant at River Rouge, also of 1927 (Sheeler was the first American photographer to use the forms of industrial buildings and processes as landscape subjects), announced that American machine art had come to maturity. Indeed, Sheeler's development away from the cubistic abstraction and manipulation of his early work and toward the precise realism of such important canvases as *Upper Deck* (1929) may be seen as the principal example of American unwillingness to romanticize the machine; American architects, lagging behind the painters, would not come to a similar point until about 1932.

A good many Americans in 1927 were reading Oswald Spengler's *Decline of the West*, the first volume of which had just been translated into English. Spengler's extraordinary comparison of the Temple of Poseidon at Paestum and the Münster at Ulm suggested to many Americans that, as George Howe put it, there was "an intimate relationship between mathematics and science on the one hand and architecture on the other, a relationship of form and spiritual content and not of dry technology."[10] Henry-Russell Hitchcock was himself in a Spenglerian mood when he wrote in 1927, in his first article in the new magazine *Hound and Horn*, that we stand "beyond the downslope of the nineteenth century and the apparent gap of the war, and regarding our architecture, we are led to demand whether the time of its discard is at hand or whether, after the superficially historical wastes of the last century, it may be reintegrated or has already been reintegrated as a sound organ in an aging body."[11]

The architectural scene in America in 1927 was electric with the spirit of "modernism," although it was in no way clear which way the profession would go. Americans were just beginning to realize that the best European architects had shed the neoclassical forms of Beaux-Arts academicism once and for all. A most perceptive American commentator on this was Samuel Chamberlain, who, after an extensive trip to Europe "in search of modernism," reported that "out of the wilderness of wails of discontented modernists, chafing at the artificiality of the academic and calling loudly for a new vision, a new era, a new impulse, there comes one strong and sonorous and uncompromising voice, setting forth the case of modernism with unexpected logic, the voice of the pensive and earnest Le Corbusier."[12] In addition to word-of-mouth reports, such as Chamberlain's, there was Le Corbusier's own emphatic polemic, *Vers une architecture*, which had just been translated by the English architect Frederick Etchells. Its awesome challenge—"architecture or revolution"—could not be ignored. The mood of the 1927 AIA national convention was one of some uneasiness,[13] but it was generally felt that hope lay in the stripped forms of Bertram Goodhue and Paul Cret or in the Paris jazz-modern of Ralph Walker, Ely Jacques Kahn, and Raymond Hood. Walker's Barclay-Vesey Telephone Building[14] in New York had been just completed and was at the forefront of everyone's imagination, just as Joseph Urban's Ziegfeld Theater[15] and James Gamble Rogers' Medical Center for Columbia would be later in the year.[16] However, Frank Lloyd Wright was at the nadir of his influence and prestige. Relegated by Thomas Tallmadge to the limbo of lost causes, along with Louis Sullivan,[17] he was without work, besieged by bill collectors and lawyers, and thought by some internationalists to be dead. But toward the end of the year, things began to look up. He was occupied with a project for Dr. Chandler at San Marcos-in-the-Desert, and Michael Mikkelsen, editor of *Architectural Record*, offered to pay him $10,000 for a series of articles, "In the Cause of Architecture," which were to go a long way toward his architectural comeback.[18] *Record* was unquestionably the most innovative among the American professional journals, and under the direction of Mikkelsen and A. Lawrence Kocher (who became managing editor late in 1927), the format was completely modernized and the magazine transformed into a sounding board for new ideas.[19]

In 1927, there was, as Sheldon and Martha Cheney put it, "a spreading machine age consciousness."[20] It was the year of the Machine-Age Exposition in New York, which, more than any other single event, opened American eyes to the wealth of new forms at their disposal. The Machine-Age Exposition was the brainchild of Jane Heap, coeditor with Margaret Anderson of the most influential of the so-called "little magazines," *The Little Review*.[21] For the first time, the American public was asked to look at machine parts, machines, and machine products and to recognize in their purely utilitarian shapes significant artistic form. In addition, models and photographs of many important European buildings were shown as well as a sizeable number of examples of Russian constructivist art, set designs, and architecture. Because of the novel Russian art, the exposition received considerable attention in the daily press and was well attended.[22] It can surely be regarded as the first major event of the Modern Movement in America.

In addition to all this intellectual agitation, there were some serious attempts at building in the International Style in 1927.[23] In New York, William Lescaze succeeded in building the Capital Bus Terminal, while in California—where Rudolph Schindler had erected his constructivist Lovell Beach House the year before—Richard Neutra built the more conventional Jardinette garden apartments with the illusion of continuous strip windows (as superficially conceived as those of Hood's McGraw-Hill Building of 1930–31), white walls, and other trademarks of the new style. Neutra's book, *Wie baut Amerika?*, was published in 1927 as well, presenting, in addition to a discussion of technology, Neutra's futurist urban vision, Rush City Reformed. The projected office tower in Rush City was to influence Lescaze and George Howe's design of PSFS (1930–32), the first significant modernist sky-scraper to be realized. Most importantly, Neutra has long claimed that the Health House for Doctor Lovell (1929) was also conceived in 1927.[24] Clarence S. Stein's and Henry Wright's City of the Motor Age at Radburn, New Jersey[25]—the first section of which was completed in 1927—was perhaps more humane in its sepa-ration of pedestrian and motor traffic than Neutra's Rush City, but it was surely less exciting in its architectural forms. Stalled by the Depression, Radburn never grew to its full size; yet its principles dominated new-town planning in America throughout the 1930s and early 1940s.

Surely other events can be added. The point is that all of these I have men-tioned belong, it seems to me, far more to the future than they do to the past. If we confine our discussion at this conference to the years after 1929, we will cut ourselves off from the roots of an era and find ourselves afloat in a phase of devel-opment already well underway.

# 13

## Television and Architecture
### *Notes on* Pride of Place
#### 1988

Although it is a cliché, it is also a truth: television is powerful. And, from my limited perspective, I am convinced that the public television audience is a serious one: people watch, they listen, and they care. I am certain Spiro Kostof discovered the same thing: the audience for public television is large and vocal—maybe not as many people watched *Pride of Place* as, say, *Dallas*, but fifteen million or more per episode is no small number.[1] Caring and involved, the audience for *Pride of Place* was also appreciative. To this day people stop to talk to me on the street about the series, and they stop to say thank you, and once in a while something less appreciative, but most of all they stop because they want to discuss the ideas on the show. *Pride of Place* pioneered the premise that people would watch a program about buildings with as much interest and commitment as they would expend on a program on sea otters or the disease of the month. The point seems to have been made: There is a hunger for discussion of the man-made environment, of architecture and urbanism.

In undertaking *Pride of Place*, we began by choosing the major themes of each episode. In the next stage, the director Murray Grigor and I crisscrossed the country to see what would fit the themes visually, and when we returned with our wish list, we sat down with the producers to face the practical and financial issues of getting a crew to all these places.

It was a collaborative process, yet I should emphasize that when I was asked to undertake what became *Pride of Place*, I was asked for a "personal view" of American architecture. Taking this mandate from the show's funder, Mobil, I not only learned a lot about myself—about what I really believe in—I also learned, to my surprise, that although many real people shared my view, or at least enjoyed having it presented to them in their living rooms, many critics had rather a different reaction. So I learned about criticism as well—I should have known better. What I learned is that many critics seem to believe that in criticizing the series, their best way to evaluate what had been done was to point out what should have been done, or more precisely, how they would have done it, if only they had been asked. Much of the criticism of *Pride of Place* took the form of idiosyncratic agendas or, more commonly, complained that *Pride of Place* was not a straightforward history of American architecture—something neither I nor Mobil had any intention of presenting.

I believe that a personal statement well argued—note that I did not say well acted—is meaningful. If you take a stand, hold a position, stick your neck out, not only will you get people to pay attention, but they will actually think at the same time. TV is not a textbook—so we set out to be interesting, entertaining even, which counts for something in this life. And if there is a good reason to tell an audience why Robert A.M. Stern became an architect, it is not just a cynical concession to a society in which everybody is shallow and would rather read *People* magazine than the *New York Review of Books*. The justification for a personal statement is that when most architects and historians speak about architecture, they seem to forget just how personal an art architecture is, personal in its sources, personal in its teaching, and personal in its practice, in which the relationship between the architect and client determines so much of the final result. It is one of architecture's little secrets, one that the high mandarins of modernism didn't want anyone to know, because it would have unveiled the modernists' pose as value-free rationalists.

From the start, we made a bold assumption: that the public television audience was not a junior high school art appreciation class. We assumed that they were educated and widely experienced. We *assumed* that our viewers knew a lot about architecture, much more than they probably thought they did, because they knew about architecture not as an art but as a setting for important historical events, or as places they visited on vacation, places, in other words, that more often than not they chose to experience for pleasure.

From the beginning, I felt that my job wasn't to simplify but rather to connect things up—to establish linkages that would help the audience realize that they do in fact think about architecture, much as most of us have at one time or another discovered that ordinary writing is in fact prose. I hoped that *Pride of Place* would encourage people to dare to speak the A-word, *architecture*; that they would become comfortable with their feelings and not feel that architecture was the sole prerogative of architects and related professionals. This I tried to do most of all by focusing on clients and real people like themselves who were decisive participants in the creative process, who not only paid the bills but frequently influenced the design as well.

While the series was not specifically intended for architects, I did hope to inspire architects to think about their role in a new way. More importantly, I hoped to jog their beliefs out of traditional ruts—for example, by presenting subjects such as the suburb as a legitimate form of urbanism, rather than an anathema; by presenting the campus as a microcosmic representation of urban ideals; by showing the importance of women in architecture—not from the now stylish sociological point of view, which traces women's influence on the domestic interior, but rather showing that women like Theodate Pope Riddle and Julia

Morgan were important as architects. Also, in what is still an unacceptable idea to many architects, *Pride of Place* tried to show how many of the best American buildings and places of the past two centuries were inspired not exclusively, nor even primarily, by their architects, but by the talents and ideas of the people who paid for them.

We decided at the outset not to use television as if it were a didactic medium. I didn't want to give lectures, and as far as I am concerned, a television show that isn't entertaining, no matter how grave the subject, is doomed to not get its point across. We were criticized for being too entertaining, or trying too hard to entertain, for being too involved with movie score soundtracks and impressive cinematography. Yet I ask: Is dry, cinema verité the most effective way to introduce viewers to the U.S. Naval Academy, Grand Central Terminal, Marble House in Newport, the Rainbow Room, or even the urban wasteland of the South Bronx? Architecture, like the other arts, is meaningful in its cultural context, in how it was used and thought of at the time. Whether we succeeded or failed, what we tried to do—with archival footage, music, interviews, whatever—was to imbue tele-versions of architecture with some of the excitement that buildings and places have when they are experienced directly. I didn't drive in my little red convertible to Jones Beach, or ride in a carriage with Léon Krier, just for kicks. I think that driving out to Jones Beach tells far more than a diagram about how Robert Moses imagined the parkways and parks of New York, and more about how generations of New Yorkers have experienced them. I think the carriage ride with Krier said more about how others see our architecture and about how most of us are capable of living in the present *and* the past than just verbalizing these ideas could do. Let's face it; there is more to television than talking heads.

In conceiving *Pride of Place* we were acutely conscious of the influence the media can have on how we perceive architecture and how, ultimately, it influences architectural design. We didn't *tell* the audience exactly how the media affects design; rather, we *showed* them. We juxtaposed footage from *Citizen Kane* with views of San Simeon, because William Randolph Hearst didn't just imagine his enchanted hill as a drawing or sketch or reality—he clearly dreamed of San Simeon as a movie set, where he ran the cameras day and night to show his wonderful life there. In the same way, the designs of Morris Lapidus for his Miami Beach hotels, and of Eero Saarinen for the General Motors Tech Center, only begin to make sense when you immerse yourself in the brave new world of 1950s consumer capitalism.

So we tried to entertain and, ultimately, to instruct. For all the jump cuts and crazy juxtapositions, we generally presented buildings in a very straightforward, informative way, moving from a general view of the exterior toward the entrance, then through it and on through the rooms and spaces in a logical sequence. In so doing, Murray Grigor and I demonstrated, to our satisfaction at least, that architecture is a subject that can be interpreted seriously and pleasurably on film.

One of the limitations of the medium, however, is just how long a viewer can watch a single person, even a star named Stern. Herb Schmertz of Mobil insisted early on in the production that there be other architects and critics on the show, and although at first I believed to the core of my psyche that the world could never have enough of Robert A.M., after watching fifteen minutes of rushes I became more Miesian than Mies—less of Stern, clearly in matters of TV, *is* more.

I hoped to make the show, like my architecture, deceptively subversive. While I argued strongly that architecture required a link to the past, I wasn't afraid to show modernist buildings at their best. Saarinen's GM Tech Center has never looked better in my view, neither has Louis Kahn's Salk Institute or Philip Johnson's Glass House than they did through the lens of *Pride of Place*. But the truth will out. The camera can bring out the best qualities in buildings but it cannot turn frogs into princes—Grigor and his cameramen, Terry Hopkins and Rob Orr, didn't try to make New York's Sixth Avenue or the Chicago Circle campus look bad—they just do. For after all, architecture is neither rampant materialism nor built ideology; it is art, and as such must be about life. So, too, must television give life as it reflects it.

# 14

## An Architect's
## Impressions of France
### 1987

In 1986, after having worked steadily for three years to take America around its own continental backyard—in the book and television series *Pride of Place*—I felt I needed to refresh myself by rediscovering some bits and pieces of our architectural past in another culture. So I embarked on a jet-age fragment of the Grand Tour, a two-week picaresque journey through France that allowed me to relax while doing what I like best, looking at buildings. It was, in short, an architectural version of a busman's holiday, and a wonderful way, as well, to do a little catching up with my life: notably with my traveling companion, my son Nicholas, then eighteen and about to become a freshman at Columbia. Although Nick is interested in architecture, he has a healthy sense of life's other possibilities, so he saw to it that my giant gulps of French towns and chateaux were washed down with a bit of scenery, some dad-son talk, and a lot of wine.

While this was to be a trip in which no angst-inspiring issues were confronted—the monuments of modernism and postmodernism were largely ignored—nonetheless there was, as I must always have, an agenda. For me, travel is architectural research; the buildings of the past are the jumping-off point for my designs. This time I had a few places I particularly wanted to see: farmhouses and chateaux in Normandy and seaside villages, each of which related to projects on my drawing boards.

A brief stop in Paris—empty that August, not only of the French but also of Americans—was like encountering a dream city waiting for its real life. A quick visit to the opera, a long walk in the golden sunshine through the courtyards of the Louvre, the Palais-Royal, and the Marais, followed by dinner in a sidewalk restaurant on the boulevard Montparnasse, ensured that the last motes of American dust were shaken off our feet.

The following day we drove immediately toward Normandy, stopping first at Honfleur, a port village popular with the Impressionists. In Honfleur I found confirmation for the direction I am pursuing at Grand Harbor in Florida—a project where, as in a typical French coastal village, the yacht harbor will be almost completely encircled by buildings in which the people live above the shops. I saw at Honfleur, and later at Vannes, just northwest of Nantes, how important it is to convey a sense of the harbor as outdoor urban theater, where the play is enacted not only in the water but along the broad quais under the sheltering sidewalk arcades and on the balconies above.

Honfleur had another lesson for me. One of the great design traditions we think of as uniquely American is, of course, the Shingle Style. But as Vincent Scully has told us, those late-nineteenth-century houses not only "recall colonial [American] practice in mass and detail" but also strains of English and French architecture. In Normandy and Brittany and even in the chateaux of the Loire, the sources of this style are everywhere: the round towers with pointed "candle snuffer" roofs; the tile-hung roofs and walls that suggest shingling; the elemental geometry of cone, sphere, and cylinder. But particularly in Honfleur, with its shingle-covered, wood-framed buildings, did I feel a special kinship between the France of the Impressionists and the Newport and Marblehead of the generation of Winslow Homer and Childe Hassam.

One of the great sights of Normandy, of course, is Mont-Saint-Michel, the medieval abbey and village built on a rock, surrounded by water at high tide. I had never seen Mont-Saint-Michel before, and for this American it took an act of will not to see the island as a fabrication of Disney. Disneyesque as well were the crowds and the bustle in the narrow street lined with souvenir shops and restaurants. But, of course, my ideal was a false one, was it not? It was I, and not Disney, who had the illusions about the past.

The tourist-trodden Mont-Saint-Michel is pretty much as it was in the Middle Ages; today's pilgrim is also in search of a transcendent experience—only now it is this world's past and not the next world's future that marshals our passions. Whether we buy a picture postcard or a piece of the true cross, most of us want a memento

*Fig. 2.* Domenico da Cortona, Château de Chambord, 1519–47

of our visit in the vain hope that the experience can be rendered permanent and tangible, that we can enrich our life in this world if not necessarily in the next.

Eventually Mont-Saint-Michel, crowds and all, had its way with Nick and me. Clambering up the main street, I had the feeling of being truly in the Middle Ages in a way I've almost never had before. Inescapably Disneyesque it may be, but this island fortress is also real and moving. And, of course, unlike Disneyland—a magic city in which the castle is unattainable—Mont-Saint-Michel has a very real abbey, where on a blustery gray day Nick and I found ourselves confronting a remarkable fusion of architecture and place. For today's traveler, Mont-Saint-Michel must be taken as a metaphor for the world as it was and is not, as we wish it had been and would become again.

From Mont-Saint-Michel, Nick and I pressed on under clouded skies through Saint-Malo, through some lovely Normandy countryside, and a corner of Brittany as we headed toward that endless source of visual and gustatory pleasure, the valley of the Loire (fig. 1). To a contemporary architect the chateaux, which developed into their present form mostly after 1500, are particularly fascinating because they represent a rediscovery and reuse of classical forms similar to the experiments that characterize architecture today.

In the sixteenth century, the Renaissance was just reaching France from Italy. François I brought Leonardo da Vinci to his court in the Loire Valley in 1516, and it was there that Leonardo died in 1519. The rich, disciplined language of architectural form based on the columnar orders—Doric, Ionic, Corinthian—and composed along lines of symmetry was adopted by the French as they turned many of their fortified castles into elegant country houses. That the chateau is part fortress, part villa, part medieval Gothic, part modern classical makes it a uniquely French contribution to architecture.

One of the most beguiling of the chateaux is Azay-le-Rideau (1518–29), half house, half boat at rest in a moat, which reflects the light along its stone surfaces and dematerializes its creamy mass. Chambord, on the other hand, is big and formidable—a child's vision of a castle made real (fig. 2). Chambord was begun circa 1519 for François I by the Italian architect Domenico da Cortona. Nick and

*Fig. 3.* Ricardo Bofill, Place du Nombre d'Or, Antigone town center, Montpellier, 1981–84

I approached it at sunset, its many turrets casting long summer shadows in the golden light. Chambord is at first glance all geometry and order. But on closer inspection, and especially after an hour spent on its roof, a counterpointing puckishness is revealed—that same wonderful sense of the absurd that transformed water spouts into gargoyles in the Gothic cathedrals of medieval France.

Chambord, like most of the other chateaux, was built to establish an image of royalty at leisure, a relatively new concept for a society only recently emerged from the puritanical constraints of medievalism. It's not surprising that when architect Richard Morris Hunt set out to create Biltmore House in North Carolina for George Washington Vanderbilt, he based it on the chateaux of the Loire. Hunt, who began the design of Biltmore House in 1888, got the chateau spirit quite right for a client who was distant enough from the source of his great wealth that he could take it for granted and enjoy it, yet was intelligent enough to realize the social obligations and responsibilities it entailed. At Biltmore and at Chambord, there is the same rational complexity and the same sense of noblesse oblige, the sense that the public rightly expects those who have money to have taste and use it to make the world more beautiful than they found it.

From the ripe summer of the Loire we headed southeast through the Dordogne, terra incognita to me but a must for Nick, who wanted to explore the prehistoric caves and the nearby wild valley known as the Gorges du Tarn. Caves bore me; on the other hand, Nick proclaimed "enough" as we cruised through innumerable picturesque farm villages and medieval hill towns. The hill towns are remarkable—not because they contain monuments, or even because they are so different from one another, but because they are so much of a type, a fusion of architecture and nature, building and landscape, that makes them seem almost one.

Villages such as Rocamadour and Conques of the Massif Central were a completely delightful surprise. Hitherto, I had had the fixed idea that hill towns were Italian, like San Gimignano, and that France was an affair of towns rising from flat plains, like Chartres. But as it turns out I'm about the only one who didn't know about the hill towns of the Massif Central. Surely all of France, and a good deal of Germany and the United Kingdom, was in Rocamadour when we arrived to have a look.

Conques, once on the pilgrimage route to Santiago de Compostela, nestles in a spectacular, very remote landscape. Its principal ornament, the Church of Sainte-Foy, is one of the most imposing small buildings I've ever seen—strong in its forms with a wonderful juxtaposition of roofs. Its beautifully ornamented façade calls every visitor to moral attention.

The last stretch of the journey took us to the Mediterranean and Provence. After the almost primordial splendors of Albi, which so inspired Louis Kahn, an ill-advised stop at Carcassonne seemed to me just so much hokum. Then on to Montpellier, whose nearest beachfront, La Grande-Motte, planned no doubt as a late-twentieth-century Rio, comes off more like Miami Beach—which is by no means all bad. We went to Montpellier to see the new town-within-a-town called Antigone, planned by the Spanish architect Ricardo Bofill (fig. 3). Breaking Nick's and my no-modernism/postmodernism pact, I wanted to see just this one contemporary project—and it was worth it.

In 1963 Bofill established his Taller de Arquitectura—a studio for architecture in Barcelona. Most of his work since 1979 has been in France, creating a series of "new towns" in which traditional urban form has been brilliantly adapted to late-twentieth-century conditions. His search for a usable past has taken him backward in time from the zany Gothicism of his immediate mentor, the Catalan Antonio Gaudí, through the medievalizing revivals of the French architect Viollet-le-Duc, to the grand classicism of the French academy.

About his Antigone project, Bofill has said, "Today's city . . . must be conceived as an ensemble of neighborhoods where different activities take place, where housing, shops, offices, workshops, and public facilities are mixed in a continuous façade." Bofill's buildings at Antigone have classical colonnades along the central street area. In the spacious quatrefoil-shaped central plaza there are great projecting cornices jutting out to frame the blue Mediterranean sky. Bofill intended these to serve as the base of a dome, formed by the sky itself, and he got it right.

After so much intense architectural tourism, a few days in Provence seemed well-advised. The classicism of Rome is so wonderfully at home in the dry, gray-green landscape of late summer. How I love Orange, with its incredible triumphal arch (fig. 4) and the ruins of a first-century BCE theater. In Nîmes it was not so much the stiffly composed Maison Carrée, arguably the best-preserved building of the ancient world, that moved me, but the Jardin de la Fontaine and the ruins of a temple of Diana. There, great vaults and a beautiful pool have been incorporated into an eighteenth-century garden that seemed intoxicating, a delicate architectural fragrance of centuries-old Mediterranean culture. In Provence the ancient classicism of the theater and the arch are the beginning of a story that Bofill's Antigone project takes up again after decades of neglect.

*Fig. 4.* Arch of Tiberius, Orange, ca. 10–27 AD

A brief stay in a still-empty Paris, where all the past—scraps of ancient buildings, the Gothic pile of Nôtre Dame, the lace-making of the squares and roundabouts and the Champs-Elysées itself, the superb renovation of the Hôtel Salé that houses the collection of Picasso's work—brought us back to the beginning in more ways than one: Nick to the great adventure of college, and I to reflect, yet again, on the power the past holds over us all, as standard-setter for the present and signpost to the future.

# 15

## Buildings and Brands

### 2001

In the summer of 2000, when the Spangler Center at the Harvard Business School had taken shape but was far from complete, architects leading our team were summoned by the school's communications staff to discuss publicity. One of the school's primary concerns was that someone involved with the project might publish the building in a way that would compromise the integrity of what they called "the HBS brand." At first my colleagues were a little confused—as architects they were not unfamiliar with the idea of branding, but associated it with commercial enterprises, not institutions like Harvard. And at first blush, the idea of an institution of higher education as a brand may seem unorthodox, if not downright unprecedented. But, in reality, such thinking has a long history. Universities compete with each other, and competition between peer institutions of learning has inspired some fine architecture. Thomas Jefferson was very much aware of this when he pleaded for funds to build the Rotunda, the centerpiece of his elaborate and masterful plan for the University of Virginia. In addressing the penny-pinching Virginia legislature, Jefferson asked rhetorically, "Had we built a barn for a college, and log huts for accommodations, should we ever have had the assurance to propose to a European professor of [first] character to come to it? To stop where we are is to abandon our high hopes, and become suitors to Yale and Harvard for their secondary characters."[1] The year was 1822.

Can a building promote a brand? And should it? After all, a lot of building is just about functional accommodation. But architecture, as opposed to ordinary building, is more than that; it is an art of representation, an art of communication. Architecture can help tell a story; it can take on a symbolic role; it can become an emblem; it can become part of a brand—and yes, to a remarkable extent, even

represent the brand itself. A building can express the identity of an institution through its stylistic language. It can express both an institution's inspirations and its aspirations. It can reflect its system of values and place those values in a continuum. The traditions of an institution become associated with the traditions of its architecture. Form and content can become one.

Brands were first developed to identify cattle as they freely roamed the prairies in the American West. Today, establishing a brand is a widespread practice and preoccupation, not only of image-conscious businesses, but also of universities, which struggle to differentiate themselves among their peer institutions so that prospective students and prospective donors perceive a clear distinction between them. A recognizable brand is necessarily a part of the process that leads to the selection of one institution over another. After all, students and teachers and even programs come and go, but the institution, identified by its name, its reputation, its setting—in short, by its brand—needs to prevail. The packaging, that is, the physical environment, matters. The architecture of a campus, the quality of its buildings, is a direct reflection of the quality of the institution and the coherence of its programs.

Before Jefferson set out to build a completely new university in Virginia, American colleges and universities were not consciously planned to be stylistically different one from another. They soon did take on different characteristics, owing to differences in local building materials and regional building practices. But with Jefferson's creation of a new university, everything changed.

Jefferson created an image of higher learning—or a brand—for his new university by adopting forms from the classical past to make a new statement. The Rotunda, for example, was a half-size version of the Pantheon in Rome. While in Jefferson's time the Pantheon was used as a church, it had been built as an all-encompassing pagan shrine, which gave it the aura of universality that mirrored his vision for the university. In founding the University of Virginia, Jefferson insisted that it be universal in outlook. The Pantheon model perfectly mirrored his conviction that secular learning, represented by the library, should usurp the spiritual focus of earlier universities. For Jefferson, the pure geometric figure of

*Fig. 1.* Thomas Jefferson, University of Virginia, Charlottesville, Virginia, 1819–26

the sphere expressed the Newtonian conception of the world to which he fully subscribed. On the other hand, the Rotunda's temple front connected the concept of the state-supported, secular, tuition-free educational enterprise with the democracy of ancient Greece. The Rotunda made it clear that the worldliness of learning rather than religion was the symbolic heart of the life of UVA, and that the new world drew strength from, and directly built upon, the history of the old. The Rotunda was the symbol of the University of Virginia, the brand, if you will; but that brand was extended by Jefferson to organize the entire university. His campus plan as a whole reinforces the image: the pavilions that border the Lawn express his pedagogical strategy of integrating the professors and students in the daily life of the campus community; professors lived above their classrooms in the pavilions; students in rooms behind the ranges that formed the connections (fig. 1).

In this way the architectural forms of Jefferson's campus truly reflected his theory of education. Form and content were one and, remarkably, remained so for about 150 years, until the university expanded in the 1960s to a new campus called the North Grounds, where it seemed to betray its brand by surrendering to another artistic vision that created what was, in terms of the historic place, an alien environment. Since the 1980s the Trustees of the University of Virginia have been systematically rebuilding the North Grounds with renovations and additions in an effort to reunite it with the university as a whole. Our campus for the Colgate Darden School of Business of 1996 is an example of this effort, extending the ideas of Jefferson to the North Grounds and the new century (fig. 2).

The University of Virginia was a completely thought-out plan; but other universities, and Harvard is among these, were not created out of whole cloth but developed more organically. These institutions grew and changed in a contingent manner. In that sense, Harvard's evolution is like that of a business that starts with one product and then diversifies, becoming more complex and, in the process, more diffuse. Although the architecture of Harvard's campus is today predominantly Georgian, that wasn't always a foregone conclusion. Harvard began with a building that looked like a modest house in Elizabethan England; as the college expanded in the eighteenth century, it established a campus—the Yard—and a coherent architecture—the vernacular red-brick Georgian of the American colonies. Then, in the nineteenth century, Harvard, along with other universities, burst in size, building in the fashionable styles of a richly eclectic era. By the mid-nineteenth century, Harvard had become a university, with undergraduate and graduate schools. In the course of this period of explosive growth, each new school—whether for law or engineering or medicine—began to build in its own individualistic way, so that the sense of Harvard as a coherent entity began to erode as the tastes and experiences of individuals—of architects, donors, and even deans—seemed to have their way. These decision-makers were not guided by a concept of institutional identity imposed, or even suggested, by the administration.

As the twentieth century dawned, Harvard came to realize that its physical identity was nearly lost, and was forced to reinvent its architectural image, in part to meet competition from a surprising variety of rivals, including a major start-up university, Stanford, which in 1886 had hired Boston-based architects and landscape architects to design an ideal campus in a new, barren part of the country.

Stanford invented its identity from diverse sources, including Romanesque monasteries, California missions, and English collegiate quadrangles. But the result was uniquely Stanford's—virtually overnight a strong and enduring image of a new brand of higher education had been created (fig. 3).

At about the same time that Harvard was being challenged by Stanford, established rivals Columbia and the Massachusetts Institute of Technology had the opportunity to rebrand themselves by building new campuses. Both institutions saw themselves as modern universities with an emphasis on graduate studies, including the Ph.D., and both, but especially MIT, which was devoted to technology and the sciences, adopted a grand classicism, which they believed reflected the goals of their programs, transcending the local vernacular styles to establish broader international appeal. Columbia and MIT succeeded brilliantly in recreating their brands through architecture long before their new programs lived up to the promises of their vision. MIT's new campus, begun in the second decade of the twentieth century, was a symbol of modern rationality that recalled Jefferson's University of Virginia but in a much bolder, more urban way, commanding a splendid waterfront site (fig. 4).

Other provincial colleges seeking to grow into universities undertook the same process of image enhancement to reinforce a brand of education. Take the case of Princeton, which in the 1890s was the very provincial College of New Jersey, a pokey, Presbyterian school. In 1896, as Princeton celebrated its sesquicentennial, Dean Andrew West persuaded the college trustees that the time had come to become a modern university. He believed that Princeton would most easily become a great and venerable institution if it looked like one, specifically like Oxford and Cambridge: the Oxbridge style, or what has come to be known simply

*Fig. 2.* Robert A.M. Stern Architects, Colgate Darden School of Business, University of Virginia, Charlottesville, Virginia, 1992–96

*Fig. 3.* Frederick Law Olmsted and Shepley, Rutan, and Coolidge, Stanford University, Palo Alto, California, 1886–1914

*Fig. 4.* William Welles Bosworth, Presentation drawing of the proposed campus, Massachusetts Institute of Technology, Cambridge, Massachusetts, 1913

*Fig. 5.* Cope and Stewardson,
Blair Hall, Princeton
University, Princeton,
New Jersey, 1897

*Fig. 6.* James Gamble Rogers,
Branford College, Harkness
Memorial Quadrangle,
Yale University, New Haven,
Connecticut, 1917–21

*Fig. 7.* McKim, Mead & White,
Harvard Union, Cambridge,
Massachusetts, 1901

as Collegiate Gothic, is an American style invented precisely to evoke an aura of
venerability on young American campuses (fig. 5).

Yale's story is pretty much the same. At Yale the red brick buildings of the
colonial campus—red brick had been a material for mill construction in greater
New Haven, thus compromising Yale's identity as a privileged educational environment—were in the mid-nineteenth century joined by battlemented dormitories
that unfortunately memorialized unpleasant ongoing conflicts between town and
gown. In the early years of the twentieth century, following Princeton's lead,
Yale rebuilt itself with brick and stone-clad Gothic residential colleges, like the
Harkness Quadrangle of 1921, which served to reassure would-be undergraduates
that once alternately belligerent and besieged Yalies were in fact genteel children
born of the marriage of American money and English antiquity (fig. 6).

Not surprisingly, Harvard took notice. To meet the challenge of powerfully
branded campuses, Harvard called on McKim, Mead & White to reinvigorate its
historic identity. For most of the nineteenth century Harvard's red-brick vintage
had been disdained for the same reason that Yale's was. But McKim and Harvard
turned things around, reinventing the brand by returning to the Georgian architecture that was embedded in the minds of many observers as Harvard's essential

image. In so doing Harvard took advantage of its greatest asset: its age, with all of the positive virtues that longevity can bring to an institution. The return to the architectural language of its earliest buildings was an expression of Harvard's pride in its past and in its present as an institution with a past—a past that provided reassurance and the confidence to allow all kinds of forward-looking experimentation.

Harvard's return to its Georgian roots can be seen in the gates to Harvard Yard, in the restoration of Holden Chapel in the Yard, and especially in the Harvard Union of 1901 (fig. 7), the first student-oriented center ever built—a bold social experiment and a conceptual model for the Spangler Center. Later, in the 1920s, the Georgian building model was dramatically extended with the River Houses and the Business School, which also transformed a stretch of the Charles River into an American Cam or Thames, using the model of the oldest campus buildings to reinforce the foundation of Harvard's image in history.

## Corporate Brands

Let us now to turn to a brief consideration of the kind of architectural branding undertaken by for-profit corporations, where brands are frequently icons for things with no intrinsic value. Before World War I, large business corporations had occasionally built great buildings to embody their brands, especially in the major cities of New York and Chicago. These corporate monuments took the form of skyscrapers, so that through much of the twentieth century, insofar as the general public was concerned, corporate identity through architecture was virtually indistinguishable from the race to build the tallest building.

Corporations took pride in their skyscrapers, which became symbols of their prominence and stability. Even today the phrase "tallest building in the world" has only recently lost its power to inspire. The Woolworth Building (1913), for example, raised the profile of the company in the public consciousness by establishing an image of financial strength for an enterprise based on five-and-dime stores (fig. 8). It also evoked a sense of higher purpose: architect Cass Gilbert turned to the Gothic style, which evoked the spiritual authority of medieval cathedrals, transferring this noble motif to what was essentially a speculative office tower, a building that would become known as "the Cathedral of Commerce." No building type more perfectly expressed America's boundless optimism on the eve of World War I than the New York skyscraper, and no skyscraper more perfectly advanced a corporate brand than Woolworth's.

In the Depression years, the Chrysler Building (1930) brilliantly represented the financial stability of its not notably stable corporate owner, and was also a very important bit of advertising and public relations. The Chrysler Building was decorated with the iconography of the automobile: the arches at the top of the building were punctured by triangular windows that suggested the spokes of a wheel; a frieze at the thirtieth floor represented a long line of Chrysler hubcaps speeding toward the corners (fig. 9), and the gargoyles were vastly enlarged radiator ornaments. The gleaming surface of the crown of the building suggested the sheet metal and chrome that were already becoming important status symbols on automobiles. When Chrysler left its building in the late 1930s, Texaco took it over and was there for forty years. Nonetheless, the building's name and its power to identify a brand of car company would not go away. Once it had not only been

*Fig. 8.* Cass Gilbert, Woolworth Building, New York, New York, 1910–13

home to the automaker but had also reflected prevailing car design. But the rapidly changing styles of automobile design and trendy building design had made the Chrysler Building and the cars it portrays period pieces; only now, as Chrysler markets its "Depression-style" PT Cruiser, do the brand, the building, and the product once again work together.

After the Chrysler Building opened, the Empire State Building (1931), in a kind of coda to the sequence of "tallest in the world" corporate skyscrapers, was dedicated not to a corporation but to the entire State of New York. Still later came Rockefeller Center (fig. 10), an entire complex that managed to combine the idea of the skyscraper with that of the campus, constructed both to celebrate a particular company—RCA—and a powerful family—the Rockefellers—who undertook the project as part of a campaign to redeem its reputation for untrammeled greed by showing that enlightened urban real estate development could lead to both public benefits and private profits. Rockefeller Center helped to rebrand the Rockefeller family in such a way that it is still identified as enlightened private wealth in the service of the public good.

At the end of World War II, the idea of buildings as the image of brands went further than ever before. Lever House, headquarters of an international soap and detergent company, was the great postwar brand building (fig. 11). The crystal clarity of its glassy walls was an exact metaphor for the company and its products, leading the distinguished architecture critic and cultural observer Lewis Mumford to ask, "What could better dramatize its business than a squad of cleaners . . . capturing the eye of the passerby as they perform their daily duties? This perfect bit of symbolism alone almost justifies the all-glass facade."[2]

Soon enough there would be a slew of "branded" skyscrapers, none greater than the Seagram Building, known to the man in the street as the Whiskey Building or the "Box the Bottle Came In" because its bronze facades recalled the transparent color of some of the company's principal products.

Nonetheless, in the years after World War II, the real action took place in the suburbs, where the idea of the campus and that of the building-as-brand coalesced

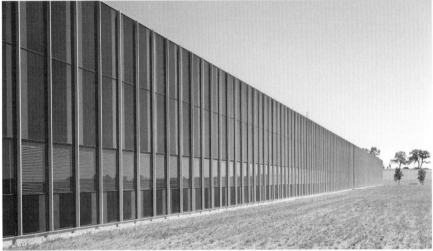

Fig. 11. Gordon Bunshaft of Skidmore, Owings & Merrill, Lever House, New York, New York, 1950–52

Fig. 12. Eero Saarinen, Styling Building, General Motors Technical Center, Warren, Michigan, 1949–56

Fig. 13. Eero Saarinen, IBM Manufacturing and Training Facility, Rochester, Minnesota, 1956–58

as the emergence of automobile culture allowed major companies to move from downtown to suburban locations. General Motors and IBM were two great corporations that made branded campus design their hallmarks.

Eero Saarinen's General Motors Tech Center in Warren, Michigan, was an entire campus of buildings meant to embody the technical prowess, the aesthetic sheen of the stylized products, and the optimism of the automobile company. The principal building in the group was the Styling Building (fig. 12), a domed rotunda deliberately conceived in direct emulation of Jefferson's Rotunda at UVA. Where Jefferson's library had transformed a pagan temple into a universe of knowledge, Saarinen's GM dome celebrated the latest styles of automobiles, which were displayed on revolving platforms.

But the great brand-maker of the postwar era was IBM, which, under Thomas J. Watson, Jr., retained Eliot Noyes, an architect and industrial designer who had attended the Harvard Graduate School of Design, to orchestrate the work of some of the leading architects and designers of the day as they shaped products

*Fig. 14.* Charles and Ray
Eames with Eero Saarinen and
Associates, IBM Pavilion, New
York World's Fair, Flushing
Meadows, New York, 1964

*Fig. 15.* Kohn Pedersen Fox,
IBM World Headquarters,
Armonk, New York, 1995–97

and buildings that would represent the no-nonsense efficiency of the company that came to be known as Big Blue. These included Saarinen's IBM building in Rochester, Minnesota (fig. 13), and facility in Yorktown Heights, New York, and Gordon Bunshaft's headquarters building in Armonk, New York. IBM was the hero of the first computer age, taming calculations that had remained insoluble for centuries by reducing everything to patterns of zeros and ones and iterated algorithms. Its buildings expressed that reductiveness, and its promise of infinity, with repetitive curtain walls that seemingly stretched to the horizons and which gave little clue to the workings inside. But IBM also sold business machines, and it projected its brand through high-style design developed by Charles and Ray Eames, among other leading designers. Together with Eero Saarinen and Kevin Roche, the Eameses designed what was perhaps the first great building of the information age, the IBM Pavilion for the New York World's Fair of 1964 (fig. 14). Here at last was the appropriate marriage between modernist aesthetics and this most modern industry.

But just as IBM reached its zenith, something happened. People began to question the company's brand. Many people, arguing that IBM was more about machines than people, rejected the company because they resented products that they saw as dehumanizing rather than empowering. The brand that had once stood for liberating the power of the intellect began to falter.

As this happened, IBM became a negative symbol, and its branded buildings a detriment to the company's reinvention. After a decade of soul-searching, Big Blue is back and is reinventing its brand. And once again it has turned to architecture to help define its corporate culture, in 1997 completing a new headquarters that was deliberately designed by Kohn Pedersen Fox to reflect the company's "looser" image (fig. 15). The new building nestles into its site; it is a nonhierarchical, employee-empowered company built around networking. The building expresses the changes in the company's culture and image with its approachable size, open offices, and pavilioned plan.

A later example of using architecture to promote the corporate brand is The Walt Disney Corporation—a very different kind of company from Big Blue, and one with which I am very familiar, having served on its Board of Directors from 1992 to 2003. The Walt Disney Company was founded in the 1930s to make

*Fig. 16.* Michael Graves &
Associates, Team Disney
Building, Burbank, California,
1986–91

*Fig. 17.* Robert A.M. Stern
Architects, Disney Feature
Animation Building, Burbank,
California, 1991–94

animated movies. By the 1950s it needed to increase the market value of these extremely expensive films by taking greater advantage of the characters they had introduced, using them to "brand" children's toys and common household objects like radios and telephones. Then Walt Disney built theme parks where the characters could be brought to life via costumed actors who walked around a dream world of castles and thrill rides. In the 1980s, when Michael Eisner and Frank Wells took over the company, they set out to grow the brand beyond the walls of the theme parks, which led to the construction of hotels and other venues that could extend the experience.

As a result, the company experienced incredible growth, requiring office buildings for administration and research. One might argue that an office building has nothing to do with a character in a movie or a theme park, and that the two shouldn't be confused—you could just slap a logo on the front door of a building and be done with it. But Eisner felt that everything about Disney should reflect and contribute to the Disney brand in a significant way. Eisner turned to some of the world's best architects to design the company's corporate facilities, but he had the courage to stick to *his* brand, not theirs. Eisner demanded that the architects use their talents to tell the Disney story, and not merely to showcase their individual talents. Architecture, he seemed to say, was not a form of artistic autobiography but one of brand extension.

The architects were challenged to create buildings that testified to the fact that the company meant serious business, but that it could do so without losing the playfulness that is its stock in trade. Team Disney, the company's headquarters in Burbank, has a pediment carried by what the architect Michael Graves calls dwarfatids (fig. 16); Team Disney in Florida, designed by the Japanese architect Arata Isozaki, features vibrant colors; and our Feature Animation Building uses the company's principal symbol for imagination as a starting point for the design (fig. 17).

### Institutional Brands

Today a new trend has arisen: the branding of cultural institutions. We have recently seen the emergence of the Guggenheim Museum as an international franchise, with Frank Gehry's masterpiece in Bilbao, Spain, building on the

*Fig. 18.* Frank Gehry,
Installation view from Project
for a New Guggenheim
Museum in New York City,
Solomon R. Guggenheim
Museum, New York, April 19,
2000–April 25, 2001

*Fig. 19.* Walter Gropius and
The Architects Collaborative,
Harvard Graduate Center,
Harvard University,
Cambridge, Massachusetts,
1948–50

*Fig. 20.* Josep Lluís Sert,
Undergraduate Science
Center, Harvard University,
Cambridge, Massachusetts,
1966–68

Buildings and Brands

brand established by its famous predecessor, Frank Lloyd Wright's Guggenheim Museum in New York. Both architects created curvilinear sculptural buildings set into an urban grid, providing dramatic views from the outside—and equally dramatic interior spaces for the display of art. Soon the Guggenheim will have both a Wright building and a Gehry building in New York (fig. 18)—but can the Guggenheim brand survive such bold but not absolutely complementary visions?

Let me conclude with a case study: Harvard in the postwar era. At the end of World War II, Harvard was confronted by the arguments of intellectuals and a new generation of European-trained architects on its faculty who insisted that a new era demanded a new architecture. Harvard's architecture school, in fact, rebranded itself as the Graduate School of Design. Once again, as in the mid-nineteenth century, the desire to be up-to-date and sophisticated challenged the desire to maintain the identity of an institution, and won. So when Harvard built its first significant postwar building, Walter Gropius's Graduate Center complex on Everett Street, it was not as an extension of Harvard Yard, but in many ways its complete repudiation (fig. 19).

*Fig. 21.* Moshe Safdie, Class of 1959 Chapel, Harvard Business School, Boston, Massachusetts, 1992

Soon, led by Josep Lluís Sert, Gropius's successor as the leading architect on the GSD faculty, Harvard built many modern-style buildings, like Holyoke Center and Peabody Terrace, which looked more like housing projects by Le Corbusier in Marseilles and Nantes, France, than like buildings in Cambridge. Sert's Undergraduate Science Center of 1968 seemed far more expressive of some ideas about science, or at least technology, than it did about its sensitive location just outside Harvard Yard (fig. 20). Each of these modernist buildings made a point about style, technology, the zeitgeist—but what did they contribute to the totality of Harvard? What did they contribute to the preservation of an identity, a sense of place, a community?

Even at the more conservative Harvard Business School, the postwar years were ones of indecision, perhaps best exemplified by the dual aspect of Aldrich Hall of 1953, with its formal, reasonably correct Georgian front facing the McKim, Mead & White campus, and indeterminate rear elevation—Georgian with a twist, some might say, facing the uncharted edge of the campus—and now facing the Spangler Center.

Soon even at the Business School the historic Harvard image was shunted aside in favor of new buildings in the 1960s like South Hall (formerly known as Teele), which represent the bleak side of modernism: all walls and windows and no big ideas; or Philip Johnson's Burden Hall, a much more important building that cloaked an idiosyncratically massed, functionally suspect shape in familiar red brick. More recently there was the Chapel (fig. 21), designed by Moshe Safdie in 1992, which somehow confused the Harvard Business School with MIT, where forty years before, a similar structure was designed by the pioneer modernist Eero Saarinen. Saarinen's chapel related to the abstract classicism of MIT's historic campus and to the brick apartment houses along Memorial Drive that MIT had taken over as dormitories. But what did the new HBS chapel refer to that was place- and institution-specific? The brand of the Harvard experience was in danger of losing its identity.

Safdie's additions to Morgan in 1992 and the construction of Kallmann McKinnell & Wood's Shad Field House in 1991 began to rebuild the brand, reconnecting the present with the past. Now, with the Spangler Center, the image of

the brand is once again affirmed (fig. 22). But it is important to remember that with the construction of the Spangler Center, more is at stake than just the identity of the Business School. With Spangler, Harvard is now not only in Boston but also open to it, so that with the Spangler Center, the brand—the ideas, the beliefs, the history, and the ideals of Harvard as the oldest American university—extend into new territories of geography and time.

# 16

## Rationalism and Romanticism in the Domestic Architecture of George Howe

### 1963

"Modernism," George Howe once said, "is not a style. It is an attitude of mind."[1] Few American architects of his time could make a similar statement with as much authority as this aristocratic Philadelphian, who understood better than most what it means to be modern.

For Howe, modernity was not a simple matter of the fashionable formal solution. His definition of modern architecture was a broad and profound one based not on a concern for new shapes but rather on a determination to find a way of building in the twentieth century that would be a "return to sound tradition . . . that is to say, to the interpretation of function, spiritual as well as material, logically and imaginatively, in terms of modern materials, internally structural as well as visible."[2]

Howe's predilections for expressive form and rational structure directly reflect his personality, which suffered from a split that was no less intellectual than psychological. He was romantic and emotional in feeling but coldly, even dryly, analytical in mind. George Howe was the perfect example of that Harvard graduate whom Henry Adams characterized as "neither American nor European, nor even wholly Yankee; his admirers few, and his critics many; perhaps his worst weakness was his self-criticism and self-consciousness."[3]

George Howe believed that "the peculiar satisfaction . . . architecture . . . can give us is the syncretism of instinct and intelligence which Bergson finds always side by side in the organic world but never coinciding."[4] The diverging strains of instinct and intelligence in Howe's personality, as they are reflected in his architecture, may be labeled romanticism and rationalism. It is their syncretistic interaction in Howe's domestic architecture with which we are concerned today.

Howe's romanticism expressed itself architecturally in two ways. The first was his desire to infuse each of his buildings with associative meaning; that is to say, form, or what he chose to call the "configuration" of a building, was intended to evoke the past without duplicating it. This brings us to the second aspect of his romanticism, which was Howe's desire to produce picturesque architectural effects through geometry. Although the configurations of Howe's buildings differed greatly in the thirty-year span of his career, they all share one thing in common: all are the result of the asymmetrical composition of clearly expressed geometric volumes.

Howe's rationalism manifested itself in a concern for "the assimilation of the spiritual significance of the program in terms of its material fulfillment."[5] Material fulfillment meant structure—not in the engineering sense but in the Beaux-Arts sense, which was concerned with visual expression. Formal intentions were not deemed sufficient; they must be given significance in a process of rationalization, which Howe described as the "ordering of [architectural] elements with due emphasis on the important and subordination of the unimportant, in such a way as to produce a work of art."[6] In this, he was merely restating the basic design philosophy of the Beaux-Arts. The architecture of George Howe was regulated by a system of checks and balances, the rationalism of his Beaux-Arts training serving as a needed corrective to his picturesque and sometimes rebellious romanticism.

Howe was born in 1886; his career in architecture began in 1913, when he was graduated from the École des Beaux-Arts, and continued until his death in 1955.

Shortly after returning to America, Howe built for his own use a house in the Philadelphia suburb of Chestnut Hill. He called it High Hollow (fig. 1). It is a direct expression of theories imbibed at the École but by no means is it a dry working out of rules dutifully learned. It is the work of a man who knew Italy well. But, beyond the languid Italianate air that High Hollow conveys, there are more fundamental qualities, which Paul Cret recognized when he wrote that it is "a very typical example of what modern art ought to be: a logical continuation of the best traditions. It is as free from archaeological imitation as it is devoid of a pretentious striving for originality."[7]

Rational in the disposition of spaces and the handling of materials, romantic in its formal configuration, High Hollow is architecture in the great tradition—a way of building, as Cret wrote, owing "so little to precedents, is true to the best traditions of art; in finding the soul of our art instead of the cast-off clothing of former time."[8]

In 1916, Howe joined with Walter Mellor and Arthur I. Meigs to establish the firm of Mellor, Meigs & Howe. The best known of their designs was the estate of Arthur E. Newbold, built at Laverock, Pennsylvania, from 1922 to 1928 (fig. 2). The size of this unusual project, a gentleman's farm on an enormous scale, should not be considered as typical of the firm's work. Rather, it is the quintessential example of their romanticism, combining generous amounts of architectural make-believe with sound building in a composition that Howe was fond of describing in his later years as a "Jumbo, Anti-Economy, Romantic Country-House Package, complete with sheepfolds, duck ponds, dovecotes and immemorial elms, transplanted at enormous expense."[9] One can easily criticize the escapist philosophy that lay behind the Newbold farm as well as the theatricality of its sagging roofline and of the other details contrived to give the feeling of age. But it would seem more profitable to seek out the virtues in its defects.

Rationalism and Romanticism in the Domestic Architecture of George Howe

Reflecting on his work of the twenties, Howe asked himself: "What were we trying to do, we Romantics and Gothicists? Were we merely trying to recreate a picturesque past without any higher purpose than to arrive at sense-soothing and soporific forms? I venture to say no.

"As I look back on the conviction with which we imposed ducks, sheep, doves and cows on rueful stockbrokers, I am convinced these animals represented to us a 'Symbol,' the symbol of the fruitful soil as opposed to the hundred-acre suburban lot with its dreary monotony of lawn and landscaping. . . . That we . . . gave these symbols a 'Configuration' out of the past shows merely our incapacity to invent a better."[10]

*Fig. 2.* Mellor, Meigs & Howe, Newbold Estate, Laverock, Pennsylvania, 1922–28

The origins of the forms of the Newbold house lie in Howe's and Meigs's interest in the peasant architecture of the Normandy region of France, which they felt derived its richness from the expression—indeed, the over-expression—of certain elements of the building fabric. The elaboration of joints and intersections as well as gates, railings, and door handles gave a richness to the strong geometric forms. At the Newbold farm, the architects sought, according to Meigs, to "bring back forgotten functions and clothe them with a form of grace."[11] Returning the animals to the main entrance and the vegetables to a position in the immediate front of the whole design, they pursued not so much the forms as the methods of the Norman builders down to the smallest detail. For example, as Meigs described it, "The door locks have been pulled out of their holes and set again where they may be seen and enjoyed. The treatment and decoration of function has been the controlling force throughout the entire design, and since function is everywhere in domestic architecture, function becomes the motif of the place."[12]

The architecture of Mellor, Meigs & Howe is also characterized by a consideration for wall surfaces as constructed space definers. At once volumetric and massive, these architectural shapes, if we imagine them stripped of their detail and textures and painted white, qualify as the cones, spheres, and cylinders so often praised during the 1920s by Le Corbusier. What is lacking in the American work is a sense of the possibilities for architecture inherent in the machine—while the work of Le Corbusier, at that early stage of his development, lacked Howe's comprehension of functional and structural relationships.

Disgusted with what he came to call his "Romantic Pastorale" period, Howe left Mellor and Meigs in 1928. This momentous decision to cast his lot in with the Modern Movement was reinforced in a year's time, when he joined William Lescaze, a modernist architect who had come to the U.S. from Switzerland in 1920. Together they established a remarkably successful practice in the newly accepted vocabulary of what William Jordy has isolated as the first, or European, phase of the International Style, and which might more easily be called the "machine style." Their great achievement, PSFS (1930–32), is a central monument in the development of the tall building. No memorable house designs grew out of this association, which was terminated in 1934. One design, however, a house for William Stix Wasserman, had been under discussion since 1929. When the partnership ended, Howe retained the commission and designed the prophetic house, called Square Shadows, which was built in the Whitemarsh Valley, just beyond Chestnut Hill (fig. 3). Completed in 1934, it is Howe's most rational scheme. It is also his protest against the skin-deep formalism of the machine style. Howe found the imitation

*Fig. 3.* George Howe, Square Shadows, Whitemarsh, Pennsylvania, 1932–34

of machine shapes in architecture as false as any of the evocations of historical forms, which he himself had indulged in only a few years before. What Howe felt missing in machine style architecture, especially in such American examples as the 1934 Richard Mandel House at Mount Kisco, New York, by Edward Durell Stone, with which Square Shadows is frequently compared, was his own highly developed sense of rationally expressed structure. Where Stone was merely typical in his willingness to ignore the demands of his discontinuous concrete block structure in favor of an applied aesthetic of sleek, continuous stuccoed surfaces painted white, Howe, acknowledging the facts of his structure, sought to express them in a modern fashion—not to gloss over them. Stone's geometry is skin deep; Howe's is a direct reflection of the way the building is put together.

Up until Square Shadows, Howe had been content to determine the formal configurations of his buildings from the program and to give those configurations significance through rationalized structure. At Square Shadows, he abandoned half of his romanticism—the direct evocation of the past—in favor of the other—a strong geometry based on the facts of a building as a constructed object. In so doing, Howe began at the beginning—going forward from structure toward a romantic configuration.

The clients wanted a modern house with the gracious air of the traditional country houses for which Howe had long been known. Specifically, they did not want a "white elephant" in the Whitemarsh Valley. The plan is baronial. In it, Howe sought to apply to the new aesthetic of dynamic movement, which Sigfried Giedion was to call "flow." Howe interpreted flow as a variation on the Beaux-Arts compositional technique called the *marche*, which had been intended to sequence movement through static spatial groupings. That is to say, spaces are defined by walls, which are considered as planes of contact between them. Their length or the size of their openings measures the openness of the spatial relationships between the various rooms. Thus, as the patterns of movement drawn on the plans indicate, individual spaces, conceived in a static fashion, are related to each other dynamically (fig. 4).

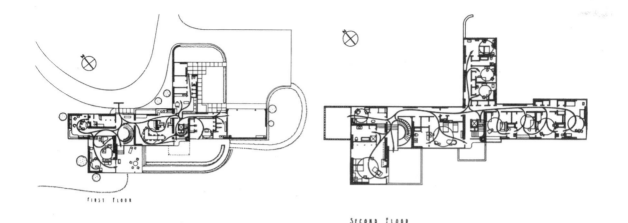

FIRST FLOOR

SECOND FLOOR

The most interesting interior space at Square Shadows is the entrance hall. Concluding that the essential characteristic of such a room is a "sense of passing through," Howe envisioned it as a point of transition between indoors and the outdoors.[13] Using a flying, semicircular spiral stairway that comes in contact with walls only once, he hoped to keep the spatial flow free and to convey a sense of walls extending beyond the stairs without interruption. The construction of the stairway was extremely complex: the close, flush, veneered railings form built-up girders that carry the entire load; treads and risers are cut between these and carry only themselves. The veneered surfaces are sleek—streamlined, to use the vocabulary of the day—and enhance the sense of movement within the space. Howe was able to take the graceful spiral form associated with traditional country house staircases and apply to it a structural system so new as to be almost unique, producing a wholly modern if somewhat glossy restatement.

It is the exterior of Square Shadows that is most revolutionary. All load-bearing walls are built of Chestnut Hill limestone in Howe's customary manner. Non-load-bearing walls, supported either by steel or concrete lintels, are built of red brick laid in a bonding pattern that emphasizes their nonstructural character. Concrete floor slabs are extended to form hoods and balconies, which, where necessary, are supported by tall pipe columns painted black and by concrete girders cast integrally with the slab.

The blunt rectangularity and the elegant fenestration of Square Shadows bear comparison with Mies van der Rohe's brick houses of the 1920s, especially with the Hermann Lange House of 1927–30 at Krefeld, Germany. But it was not until after World War II that Square Shadows found its proper descendant in Le Corbusier's Jaoul Houses, where a comparable structural system combining brick bearing walls and arched concrete floor slabs produces a composition of tremendous force. More importantly, Le Corbusier's own integration of passionate romanticism with rigorous logic—an integration at once more complete and more intense than Howe's—at last seems to have brought to maturity within modernism that highly expressive way of building with simple materials first explored in

*Fig. 4.* George Howe, Square Shadows plans showing spatial flow diagrams, Whitemarsh, Pennsylvania, 1932–34

1923 by Hugo Häring at Garkau. In a fundamental sense, Howe's work had always been part of this movement, which, for many architects today, appears to hold within it the possibility for a modern vernacular.

Square Shadows is little known today but its rigorous logic may yet earn it its proper place in history. Caught between the old and the new—the machine style and the still unlabeled present—and with no ready-made set of formal images yet available, Howe was, typically, ahead of his time but unsure of himself.

Howe once told a group of students at Yale that "architecture . . . though produced by man, resembles more a natural phenomenon than an artifact."[14] This would seem to be the case in the weekend cottage called Fortune Rock, which was designed and built for Mrs. Clara Fargo Thomas at Somes Sound, Mount Desert Island, Maine, from 1937 to 1939 (fig. 5). With its living room wing thrust out on giant double cantilevers, Fortune Rock is both romantic and rational. The forms, no less than the materials, make Fortune Rock an authentic essay in regionalism. Its boldly proportioned, simple rectangular masses with their pitched roofs seem at home in the rugged Maine landscape.

The house is almost entirely the product of native craftsmen. To satisfy Mrs. Thomas's vision of a room that would ride above the waters of Somes Sound at high tide, one that would project itself out over the land and into the enveloping panorama of sea and sky, Howe designed boldly scaled cantilevered beams that were fabricated by a local bridge contractor. Howe himself, with his Beaux-Arts sense of static shapes, had intended to support the living room on columns. His instinct was in one sense correct—as far as his original training was concerned—since this building did more to enrage Howe's academic contemporaries than any other. It is reported to have inspired the eminently Beaux-Arts Everett Meeks of Yale to exclaim, "This, gentlemen, is an example of the cantilever gone mad!" Indeed, the use of such large structural members in residential design is unusual.

Frank Lloyd Wright also made extensive use of the cantilever at Fallingwater in 1936, but there is little structure visible because, as analyzed by Vincent Scully, the architect's concern for horizontal spatial continuity is made to triumph over an expression of vertical support. In addition, the cantilevered decks are simply extensions of the interior spaces, while at Fortune Rock it is the living room— indeed, the whole volume of this wing of the house—that is lifted above the void.

Fortune Rock exemplifies the renewed interest in native building forms and construction techniques that comprised an important part of American architecture during the late 1930s and produced a number of regional movements. The best known of these could be found, ironically, at the geographical extremities of the continent where Native American traditions are most self-consciously cultivated. In New England, Walter Gropius and Marcel Breuer attempted to Americanize European modernism using wood siding and fieldstone, while the pragmatic informality of William Wurster in California gradually grew more Japanese in its handling of shapes and materials. Fortune Rock stands apart from the work of these men. It is comparable, however, to the house for Weston Havens, designed by Harwell Hamilton Harris in 1940. The dramatic siting of this bold house and the interesting use of inverted gables come close in spirit to Howe's design.

There is a haunting quality of loneliness about Fortune Rock that reminds one of the paintings of Edward Hopper, especially his *Rooms by the Sea*. As in

*Fig. 5.* George Howe, Fortune Rock, Mount Desert Island, Maine, 1937–39

Hopper's painting, there is at Fortune Rock a strong tension between the man-made and the natural; the hard clear lines of the window frames and the deep blue waters of Somes Sound below.

With barely a toehold on American soil, Fortune Rock is both American and modern. Here, on the Maine seacoast, George Howe, that lonely Harvard graduate, neither European nor American nor even wholly Yankee, fulfilled his architectural search. We see him here, standing on the balcony—so like the bridge of a ship—looking back toward Europe, where he had learned so much. He had succeeded in dumping overboard the excess baggage of the past without losing sight of the lessons it has to teach. Here, at Fortune Rock, the interaction between Howe's romanticism—the memory of the past expressed geometrically—and his rationalism—the action of the present expressed structurally—seems to have transcended the syncretism of Bergson and become a synthesis.

Howe's importance lies, finally, not so much in his buildings as in their relationships to the time in which he lived. In another talk to Yale students, Howe said, "Our aim must be to contribute . . . to the creation, not just of architecture, whether good or bad, but of *an* architecture, an architectural *style*, expressive of and worthy of our time.

"A *great style* is not made by uttering great words. . . . A *great style* is not made at all. It is discovered by a host of explorers with their minds and hearts full of the thoughts and feelings of their day. When it is discovered it becomes the property of a whole culture, to draw on as it will, until it has been sucked dry of meaning in its turn.

"The time for the discovery of a great style may be ripe. The opportunity, not only to share, but to lead in the exploration is ours. . . . This task we shall share together."[15]

Rationalism and Romanticism in the Domestic Architecture of George Howe

# 17

## Robert Moses as Architect
### 1989

Robert Moses never trained as an architect or as an engineer, yet he was the principal in a massive enterprise of public works, conceptualizing and realizing a synthesis of roads, buildings, and landscape that would define New York City's form for the better part of the twentieth century.[1] To understand Moses as architect—by the mid 1930s many called him "the greatest architect in New York"—it is important not only to look at the work of Moses's chief consulting architects and engineers but also to consider his own beliefs about architecture. Moses's principal architectural achievements extend from the late 1920s, when he masterminded Jones Beach, to the early 1940s, by which time he had completed his parkway system and the 1939 New York World's Fair. From the point of view of architectural aesthetics, it was an important time of change, when architects took sides in the struggle between traditionalism and modernism.

Moses was no casual observer of this battle of styles. He was a full-fledged combatant who remained openly and consistently contemptuous of modernism. His view of architecture mirrored his overall philosophy. Moses was a reformer but not a radical. He was interested in adapting the best ideas of the past to the realities of his own era. In 1940 he sought to reassure the readership of *Architectural Forum* that his program for the physical transformation of New York did not embody radical change. "We are the apostles of change but not of revolution," he wrote. "We do not advocate change as a philosophy. We are not iconoclasts by profession nor breakers of tradition by temperament nor, on the other hand, have we any predilection for keeping things as they are because they have been so for a long time."[2]

Robert Moses felt he had a public obligation not to stand on the cutting edge of architecture, but rather to adapt the possibilities of modern materials and the realities of modern scale to what he called "the standards which have pleased the eye and worn well for centuries."[3] In 1940 he stated that "public officials have no right to experiment beyond a reasonable point with new forms in architecture. . . . A public building has to last a long time. It has to wear well not only physically but esthetically. It is not a thing which can be lightly torn down if in a comparatively short time it proves objectionable, clashes with surrounding buildings or does not continue to be useful."[4]

Perhaps nothing contributes better to an understanding of Moses's aesthetic traditionalism than his attack on modernist design, published in the June 1947 magazine section of the *New York Herald Tribune*. In it he wrote, "The *functionalist* or *modernist*, having cut himself off from the lessons of the past, is untrammeled, iconoclastic, revolutionary, out of breath and in a great hurry to go for the sake of going. He claims that his great objective is to adapt form to use. His real ambition is to be a few steps ahead of his unborn grandchildren."[5]

And perhaps no building epitomized what Moses vehemently detested about modernist design more than the Municipal Asphalt Plant, completed in 1944 by the firm of Ely Jacques Kahn and Robert Allan Jacobs and now serving as a community building. The asphalt plant, loosely based on the work of the French engineer Eugene Freyssinet, was constructed of exposed concrete over an arched steel frame on a bend of the East River just north of Carl Schurz Park (1935), one of Moses's favorite projects. Shortly after its completion Moses wrote a letter to Manhattan Borough President Edgar J. Nathan, Jr., in which he asked, "Is this architecture or what? I suppose the explanation is that these things are functional. Who had the idea of the Cathedral of Asphalt and the Corrugated Shoe Box? . . . These things are unnecessarily ugly and obtrusive. They interfere with residential development to the west. If we must have freakish experiments, why shouldn't they be privately financed? After all, we will have to live with these monstrosities a long time."[6]

Yet, even under the umbrella of traditionalism, Moses did not advocate a particular style or a singular approach to form. His tastes were, in his own words, "varied and catholic."[7] Arnold Vollmer, a landscape architect and engineer who was a friend of Moses from 1935 until Moses's death in 1981, writes, "There was no such thing as a Moses style in design other than in a social sense. It is the quality of function, durability, and public use that characterizes his works, not uniformity of architectural design."[8] Nevertheless, I believe we can distinguish some common threads of design that help stitch together the fabric of independently designed beaches, parks, swimming pool complexes, parkways, and bridges of the Moses era. The public architecture in which he had a decisive influence was as a whole governed by the grand axiality and attention to detail characteristic of the Franco-American tradition of classical planning generically known as the Beaux-Arts. For Moses, architecture, landscape, and engineering were all disciplines within the larger context of the physical structuring of urban form.

Throughout his career Moses for the most part relied on the combined or singular efforts of three men to design the vast body of work, which, by virtue of its widely celebrated marriage of social concern and architectural excellence, had less-informed observers thinking that Moses was some sort of architectural deity. These three men were the engineer Othmar Ammann, the landscape architect Gilmore D. Clarke, and the architect Aymar Embury II. Two of them, Clarke and Embury, were certainly not the "giants of their profession" that Robert Caro calls them in his book *The Power Broker,*[9] but Ammann was, and all three were distinguished, well known, and respected in their fields. While there were many lesser-known architects and engineers working on Moses's staff, Ammann, Clarke, and Embury led a team whose collective genius was demonstrated not by its stylistic innovations but by the usually more than competent, sometimes glorious architecture it created. Together, they married traditional form to modern programs and materials; together, they created a public landscape of enduring utility and visual appeal.

Before looking at some of Moses's projects it is useful to consider the work that Ammann, Clarke, and Embury each produced before their association with Moses's programs. Othmar Ammann worked on nearly every one of Moses's major bridges for a period of over thirty years, beginning with his appointment as chief consulting engineer for the Triborough Bridge and Tunnel Authority in 1934. Ammann was trained in his native Switzerland at the Swiss Federal Polytechnic Institute of Zurich, and soon after his arrival in New York in 1904 he began his career assisting Gustav Lindenthal, one of the greatest bridge builders of the early century.

Lindenthal believed that bridge design was not simply a matter of civil engineering but also a problem of civic design, preferring to collaborate with architects in designing his bridges. Ammann assisted Lindenthal on the design for the Hell Gate Bridge, which, when completed in 1916, was the largest steel-arch bridge in the world. Henry Hornbostel, the architect, worked with Lindenthal on this bridge to create an eloquent dialogue between stasis and fluidity. In 1920 Ammann helped Lindenthal develop plans for an unrealized Hudson River Crossing at Fifty-ninth Street, a project Lindenthal had been working on since the late 1880s.

Ammann went into business for himself in 1923, and just one year later began to establish an independent reputation with his work on the George Washington Bridge (1927–31), a project that triumphantly rendered Lindenthal's long-standing and widely publicized dream of spanning the Hudson River at its mouth a *fait accompli.*

The construction of the George Washington Bridge was heralded not only as a technological feat but also as a magnificent work of architecture. Significantly, the stone casing designed by Cass Gilbert for the bridge towers was left off, not only for economic reasons, but also for aesthetic ones. Reflecting the growing influence of modernist functionalism, Ammann's structure was so admired during construction that it was left unsheathed. Today, almost through inadvertence, it is regarded as an important manifestation of the modernist spirit in America.

Ammann once made an assertion about bridge design that could have been Moses's own. He said that "economics and utility are not the engineer's only concerns. He must temper his practicality with esthetic sensitivity. His structures should please the eye. In fact, an engineer designing a bridge is justified in making a more expensive design for beauty's sake alone. After all, many people will have to look at the bridge for the rest of their lives. Few of us appreciate eyesores, even if we should save a little money by building them."[10]

This assertion could also have been made by Gilmore Clarke, the second of Moses's collaborators. A native New Yorker, Clarke obtained a Bachelor of Science degree from Cornell University in 1913. Before working as consulting landscape architect on nearly every one of Moses's road and park projects, Clarke was superintendent of construction for the Bronx River Parkway, the success of which led to the creation of the Westchester County Park Commission, which he served as chief landscape architect from 1923 to 1935. By that time Clarke had established a national reputation. He founded the civil engineering firm Clarke & Rapuano with partner Michael Rapuano in 1937, served as the dean of Cornell's College of Architecture from 1938 to 1950, and from 1937 to 1950 was chairman of the National Fine Arts Commission, a position to which he was not reappointed because of his sharp disagreement with President Truman about the architectural appropriateness of the balcony Truman added to the south portico of the White House.

Clarke was responsible for a series of brick and stone bridges and naturalistically landscaped rights-of-way for the pioneering Bronx River Parkway. In 1922, near the parkway's completion, Clarke published an article on bridge design in *American Architect*, in which he observed that "most small highway bridges in this country are designed with only a utilitarian idea in mind; seldom does the architect lend a hand in the design of these structures, for the engineer assumes that art is not a consideration. As a result we have the ugly concrete bridges which adorn our highways. . . . Why should we not add a touch of the artistic to our highway bridges; why not add charm to our country highways by the addition of structures fitting to the surroundings, structures in tune with nature, rather than adopt the hideous concrete designs of the engineer, who seldom knows art?"[11]

In 1933, just one year before architect Aymar Embury II was asked to serve as consultant to Chief Engineer Othmar Ammann on the Triborough Bridge, Clarke wrote another article for *American Architect and Architecture* titled "New Bridges Mean Opportunity for Architects," in which he again stressed the need for "architectural skill in development of all types of bridges."[12] Clarke blamed the poor attitude of technically minded public works commissioners for what he thought were purely utilitarian, banal bridges. He quoted one as saying, "Architects are not necessary. We can design bridges as well as they can. We don't need any help from them!"[13]

Fortunately, Moses was never so narrow-minded. For the design of the Triborough Bridge and many bridges thereafter, Moses himself engineered the brilliant collaboration between engineer and architect. Aymar Embury II, who, ironically, never attended architecture school, was the most influential of Moses's aesthetic guides. A native New Yorker and life-long city resident, he earned a civil engineering degree from Princeton in 1900 and an M.S. degree in engineering from Princeton a year later. He began his career as an apprentice with the architectural firm of George B. Post & Sons. Post, also trained as an engineer, had been one of Richard Morris Hunt's students in the famed Tenth Street Studio and was a direct heir to Hunt's grand vision of architectural urbanism. Post's New York Stock Exchange (1903) was representative of his mature work. After eight months with Post, Embury went on to work with a succession of distinguished architects, including Cass Gilbert, Howells and Stokes, and finally Palmer and Hornbostel, the latter the very same architect who worked with Lindenthal, not only on the Hell Gate Bridge, but also on his 1903 proposal for the redesign of the Manhattan Bridge. Hornbostel also worked with Lindenthal on the remarkable Queensboro Bridge (1909), which was a superb fin-de-siècle synthesis of the Gothic and the classical in metal. Lindenthal and Hornbostel's work represented a high level of

*Fig. 1.* Aymar Embury II, Guild Hall, East Hampton, New York, 1931

collaboration between engineer and architect, which must surely have impressed Embury and influenced his later collaboration with Ammann.

In 1906 Embury won first prize in a competition for a modest double house sponsored by the Garden City Company of Garden City, Long Island. The publicity from the competition brought with it many commissions that would establish Embury's reputation as a leading architect of modest suburban houses as well as somewhat more lavish country houses. He compiled photographs of similar work by other architects and published several books, including *One Hundred Country Houses* in 1909, *The Dutch Colonial House* in 1913, and *Country Houses* in 1914, which showcases his own work. Typically, Embury's early houses adapt the Dutch colonial mode, but bring to it a heightened sense of monumentality through the use of overscaled moldings and porch columns. Embury was selected to design East Hampton's library in 1910. Later, as a summer resident of the village he designed its Guild Hall (fig. 1), completed in 1931, just before he began working for the New York City Park Department. That design, which can be seen as a jumping-off point for much of Embury's subsequent park architecture, was an abstracted federal-style composition of simple, geometrically distinct volumes, rendered in white painted brick, and incorporating a charming walled garden planted by his wife, the landscape designer Ruth Dean.

Though open to the evolving aesthetic of twentieth-century modernism, Embury, like Moses, was fundamentally a traditionalist. By virtue of his training as an engineer, his work with Hornbostel, and his marriage to Ruth Dean, he was also clearly sensitive to the interrelationship of buildings, technology, and landscape that would be the hallmarks of Moses's style. As Moses put it in 1951, Aymar Embury II was "a living link between two centuries."[14]

Embury, again like Moses, had little tolerance for modernist theorizing. "If an architect has any function," he told an interviewer in 1938, "it is to coordinate units so that they do a required job and at the same time create a pleasant emotion. Modernists believe that the essence of their work is to do something that has never been done before. They leave off all ornamentation because, they say, the ornaments do not aid the structure to do its job. I suppose some of these architects do not use neckties or buttons when they dress."[15]

It was not Embury but Herbert Magoon who was credited as the architect for Moses's first and most acclaimed public project, Jones Beach State Park (1926–29). Along with John Matthews Hatton, who was actually the designer of several works credited to Embury, Magoon was one of many unknown but skilled architects who, unable to find work in the private sector during the Great Depression, went to work for various of Moses's enterprises. Nevertheless, according to the article "Pattern for Parks" in the December 1936 *Architectural Forum*, it was Moses who initiated many of the design ideas that make Jones Beach so extraordinary. Jones Beach, the editors pointed out, "was a project which had burgeoned in the Moses mind even before the creation of the Long Island State Park Commission, and his faithful lieutenants take pleasure in pointing out that in its final plan, Jones Beach deviates in no important respect from the original sketches made by Moses. Certainly he staked his personal reputation a thousand times on the success of the idea."[16] The article also noted that Moses, exasperated with his architectural staff's lack of imagination, sent them all the way to Florida to show them how banal one of their designs was.

*Fig. 2.* Herbert Magoon,
East Bathhouse, Jones Beach,
New York, 1929

*Fig. 3.* Herbert Magoon,
West Bathhouse, Jones Beach,
New York, 1931

Caro has written that Moses's admiration for Murgatroyd and Ogden's 1927 Barbizon Hotel prompted his choice of stone and brick for the facades of the Jones Beach bathhouses. According to Caro, Moses thought that the Ohio sandstone, with its traces of tan and blue, and the Barbizon brick, with its varying hues of sandy brown, would best harmonize with the colors of the sand and the ocean.

Though the palette of materials is similar in each of the bathhouses, the designs are quite different. In 1940 Moses compared the two, writing, "I think they represent a reasonable compromise between modernists and traditionalists. . . . If an illustration is needed of the limits of ultra-modern design as applied to structures of this kind, it is only necessary to compare the original East Bathhouse [1929] at Jones Beach with the later West Bathhouse [1931]. The West Bathhouse . . . lacks the dignity, simplicity and beauty of the original East Bathhouse. The architect was just a little too gay and playful with the West Bathhouse, especially with the facade toward the ocean. It is interesting but not first rate, and it would have been better to have followed the severer lines of the earlier structure than to try to do something entirely new and different."[17]

The East Bathhouse (fig. 2) was the premier building at Jones Beach. With its simple masses of brick and stone and its crisply rendered planes, it owes quite a lot to the simplified Gothicism of the 1920s, as seen in the work of Giles Gilbert Scott, Bertram Grosvenor Goodhue, and Sir Edwin Lutyens. The West Bathhouse (fig. 3) is more directly linked with the landscape and, in this aspect, also is indebted to Lutyens's example.

In order to transform a necessary feature, the water tower, into an amenity, Herbert Magoon suggested that it be designed like a lighthouse. But Moses thought that too prosaic and proposed instead a streamlined version of the campanile at San Marco, with which Magoon obliged him (fig. 4). The design evokes both the campanile and Walker & Gillette's Playland Music Tower at Rye, New York, a project with which Clarke and the Westchester County Park Department were involved until the late 1920s. A closer look at the water tower reveals how Moses was able to instill the spirit of craftsmanship in his architects.

It is at Jones Beach that the breadth of Moses's vision is most completely visible. He may not quite have been God, but he was certainly everywhere to be seen in the details. At Moses's suggestion the directional signs were decorated with ironwork puckishly depicting various waterside activities. Moses's boardwalk was modeled after the promenade deck of a great luxury liner, a nautical theme that was carried down to the waste receptacles placed in mock ship's funnels.

Robert Moses as Architect

*Fig. 4.* Herbert Magoon, Water Tower, Jones Beach, New York, 1934

*Fig. 5.* Gilmore D. Clarke, Bronx River Parkway, New York, 1917–25

Coinciding with the construction of Jones Beach State Park was the design of the Long Island State Parkways, one of the most dynamic syntheses of architecture, engineering, and landscape architecture during Moses's career. As the philosopher Marshall Berman observed in 1975, "These roads, still among the most beautiful in the world, do not (like California's Coast Highway) cross or adjoin or highlight a beautiful environment: the point about them is that they are *in themselves* a beautiful environment. Even if they adjoined nothing and led nowhere, they still would be, as we said in the Sixties, a trip. Thus Moses, who never learned to drive, inspired what has since become one of the basic (and, alas, costly) American experiences: driving as an end in itself. He became a national hero."[18]

The parkway concept grew out of a tradition of road building that goes back to Frederick Law Olmsted. Its specific precedents were the Vanderbilt Parkway on Long Island, completed in 1911, and the Bronx River Parkway, completed in 1924. The Vanderbilt Parkway, a toll road, constituted the first crossing-free automobile road in America, complete with gatehouses and an inn designed by John Russell Pope. Initially designed for William Vanderbilt to accommodate the Vanderbilt Cup Auto Races, it came into its own as a recreational parkway in the 1920s because it gave the automobile an uninterrupted right-of-way similar to that which only the railroad had previously enjoyed. In the early 1930s Moses absorbed stretches of the Vanderbilt Parkway into his Northern State Parkway. However, the better known Bronx River Parkway (fig. 5) offered the recreational driver the pleasure of travel along a longer and more scenic stretch of roadway. Here Gilmore Clarke adapted the curvilinear road and bridge designs to the existing topography with such skill that it prompted Moses to enlist his talent for the design of the Long Island State Parkways, where his bridge designs recall early European highway bridges, which he admired for their seemingly craftsmen-inspired charm, and for their beauty of color and texture made possible by the use of native stone.

Moses prohibited commercial development and the use of billboards along the parkways and commissioned his architects to design fencing, signage, light-posts, and police barracks. The filling stations (fig. 6), designed by Embury, even more than Clarke's bridges, show how far Moses was prepared to go in elevating the banal elements of everyday life into enduring works of architecture.

Moses understood that the aesthetic of his parkways had to be different from that of the metropolitan expressway. No facility was more critical to the city's suburbanization than Ammann and Embury's Triborough Bridge (1936), which constituted a complex system of bridges and connecting roadways that tied together upper Manhattan, the Bronx, and Queens. Moses conceived of bridge construction as a synthesis of architecture, engineering, and landscape architecture. Embury told the American Society of Civil Engineers in 1944, "It is only within the last few years, particularly because of the vision of Mr. Robert Moses, that the bridge approaches have been made ornaments to the neighborhood in which they occur, rather than detriments to them. . . . There is no excuse for ugly engineering structures. Ugliness and economy by no means march hand in hand."[19]

Assisted by the talented architect and renderer A. Gordon Lorimer, Embury created a stylishly modern bridge complex with the lines of force captured in the shaping of the massive cable anchorages; also of interest are the streamlined toll booths and the lighting pylons.

From the point of view of architecture, Moses's most elegant bridge was the Bronx-Whitestone Bridge (1939) (fig. 7), designed by Ammann and Embury to coincide with the opening of the New York World's Fair. The Bronx-Whitestone

*Fig. 6.* Aymar Embury II, Filling station for the New York Park Department, ca. 1940

*Fig. 7.* Othmar Ammann and Aymar Embury II, Bronx-Whitestone Bridge, New York, 1939

*Fig. 8.* Calvert Vaux with Jacob Wrey Mould, Central Park Casino, New York, New York, late 1860s; interiors redesigned in 1929 by Joseph Urban; demolished 1935

*Fig. 9.* Aymar Embury II and Gilmore D. Clarke, Central Park Zoo, New York, New York, 1934

Bridge was the undisputed favorite of Moses, Ammann, and Embury, even after plate girders were added to lessen widespread fear about the streamlined bridge's stability. Moses reflected in his 1956 book *Public Works: A Dangerous Trade*: "The lesson of the Bronx-Whitestone plate girders is that although the quest for beauty as such is never to be scorned, it must not be pursued to extremes but subordinated to practical considerations. . . . Let me add that in my book, the Bronx-Whitestone is *still* the most beautiful suspension bridge in the world."[20]

Moses's appointment as the commissioner of the New York City Park Department in 1934 enabled him to focus his vision on the city at the height of the Great Depression, which ironically turned out to be the means to rescue a demoralized staff and an abused system of open spaces, using federal funds available from newly established relief agencies. In 1934 Central Park was dilapidated, home to many unemployed who lived in shantytowns that were derisively called Hoovervilles. Within the first five months of his appointment Moses completed no less than 1,700 park renovation projects across the city. Although the financial constraints of the period required Moses to use less expensive materials with less embellishment than was allowed at Jones Beach, the results were sometimes no less inspired.

A potent symbol of Moses's intention to separate the Park Department from its demeaned state under the fun-loving but corrupt regime of Mayor Jimmy Walker was his demolition of Joseph Urban's extraordinary 1929 Casino (fig. 8), replacing it in 1937 with the archetypal Rumsey Playground, similar to 255 other such facilities constructed in New York City between 1931 and 1935.

One of Moses's most dramatic projects was the transformation of Central Park's run-down Menagerie, the nation's oldest zoo, into a cluster of charming small-scale red-brick buildings designed by Embury and containing a cafeteria as well as animal houses (fig. 9). Completed in 1934, Embury and Clarke's zoo incorporated Martin Thompson's adjoining arsenal of 1848, which Moses refurbished to serve as the Park Department headquarters.

A year later Embury and Clarke collaborated on the redesign of the Prospect Park Zoo in Brooklyn, arranging buildings in a semicircle, with the domed

Elephant House in the middle of the arc and a pool for seals at the core (fig. 10). Despite the refusal of the Civil Works Administration to approve the use of anything other than the most inexpensive materials, Embury added delightful touches of ornamentation to the buildings of both zoos, including friezes on the animal houses depicting the activities of their occupants.

Bryant Park was perhaps the most drastic of Moses's park renovation projects. Here his urban vision is clear; formal plantings replace the Victorian informality of the original park, which had, in the words of *Architecture* editor Henry Saylor, become "one of the most disreputable . . . in the city."[21] The highly formalized scheme, outlined by Lusby Simpson and executed by Embury and Clarke, was designed to include a wide lawn flanked by rows of trees (fig. 11). A terrace, punctuated by the Lowell Memorial Fountain designed by Charles Platt, could be reached by a broad flight of steps leading up from Sixth Avenue.

Moses's most inventive park developments in Manhattan were located in the residential areas along the Hudson, East, and Harlem rivers, where new facilities for active recreation were made possible by the construction of peripheral highways that formed the basis of his ultimate plan to provide a continuous New York parkway system linking the inner city to the outer boroughs and to the growing suburbs beyond.

On the West Side of Manhattan, Moses brought to fruition plans for improvements that had been proposed as early as 1885, including the covering of the New York Central railroad's tracks and the creation of a limited-access water-level Henry Hudson Parkway at the edge of a revitalized Riverside Park. The Parkway's highlight, completed in 1936, was Clifton Lloyd's traffic rotary at Seventy-ninth Street, which doubled as the inner courtyard for a grand park and marina complex Moses had envisioned years before (fig. 12).

According to Caro, Carl Schurz Park, on the East River, represents one of the few smaller projects in which Moses took a personal interest because he passed it during his evening walks from his Gracie Terrace apartment. Here again, "Moses is in the details." The park's elaborate reconstruction by Harvey Stevenson and

*Fig. 10.* Aymar Embury II and Gilmore D. Clarke, Prospect Park Zoo, Brooklyn, New York, 1935

*Fig. 11.* Lusby Simpson, Aymar Embury II and Gilmore D. Clarke, Bryant Park, New York, New York, 1934

Robert Moses as Architect

Cameron Clark included a waterside promenade, John Finley Walk, perched above a double-decked stretch of the East River Drive.

The idea of integrating inner-city parks and roadways reached an apotheosis with the esplanade on Brooklyn Heights (1945–50) where two levels of express roadways are tucked beneath a broad harbor-facing pedestrian promenade, marking the culmination of the glory days of Moses's public works.

### The Neighborhood Pool

As pressing as the need for restored parks and new parkways was the need for active-recreation facilities in densely populated neighborhoods. To this end, Moses, who had been a member of Yale's swim team, constructed ten neighborhood swimming pool complexes in 1936. These structures, even more than Jones Beach, represented the extent to which Moses could combine a social concern with architectural excellence.

Moses's pools went far beyond their function to become grand urban landmarks—through their triumphal arches lay physical health and social wellbeing. The comparison between Moses's pools cannot be made with similar facilities; among American sports buildings of the period they are in a class by themselves. They can only be contrasted with grand Olympic facilities realized in Berlin and Amsterdam, or monumental structures such as war memorials. For example, Herbert Magoon's Crotona Park Pool (fig. 13) seems to have been influenced by Lutyens's War Memorial at Thiepval, France (fig. 14), completed in the late 1920s, while Embury's McCarren Park Pool (fig. 15) seems to have been based on Karl Ehn's triumphantly proletarian Karl Marx Hof in Vienna, completed in 1930 (fig. 16). We can assume that with the Astoria Park Pool Bathhouse Moses himself opted for a more modernist expression, given that the individual architects involved in this swimming pool project—Hatton and Embury—had no particular association with modernism.

Moses also sought to bring the kinds of facilities that had earned him international fame at Jones Beach closer to home, where they would be easily accessible

*Fig. 13.* Herbert Magoon, Crotona Park Pool bathhouse, Bronx, New York, 1936. Rendering of main entrance by J. MacGilchrist.

*Fig. 14.* Sir Edwin Lutyens, Memorial to the Missing of the Somme, Thiepval, France, 1928–32

*Fig. 15.* Aymar Embury II, McCarren Park Pool Bathhouse, Brooklyn, New York, 1936

*Fig. 16.* Karl Ehn, Karl Marx-Hof, Vienna, Austria, 1927–30

Robert Moses as Architect

*Fig. 17.* Aymar Embury II and Gilmore D. Clarke, Orchard Beach Bathhouse, Bronx, New York, 1936

*Fig. 18.* John Matthews Hatton, Pelham Bay Golf Clubhouse, Bronx, New York, 1936. Rendering by Eugene Marugg.

to city dwellers using mass transit. According to Caro, Moses informed Embury and Clarke that their work at Orchard Beach (fig. 17), located in Pelham Bay Park in the Bronx (1936), should be less horizontal than at the Jones Beach bathhouses, and that they should start thinking about incorporating columns or a colonnade. The plan for Pelham Bay Park incorporated a golf course serviced by a clubhouse designed by John Matthews Hatton in 1936 (fig. 18). Here a movie-set-influenced American version of the Regency style created a sophisticated setting for public golfing comparable to that of any private membership club. Moses did not believe that public architecture should talk down to the public, who, he seemed to be saying, deserved the very best.

As proposed by Gilmore Clarke in 1937, Flushing Meadows Park (fig. 19) was meant to be the capstone of Moses's park system. It is the ultimate expression of Moses's professed goal of achieving *rus in urbe*, which he claimed was the goal of the Greeks and Romans. He sought to use the 1939 New York World's Fair as an excuse to completely transform the site from, in Moses's words, a dump to glory. Moses began thinking about Flushing Meadows' possibilities in 1934, when he was appointed park commissioner. He was very impressed with the vivid image of the site in *The Great Gatsby* and frequently quoted F. Scott Fitzgerald's description of it:

> About half way between West Egg and New York the motor road hastily joins the railroad and runs beside it for a quarter of a mile, so as to shrink away from a certain desolate area of land. This is a valley of ashes—a fantastic farm where ashes grow like wheat into ridges and hills and grotesque gardens; where ashes take the forms of houses and chimneys and rising smoke. . . . The valley of ashes is bounded on one side by a small foul river, and, when the drawbridge is up to let barges through, the passengers on waiting trains can stare at the dismal scene for as long as half an hour.[22]

### Postwar Decline and Fall

The post–World War II work brought with it a definite collapse of standards. Surely Moses tried to get the best work he could, but something drastic had happened. Virtually none of the plastic texture and detail, the classicized form, or the sense of place that characterized his early projects appears in the housing and slum clearance projects that occupied his late career. Nevertheless, while many of these projects constitute social and architectural failures, they still powerfully symbolize Moses's earnestly felt idealism. In his book *All That Is Solid Melts Into*

*Air*, Marshall Berman suggests that by the 1950s Moses "was no longer building in accord with his own visions; rather, he was fitting enormous blocks into a pre-existing pattern of national reconstruction and social integration that he had not made and could not have substantially changed."[23] Ironically, Moses himself was highly critical of the sometimes brutally utilitarian architecture that characterized new public housing across the country. In 1947, just one year before taking on the position of chairman of the Mayor's Slum Clearance Committee, Moses wrote:

*Fig. 19.* Gilmore D. Clarke, Proposal for Flushing Meadow Park, Queens, New York, 1937. Aerial perspective by J. MacGilchrist.

> Some of our great housing projects, because of high land values and building costs, must go up into the air ten or more stories. But need they look like prisons? Here and there we find an apologetic, ectoplasmic figure to break the endless expanse of brick, a meaningless statue which looks for all the world as if it were about to ooze back into the wall. . . . Why not ornament? Because we are told it is neither economical nor functional and spoils the mass effect. What rubbish! Does not the human eye delight in ornament? Is landscaping to be our only relief from the monotony of repetitive design?[24]

Clearheaded as he was about most architectural issues, Moses was not very clear about those of housing. For example, he ridiculed the concept of Clarence Stein's excellent Hillside Homes development of 1934 as a form of urbanism that, in his words, "should come under the head [sic] of research and trial and error, not touted as successful achievements."[25] But in saying this, I think Moses was not quite honest even with himself. He wrote this critique of what he called "community architecture" in his defensive book, *Public Works: A Dangerous Trade*, which he published in 1956 amid the storm of protest that surrounded such of his projects as Washington Square Village and Manhattantown. It was a bad time for Moses, whose urban renewal projects were being assailed by the press and public as "dull utopias." But in his more candid moments Moses was not insensitive to

*Fig. 20.* Proposed Lower Manhattan Expressway, Rendering of view to the east, 1950. Moses began promoting the highway in 1940, beginning a twenty-nine-year effort that eventually was defeated in 1969.

*Fig. 21.* Wallace K. Harrison, Max Abramovitz, Philip Johnson, Eero Saarinen, Gordon Bunshaft, Pietro Belluschi and others, Lincoln Center, New York, New York, 1959–69

the banality of the postwar housing projects. Tragically, he just seemed unable to see his way toward an imaginative solution comparable to what he had realized for the south shore of Long Island or Flushing Meadow. Instead, for the first time in his career he fell back on utilitarian functionalism as an excuse for bad design. In an August 1957 letter, Moses asked James Dawson, director of development for the New York City Housing Authority, to respond to the overwhelming criticism of his Title I Slum Clearance projects, stating that "no doubt the design is repetitive and monotonous but there is a reason for tall buildings and someone in authority ought to state it."[26]

When Moses proposed the Mid-Manhattan and Lower Manhattan Expressways in the 1960s (fig. 20), it was clear that he had completely subordinated architecture to what he thought were more important concerns, namely, to address what Berman called "the technological and social responsibilities of modern life."[27] This is a challenge to which Moses had already responded outside of the city with the creation of his Long Island State Parkways. Moses no doubt believed, as the Swiss engineer and architectural historian Sigfried Giedion had observed in 1941, that "the parkway is not an isolated traffic lane independent of the organism of the city. It simply has a different scale from that of the existing city with its *rue corridor* and its rigid division into small blocks. No facilities of approach can really accomplish anything unless the city changes its actual structure."[28] But whereas Moses's suburban parkways had a comprehensive order of their own, his urban expressways, cut through a dense urban fabric, have none of the grand social and planning vision about them. Rather, they seem to take cues from the old elevated trains of Manhattan, or from postwar highway design, on which he consulted in Tokyo, Japan. Moses had altogether lost his large vision.

Clearly the cross-Manhattan expressways went too far; the citizens, alert to the destructiveness of Moses's power, rejected his plan and turned their back on the man who had once been their hero.

Moses did have one great triumph in his late career. Although he was not directly involved with the architecture of Lincoln Center, he was sympathetic to the classical grandeur of the collaborating architects' conception (fig. 21). When Lincoln Center opened in 1964, its architecture, urban planning, and social engineering were widely derided. But now, twenty-five years later, while the architecture may not exactly be deemed good, Lincoln Center and its great plaza have become a major democratic gathering place. Perhaps, in the end, Moses knew what he was doing after all.

# 18

## On Philip Johnson
### 1996

On a recent BBC documentary, *Philip Johnson: Godfather of American Architecture*, Peter Eisenman was asked to identify the greatest living American architect. Looking very uncomfortable, smiling nervously, placing a hand in front of his mouth, and then rubbing his hands together, Peter hedged the question by replying that he found "it difficult to answer questions about whether people are great architects or not," and going on to say that he found "Philip Johnson to be . . . a . . . a very powerful architect . . . ah . . . and a very powerful and diverse and wonderful human being."

John Brodie, a journalist who was also on the show, attributed Eisenman's clear dodge of the question to the typical mean-spirited inability of one architect to acknowledge the gifts of another. But I think there's more to Eisenman's smiling cringe than petty jealousy. What I think is that Philip has not been granted his due by very many of his colleagues because he has dared to be an architect engaged with the larger world, not only of ideas but of political action. As a fixer, polemicist, historian, critic, Philip Johnson is at the top of most lists. But the price for this real-world life is that his very considerable achievements as an architect qua architect have been seriously undervalued.

There are other reasons why the profession fails to recognize Philip's contributions as a leading architect. The reasons reveal a lot about the limited horizons architects have for their profession: in an age obsessed with self-referential object making, Philip Johnson, who is nothing if not an object maker, has committed the cardinal sin of not being self-referential. He is one of the few of his generation, or mine, for that matter, who has made a genuine effort to connect and to comment—to connect with and comment on the past, to connect with and comment on the work of his contemporaries (and rivals), to connect with and comment on the client's goals.

Philip has not seen architecture as autobiography or as an *explication de texte*. Daringly, he has seen architecture as it was always seen before the modernists, as a service to the king in the time of kings, to rich patrons and developers and the like in the time of democratic capitalism, which is our own. And Philip has served his clients very well—and served the public very well, also, with buildings that are outstanding exemplars of their genre. His work for the Rockefellers includes the best urban garden of our time at the Museum of Modern Art, and one of our era's great public places, the plaza at Lincoln Center; the plaza is in turn faced by Philip's New York State Theater, a superb building in terms of its moment and ambitions, and far and away the only successful recapitulation in our time of the grandeur, clarity, convenience, and atmosphere of the great opera houses of the nineteenth century. For another important patron, William Paley, he designed on an inconsequential mid-block site an office tower-cum-archive, the Museum of Television and Radio, which despite its comparatively minute size is one of our most beautifully proportioned and detailed skyscrapers. The work of another frequently overlooked master, Bertram Goodhue, is behind Johnson's design for the museum, gloriously realized in Wisconsin limestone.

For developer patrons Johnson has excelled—he is the Raymond Hood of our time. The IDS Center in Minneapolis realized in one stroke the unbuilt glass tower proposed by Mies van der Rohe fifty years earlier, and married it to a base with an interior court and bridgelike walkways that brought the futurist, dynamic urbanism of the 1910s to life in ways that two generations had dreamed about but never convincingly realized. For Gerald Hines, Philip has built glories of the sky-scraper art: my favorites are the Republic Bank in Houston, with its concatenated gables and Piranesian lobby, and Transco, another Goodhue-inspired design, as much a skyscraper on the plains as the Nebraska State Capitol.

I could go on listing the buildings that Philip Johnson has designed that make a real contribution to architecture. The point is not that Philip has designed so much so very well, but that each building is about something—something in the past, something happening on the local scene, something. Philip Johnson extends architecture by showing us, through his buildings, his love for architecture. For this reason he scares other architects whose love of architecture, however strong, does not usually grow out of anything like the depth of Philip's passion for his art. Moreover, as I look around at the important buildings by other masters and would-be masters of the Johnsonian age, I begin to think that, for the most part, it is not so much the love of architecture but the love of self that governs our best talents. Philip, thank you for showing those who would look to your example how to build beautifully with ideas, to build with force, conviction, passion, and a genuine understanding of what architecture can—and cannot—do.

# 19

## Remembering Louis Kahn
### 1986

I knew Kahn while a student at Yale; he was no longer on the faculty there but at the University of Pennsylvania. In my article "Yale 1950–1965," published in *Oppositions* 4, there is some material about Kahn's departure from New Haven.[1] By the time I started to study architecture there in 1960, Kahn's influence at Yale was on the wane. Already a kind of myth, he seemed a bit remote. He came to the school once or twice to deliver a formal lecture but never, that I can recall, to teach or sit on a jury. Many students first heard about Kahn and his work through Vincent Scully's lectures. Scully frequently presented recent, as yet unpublished projects, so for us students his interpretation of Kahn preceded the projects in a certain way. Certainly Kahn was incredibly important because at that time, in April 1961, the famous issue on the so-called Philadelphia School appeared in *Progressive Architecture* magazine.

I knew Kahn better than other students in the school for two reasons. One was because I was editing *Perspecta* 9/10, and I got him to commit one of his talks to the magazine; as a result, I helped with its transcription from audio tape and worked with him to adapt it to a written format. Kahn was an unclear speaker, given to aphorisms. On the platform his approach to architecture was at best poetic, at worst a kind of sermonizing. In this respect, the nearest thing to him today is John Hejduk. But Kahn refined his style a lot and tried to make it clearer as he translated his transcribed spoken words to the format of the printed page. Another way I got a bit closer to him than my fellow students was in connection with the book on George Howe that I had begun in 1961. I spent quite a number of hours in Philadelphia with him on two or three occasions, discussing Howe and Philadelphia's architectural milieu in the 1930s and '40s. Sharing his rather unfocused reminiscences of Howe gave me a certain insight into Kahn and his background. But in the end I was not an intimate of Kahn's point of view. I was quite distant from his architecture, which seemed profoundly unattainable and, when emulated by others, gauche. Perhaps, as I reflect on it now, the callowness and impatience of my youth led me to reject Kahn's direction as a bit impractical—it took so long for those ideas about form to become tangible designs.

Somehow Paul Rudolph's architecture, with its ambitious synthesis between Le Corbusier and Frank Lloyd Wright and its greater flashiness, was more popular and more important as a learnable model. Besides, Rudolph was there in the studio three afternoons a week; he was our resident star, if not necessarily our guru. Kahn seemed old; Rudolph young—in fact, I felt young with Rudolph; he made us all seem part of one great joyous struggle for design. And also there was a sense of "Philadelphia School Architecture" at the University of Pennsylvania being different from the less inner-directed but also less dogmatic work coming out of the program in New Haven. This was not a silly Harvard-Yale football game type of rivalry but a serious distinction based on the Philadelphia belief in the primacy of form over design—to use these terms in Kahn's sense—and a more visual, and yes, more pragmatic sense of design as fulfillment of form in New Haven. That was a nice dialogue, or rivalry, if you like. A real conversation.

So that is what I know of Kahn, from my student days. Years later, after I began to teach at Columbia in 1970, I found myself part of a field trip to Philadelphia. Alex Kouzmanoff, my senior colleague, had made arrangements for the class to visit Kahn in his office. I don't much like that sort of thing since I think it is a false situation: thirty people barge into a workshop, disrupting its orderly processes. But when Kahn started to talk I was astonished: it was as though he had not changed in the intervening six or seven years. In a way, time had stopped. All the sentences were the same and so were his aphorisms. It was like a rerun of earlier lectures. Here, in the intimacy of his office, Kahn proffered the same experiences he had proffered on the platform years before. This was not the Kahn I remembered sharing pastrami sandwiches with in a delicatessen he liked near Rittenhouse Square as we talked about Howe: very cutting and very direct and very gossipy. Over pastrami, he could range from gossip to poetry and back in a handful of sentences. But when he was with the students, whether on the platform or in his own office, he assumed an awesome, ministerial distance; he dropped conversational English and spoke in grandiloquent generalities that I found more like linked platitudes—interspersed, of course, with some wonderful things. But so much of his "conversation" that day was pure Sunday sermon. It was really incredible. I had this terrible sense of déjà vu and disappointment. So much self-important mythmaking. That was the last time I saw Kahn; it must have been 1972. Two years later he died.

A few thoughts about styles of work. Kahn's office was wonderfully unimpressive in its urban grittiness, quite different from the sky-lit attic that housed Rudolph's office in New Haven, though each was deliberately distanced from the corporate imagery of Philip Johnson's or I.M. Pei's offices housed in New York high rises. Johnson's office, which I knew well, was at the top of the Seagram Building. It was not what one expected an architectural office to be: it could have been an advertising agency. As a visitor I never saw the drafting tables. Pei's office was like that but even more so: conference rooms, secretaries, very impressive lobbies concealing messy drafting rooms behind. Kahn's office is very much on my mind because I am just about to take a space for my own office on another floor, and like Kahn I'm located in a nondescript building at a lively urban corner. Kahn's was just a workshop, a place to work, with no fancy secretarial stations or elegant lobbies. And it was a twenty-four-hours-a-day workshop! He was a very demanding employer, even worse than I am. He never knew the difference between morning, noon, night, and weekends. I imagine all this has been said by people who worked there and know much better than I about these things.

Kahn was amazing. When I would come to see him about the *Perspecta* article he virtually stopped everything, whatever he was doing, and spent an hour or two or more with me. Conversation would quickly shift from the ostensible purpose of the meeting to his current projects—which we were both more interested in. I haven't got that kind of patience with visitors. But Kahn loved to talk; he loved to muse, to philosophize, and to speculate. Of course, his assistants would go crazy; they'd pop into his office to say, "Lou, we need you, we need a decision. These drawings have to go to Pakistan"—or wherever! And he would reply, "I'll be there in a minute. I just want to finish this thought, this conversation." What was so nice for a young visitor like me must have been hell for the staff. Given my youthful naiveté, I had the sense in that office of Kahn as a great master and everybody else as an acolyte. At that time, I smugly believed that many there really didn't know how to do anything of value if Lou didn't tell them what to do. But now I understand how essential it is to be surrounded by dedicated, inspired assistants, without whom probably no forms can evolve into convincing, realizable designs.

I think it would be interesting to talk a bit about Kahn in terms of the present and not the past. It is incredible how Kahn's influence is and isn't felt in architecture today. One thing I think Kahn pointed out was a way to return classical order to architecture. The tendency to classicism was so very clear in his work; yet it was not properly understood or even honestly acknowledged by his epigones. Today there is a certain sense of classicism in most interesting work: Allan Greenberg, Aldo Rossi, many people. But Kahn's classicism did not have about it that sense of liveliness essential to great art. On this I always have an argument with Scully; for me, Kahn never could bring to his architecture that life, that empathy, that sense of mass, of weight and activity, that any ordinary, true classical building has. His buildings are always inert, frozen, cold. That side of Kahn, strangely enough, is picked up by Mario Botta. (But then Swiss architecture has always been lacking in joy, has it not?) People say that Botta is like Kahn, yet I do not think he is like Kahn at all. I think he is in no important way like Kahn except in certain superficialities of shape and in the sense of the building as a frozen, inert mass—an iceberg rather than an icicle, if you will permit the analogy.

What amazes me is that Kahn is not a reference in today's student work. Students don't perceive him as a link between the modernist and the classical sensibility. In less than a generation, judging from the work of today's students, not to mention many of his close colleagues and disciples, we are about to lose the vocabulary that was so important to Kahn and that he helped us to see: order and design, servant and served spaces—each pair a true distinction, which has evaporated in the false poché of the revivalist-modernists who espouse a kind of classicism without the orders. It is not yet seen in the more stimulating true classicism of others either. So Kahn was a very important transitional figure and a very important architect, but he is not yet a very understood or honored or even much copied architect. Too bad.

The other thing about Kahn is that some of his presumed great buildings are not as great as they could have been or as they are deemed by critics. Despite the brilliant light of Southern California, the Salk Institute is cold and mechanical; besides, it is an extremely problematic composition with no clear entrance and no clear hierarchy or sense of procession. The British Art Center at Yale also does not have a very good entrance. On the other hand, the Kimbell Museum in Fort Worth is a wonderful building—but nobody seems to pay much attention to it. I find it his best building.

I don't know what to make of Kahn. In a certain way he was a loner. His buildings were the buildings of an ascetic. They were cold and of ugly materials, except the Kimbell. Take the library at Exeter: the outside is wonderful—red brick; they may have told him to use it. But inside the building is visually cold with all that concrete.

As an artist you have to be in a milieu. Even an artist as unique and seemingly self-motivated as Michelangelo operated in a milieu and was surely stimulated by others. Yet Kahn, like Wright, was a loner, not in a milieu, and finally his work suffered, just as Wright's did, as each man increasingly believed his own myth. The problem with Kahn was that a lot of weak people copied his mannerisms, just as they unquestioningly imitated his epigrams—some are still writing not very good books. Part of Kahn was surely mystical; but more importantly, he adopted the mask of an ascetic. In many ways he was a hedonist. He would talk about beautiful buildings and making them out of marvelous materials. In no way was he moralistic about beautiful, voluptuous architecture; he loved beautiful things, yet Kahn was in part the victim of his discovery by the angry young British architects who trapped him in a development that he was not completely comfortable with. In a sense, he couldn't get beyond the brutalist label, which had brought him his first whiff of fame at the advanced age of fifty, yet he never built anything that could be described as embodying delight. Do you remember that when he was commissioned to design a barge for the American Wind Symphony, he made a very ugly thing? I never saw his drawings for the chemistry building at the University of Virginia so I do not know what he proposed, but I wonder how much he could rise to the sensuousness of that place? Once famous, Kahn enjoyed an enviable amount of success—when you think about it, his role was incredibly important in the late 1950s. His Richards Medical Building at the University of Pennsylvania was highly publicized and frequently visited. The Salk Institute was certainly a major opportunity, and the museums were too. He had special sites, special clients, and the universities were fantastic to him—very supportive. He had wonderful opportunities to do great work in the grand manner of the past—not least of which was the Capital Complex at Dhaka in Bangladesh. So Kahn, a man who didn't get any recognition until he was fifty, had twenty-five years of enormous success, power of a certain kind, adulation.

Yes, it is very complicated, for while Lutyens and Le Corbusier were grand heroes of the Indian subcontinent, Kahn began his work there portrayed as an artist against the world, a discoverer not of fundamental truths but of new truths, Lord help us. Pegged as an oddball; perhaps he was.

His limitations as an architect came through most clearly in his houses; they are very abstract and unloving. He made many big buildings, but with the exception of the Kimbell and the British Art Center, there are no wonderful places in his buildings, despite all of his talk. Even the institutions—Salk is the most revealing in this respect—fail to have a place, or core, that brings people together. Kahn recognized the need for such places in his writings, but he never seemed to achieve them in his architecture because he always made the buildings so brutal, so abstract. I don't like all those books that make him into a sort of god figure; they're revolting, just revolting.

# 20

Charles Moore
*The Architect
Running in Place*
1986

Among the leaders of America's architectural revival in the 1960s, Charles Moore had the clearest understanding of what had gone wrong with modernism: the God that Failed, it had never offered the public the fundamental gift of architecture—a sense of place.

To Moore, the architect's most important role was as a maker of places, not as an elaborator of forms, although he has from the first been a brilliant shape maker. In his 1967 essay "Plug It in, Rameses, and See If It Lights Up, Because We Aren't Going to Keep It Unless It Works," Moore defined architectural responsibility and, by implication, the irresponsibility of architects of the immediately preceding generation: "If architects are to continue to do useful work on this planet, then surely their proper concern must be the creation of *place*—the ordered imposition of man's self on specific locations across the face of the earth. To make a place is to make a domain that helps people know where they are, and by extension, know who they are."[1]

As a writer, architect, and teacher, Moore has discovered, designed, and taught an architecture of American places, and has taught that the creation of American places is an arduous and ironic task. The arduousness comes from the newness of the continent, the difficulty of creating a place from scratch. The irony comes from the embarrassing recognition of how contrived such a place must necessarily be, especially in a nation of nomads. A further irony is Moore's own life, in which he rarely stays in place but, as a professor and architect, is constantly traveling—to California, Texas, New York, Connecticut, Berlin, in short, the world. In his essay "The Temple, the Cabin and the Trailer," Moore brings the concept of hyphenated Americanism up to date: "Almost all of us are newcomers in the place where we are, wanderers bringing what used to be called a Yankee ingenious responsiveness to our dealings with a new place but we also bring dreams and maybe even homesick fantasies about some place far away from which we've come or some place far away in both time and space about which perhaps we've read (some generations of Americans have been far more bookish than others)."[2]

Moore inspired a generation of architects in the 1960s, a generation to which I belong, to practice architecture as an inclusive art. He showed us that we could put in as much as an earlier generation had taken out. The Modern Movement had declared its greatest ambition the public good but had never shown much interest in the reality of the public's world as it was and openly despised the public's dreams and fantasies—bookish or otherwise—of the world as it had been or might be. All that had to be excluded in favor of pure form. Moore welcomed it all, albeit critically. He condemned the American scene as it was: "I think that the environment is lousy, and there is hardly any place in North America that the hand of man has touched that it hasn't ruined."[3] Moore had no illusions that the solution was sociological. "I get very upset at the standard student approach now, which supposes that if you interview enough housewives in a housing project, and write down what they like best about where they live, you'll know what the solution ought to be."[4] Yet at the same time, Moore believed that the best architecture, an inclusive architecture, required listening to those housewives, including their dreams and homesick fantasies. In one of his most direct experiments in participatory architecture, he led the first-year students of Yale's architecture school to Appalachia in 1967. In eight weeks, New Zion, Kentucky, had a new community center, designed and built by the Yale students and professors in accordance with the local wishes and dreams of what a building should be. The building wasn't bad as a work of architecture, either.

For young architects, the first lesson of New Zion, which Moore had really begun to teach in the early 1960s, was one of exhilarating power. They didn't have to be old and hoary to build; they could make things now. The second lesson was that each time an architect undertook a design, he didn't necessarily have to begin a heroic quest for "original" or even "significant" form, the latter of which had been the approach of one of Moore's most important mentors, Louis Kahn. Architects could use what was available from the past and present: good and even bad buildings could stimulate new production; ornate Victorian details and contemporary advertising graphics could be served up with classical columns and subtle compositional moves from mainstream modernism to result in buildings that were pleasure-giving and life-enhancing. Moore showed that the familiar and the ordinary could be raised to the level of the extraordinary. America's built environment, however "lousy," was an inevitable and appropriate sourcebook for him: "My particular interest is in using familiar pieces, mostly cheap pieces, putting them together in ways that they have never been before, so as to get something that's strange and revolutionary and mind-boggling and often uncomfortable, but only using the ordinary pieces. I think that's a better way of making a revolution than just inventing a whole new crazy set of shapes."[5]

In a sense, the revolution had already occurred—in Disneyland, in Las Vegas, in Solvang, a Danish village in Southern California, and in the movies—but the most successful American places were outside of the architectural canon. It was up to teachers like Moore and Robert Venturi to bring them in. In 1964 Moore went

in search of monumental architecture as part of the urban scene in California. He came back with startling news. The private realms of the air-conditioned house and the air-conditioned car had triumphed over any traditional notion of monumental, urban architecture in California, but the public realm, the place where civilization had traditionally flourished, was somehow surviving in an animator's amusement park: "In as unlikely a place as could be conceived, just off the Santa Ana Freeway, a little over an hour from Los Angeles City Hall, in an unchartable sea of suburbia, Disney has created a place, indeed a whole public world, full of sequential occurrences, of big and little drama, of hierarchies of importance and excitement."[6]

Moore was percipient enough not to underestimate Disney. Walt Disney had not only marketed a place, he had marked a place. As Moore writes, "This process, the establishing of cities and the marking of important places, constitutes most of the physical part of establishing civilization. Charles Eames has made the point that the crux of this civilizing process is the giving up by individuals of something in order that the public realm may be enhanced."[7]

In 1964, in California, the crux of the civilizing process, the notion of sacrifice to the common good, had come down to buying a ticket at the gate of Disneyland. As Moore put it, with and without irony, "You have to pay for the public life."

In America, the proprietors of the private realm, like Disney, have most often paid for the manifestation in brick and mortar of something resembling a public realm. The putative representative of the public realm, the government, has had to be dragged kicking and screaming toward that "physical part of establishing civilization"—making places. Witness the stingy public subsidy for Moore's own Church Street South Housing in New Haven (fig. 1). Although the project was ultimately unsuccessful, Moore made a heroic effort to raise ordinary building materials and uniform facades to extraordinary levels by using siting and surface color as sufficient stimuli to make the residents feel at home. What a remarkable idea in 1966, building housing for the poor that wasn't designed to discipline them to the cruel geometries of some brave new world. For Moore, "The place that you live should allow for the everyday to become the exceptional. It should lead your mind to multiple associations."[8]

Given sufficient budget and freedom, Moore has built exceptional places that are rich in multiple associations. The year before he began Church Street South,

*Fig. 1.* MLTW/Moore-Turnbull with Marvin Buchanan and Donald Whitaker, Church Street South, New Haven, Connecticut, 1966–69

*Fig. 2.* MLTW, Sea Ranch Condominium, Sea Ranch, California, 1963–65

Charles Moore

149

Moore and his associates completed Sea Ranch. It was fundamentally vernacular, a shack-style assemblage of shed roofs and walls sheathed in the traditional local building material—rough redwood boards (fig. 2). The architects responded to the specific coastline site and, more generally, to northern California. Yet more than merely acknowledging the place where they were to build, they managed to make Sea Ranch itself a place. The architects were able to compose—not merely cluster or group—condominium units into a single building, bold enough in its overall shape to command its site. Yet they were able to compose them with enough diversity to satisfy the need for individual identification.

Moore took on that characteristically American place, the campus, beginning in 1966. For Kresge College, at the University of California at Santa Cruz (fig. 3), Moore set out to provide a stage for what he called "an urgently important four-year-long operetta."[9] The college turns an earth-colored wall to the exterior to blend its architecture with the surrounding forests and create an enclosure and a suggestion of remarkable secrets for those permitted to enter. Inside, an eclectic array of building forms is disposed to create as richly articulated a stage set for human action as any ever offered by Hollywood. Kresge is a self-contained village within a larger university, lacking only a chapel, a major library, and a gym to achieve complete independence. Without these symbolic and functional foci, Moore aggrandized the laundry and canteen, which later became a Chinese restaurant, to provide moments of architectural grandeur. An amphitheater, a red-white-and-blue rostrum, two-story dormitories that vaguely resemble roadside motels, administrative offices, shops, and a mailroom—all decorated with strips of neon—and freestanding walls with rectangular openings that visually frame the sky complete the assembly. The buildings are arranged along a grand thousand-foot-long street—the thoroughfare of the college, intended to serve as its symbolic and functional nexus, the sort of linear quadrangle guaranteed liveliness by the movement of students along it.

The use of highly abstract forms robs the scheme of much of its power. The sense of street and shelter were derived from a careful study and evocation of historic precedent—a more literal translation would have been wildly daring at the time. Moore displayed that kind of daring in a later project, the Piazza d'Italia in New Orleans (fig. 4). It is perhaps the fullest expression of his inclusivist philosophy

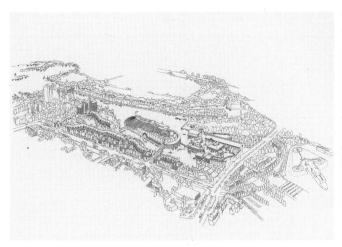

*Fig. 5.* Moore Ruble Yudell, Bird's-eye view of revised competition scheme, Tegel Harbor International Competition, Berlin, Germany, 1980

*Fig. 6.* Moore Grover Harper, Wastewater treatment plant, Cold Spring Harbor Laboratory, Cold Spring Harbor, New York, 1976

to date, combining architectural allusion of the highest level with kitsch. The reason for the piazza was to symbolize New Orleans' Italian-American community. Moore and his associates provided a dream of Italy (perhaps what he would call a "homesick fantasy") made of both cheap, ordinary materials and expensive, inherently luxurious ones: steel frame and stucco, slate, marble, granite paving stones, stainless steel, tile, water, and neon. The overt staginess and deliberate mockery of architectural tradition seem enough to appall even Morris Lapidus's sensibilities. As Lapidus often did, Moore created a sensual, exciting place to be, as close to the stagy Trevi Fountain as anyone was willing to go in 1975. The classical architecture, the earth-colored walls, the Latin inscriptions, and the eighty-foot-long relief map pool of Italy are explicit references to the collective past of the piazza's sponsors. To place the project even more specifically, Moore put Sicily, the original homeland of most of New Orleans' Italian-Americans, in the bull's-eye center of the project.

The Piazza d'Italia is representative of Moore's aggressive playfulness, an attitude that has occasionally put his status as a serious architect in question among architectural pundits. But it is Moore's capacity for finding the serious meaning in play, whether at Disneyland or in his own work, that marks his place in the history of architecture. Moore Ruble Yudell won the competition for Tegel Harbor in Berlin because it offered one of the few proposals that looked as though anyone could have fun at the recreation center, a barge resembling a huge toy boat (fig. 5).

Moore's best humor is subtly instructive as well. At Cold Spring Harbor Laboratory, Moore Grover Harper was commissioned to renovate and design several buildings for the hundred-acre campus on Long Island Sound, which had a score of nineteenth- and early twentieth-century structures. The new wastewater treatment plant (fig. 6) could have been the most banal building at the laboratory, but Moore and his associates designed it as a focal point. The main concrete structure, invisibly tucked into the hillside when seen from above, but visible from the harbor side, is sheathed in shingles and scrollwork. The shingles continue upward onto a gazebo that sits atop the plant. On the campus side, the gazebo is set at the edge of a landscaped terrace. A typically Moore-ish witty extra, this shingled architectural folly, with its spire topped by a model of adenovirus, has come to symbolize the laboratory and its dedication to research in molecular biology.

Charles Moore

Moore is a very modern, very American architect, a maker of places that correspond to the very American fluidity and restlessness of his mind. He transformed a profession by reintroducing the reality of architectural experience into the ideality of the Academy. Traditional materials and the craft to use them began to be taken seriously by a generation of architects weaned on steel and glass. Architecture could once again give pleasure, whether in a theatrical composition of staircases, balconies, cutouts, and skylights or in a sensual use of colors and materials. Architecture could also give the pleasure of memory, informed by an awareness of context and of history. The radical pluralism of Moore's art can push it to the outer reaches of coherent design, but it is always held in place by Moore's sly serenade of communality.

# 21

## Norman Foster at Yale

### 2000

Norman Foster is without question one of the most accomplished and most influential architects of our time. What interests me in particular about Foster's career is the continuing exchange of English, European, and American ideas and techniques. The Anglo-American part of this exchange has its practical, experience-based beginning in 1961 at Yale University, where both Foster and I were architecture students. Our time at Yale had a profound and different effect on each of us, leading me to question the then "constituent facts" of modernism and modernity, and Foster to open his work up to the various "constituent facts" of the American experience, including its vast landscape and its unabashed commercialism.[1]

In 1951, ten years before going to Yale, Norman Foster, then aged sixteen, had already begun to develop a healthy interest in architecture, in part stimulated by trips to the local public library in Levenshulme, the Manchester suburb where he grew up. It was there, as he recalled recently, that he "discovered the different worlds of Frank Lloyd Wright and Le Corbusier. Imagine the contrast of a house on the Prairie with a villa on a Paris boulevard. Yet I remember being equally fascinated by both at the time."[2]

At just the moment that Foster was educating himself in the history of architecture, however, he was called up for two years of mandatory National Service, which he elected to serve in the Royal Air Force. Following his return to civilian life and his subsequent graduation from Manchester University School of Architecture, Foster arrived in New Haven in the autumn of 1961 aided by a Henry Fellowship, which each year enables selected British students to study either at Yale or Harvard universities while their opposite numbers study at Oxford or Cambridge. Foster was a Guest Fellow in Jonathan Edwards College, one of Yale's residential colleges modeled on those found in Oxbridge. Interestingly, Foster had been offered a Fulbright Travel Scholarship, but declined the award because it would have inhibited his freedom to work in the United States.

Foster's decision to go to Yale was not easily arrived at, nor did the value of the place immediately manifest itself to him. For a time he wondered if he might not have done better to have gone to the University of Pennsylvania and studied under Louis Kahn. Soon enough, however, Foster found Yale to be a liberating place, alive to the possibilities of architecture as an art and to the crosscurrents of prevailing styles, ideologies, and passions.

A small school at the time—really a department in the School of Art and Architecture—Yale was dominated by two great teachers: the architect Paul Rudolph and the architectural historian Vincent Scully. There were, of course, other permanent faculty members, but the great strength of the school lay in the interplay between Scully and Rudolph and, in turn, in their interplay with a host of visiting critics, including American architects such as Philip Johnson, Henry Cobb, Craig Ellwood, and Ulrich Franzen, to name a few. They were joined by Europeans such as Frei Otto, Henning Larsen, and Shadrach Woods, and especially the British architects James Stirling and Colin St. John Wilson.

In Foster's year at Yale, the master's class benefited not only from his presence but also from that of two other brilliant English students: Eldred Evans and Richard Rogers. The confluence at Yale of the three—who had not known each other in England—proved to be remarkably important for the future of architecture, as was their interaction with American students in the class, such as Carl Abbott, as well as others in the four-year-long baccalaureate program, including Charles Gwathmey, Jonathan Barnett, M.J. Long, David Sellers, Peter Gluck, and David Childs.

Paul Rudolph's Yale was a phenomenon, a surprise newcomer on an American architectural scene that had been dominated by Harvard since the late 1930s when Walter Gropius took over as chairman of its architecture program. When Rudolph became head of the Yale program, in 1958, it was in a state of disarray, despite a burst of energy in the early 1950s when George Howe—assisted by Louis Kahn and Philip Johnson—had revived it.

Following Howe's retirement, in 1954, the school became rank with contentiousness under his short-term successor, Paul Schweikher; but Rudolph's regime changed all that. By the time Foster arrived, Yale occupied a position of international prominence in architectural education. It was arguably the most talked about architecture program in the world.

Rudolph's appointment had required a great leap of faith. He was no "educator" in the generally accepted sense of the term, but he was a brilliantly talented architect whose reputation rested on a dazzling series of small houses, mostly in Sarasota, Florida. In the late 1950s Rudolph's practice was blossoming. His first major work, the Jewett Arts Center at Wellesley College, was nearing completion and was already regarded as a serious challenge to the uniformity and placelessness of the American version of the International Style that Gropius and Marcel Breuer had advocated at Harvard in the 1940s.

Rudolph was not only not an educator, he was not very well educated himself. He was in no way like his courtly and well-connected predecessor, George Howe, who had come from wealth, attended Groton and Harvard with Franklin

*Fig. 1.* Paul Rudolph, Perspective section of Art + Architecture Building, Yale University, New Haven, Connecticut, 1959–63

Roosevelt, and spent four years in Paris at the École des Beaux-Arts. Rudolph, a Methodist minister's son raised in a variety of Southern towns, lacked cultivation and was brusque in a way many found refreshing—and many did not. He had studied at Alabama Polytechnical Institute (now Auburn University), and although he had gone on to complete two years in the master's class at Harvard, at the time of his appointment to Yale his professional academic experience was confined to a succession of posts as visiting critic at a dozen or more provincial universities.

Rudolph, forty years old when he took over Yale, was not that much older than some of his students, whose education had been interrupted by the Korean War. He lacked a theory of education and did not seem particularly interested in developing one. But he was intensely interested in the "learning process." He viewed the art of building in strictly heroic terms and passionately believed in the capacity of the architectural idea—and the architect—to prevail over day-to-day circumstances. For him theory was synonymous with the big idea that carried the day. "Theory," he argued, "must again overtake action. . . . Architectural education's first concern is to perpetuate a climate where the student is acutely and perceptively and incessantly aware of the creative process. He must understand that after all the building committees, the conflicting interests, the budget considerations and the limitations of his fellow man have been taken into consideration, that his responsibility has just begun. He must understand that in the exhilarating, awesome moment when he takes pencil in hand, and holds it poised above a white sheet of paper, that he has suspended there all that will ever be. The creative act is all that matters."[3]

The zenith of Rudolph's effectiveness as a teacher can be said to be the years 1960 through 1963, when his career as a practicing architect was in full flood and he worked intensely on the design of the watershed building that would become the new home of Yale's School of Art and Architecture (fig. 1).

Norman Foster at Yale

Vincent Scully was the other important guiding force at Yale at the time. Scully played a key role not only as a brilliant professor of art history, but also as an active participant in the crits and juries in the design studio. Cut from the same cloth as Malraux or Camus, Scully was an engaged intellectual. Typical of his often controversial stands on contemporary architecture was his endorsement of the then vigorously debated late work of Le Corbusier.

Scully, a local boy from New Haven, was a graduate of Yale College and its graduate school. He had seen active service in World War II and had been teaching at Yale since the late 1940s. By the 1960s, Scully's lectures were the stuff of legend; indeed, he was among the first of the academic media stars, working with filmmakers and frequently quoted in the press.

David McCullough, in a profile in 1959 in *Architectural Forum*, dubbed Scully an "architectural spellbinder."[4] Scully's theatrical lectures electrified his audiences, challenging architects and would-be architects while fostering a profound interest in the built world among Yale's other undergraduates, who would carry this newfound awareness to their work in different fields.

Scully taught a generation to view buildings as the embodiment of ideas and ideals. He also taught them how to see, bringing inert matter to life as—with a scholar's knowledge and an actor's passion—he brought out the empathetic relationship between mankind and masterworks of the built environment, be they Greek temples sited in the landscape or the taut abstractions of postwar industrialization. To a remarkable extent, Scully's perceptions helped to shape those of his most talented students—including Foster—and his powerful convictions became central to his students' own concerns about architecture. At the deepest level, Scully's influence was based on his feeling for the interrelation of man, building, and place. And his reach extended far beyond the lectern; he published prolifically in the early 1960s, completing monographs on Frank Lloyd Wright (1960) and Louis Kahn (1962), as well as *Modern Architecture: The Architecture of Democracy* (1961) and *The Earth, the Temple, and the Gods: Greek Sacred Architecture* (1962).

In specific historical terms, Scully stressed the great differences between European and American architecture, elevating the latter from its then lowly status as a mere footnote to the former. He dramatically and memorably presented the work of Henry Hobson Richardson, Louis Sullivan, and particularly that of Frank Lloyd Wright, as part of a continuum across national borders yet uniquely expressive of American issues of landscape and culture. In 1999, when accepting one of the architectural profession's highest honors, the Pritzker Prize, Foster pinpointed a key aspect of this teacher's impact, asserting that "Vincent Scully's insights opened my eyes to the interaction between the old world and the new."[5]

Louis Kahn was another highly consequential force at Yale when Foster arrived, although he was no longer teaching there. Kahn and Rudolph did not get on, and the University of Pennsylvania, Kahn's alma mater, offered a more convenient and, to his mind, congenial setting. Kahn nonetheless seemed ubiquitous. Scully had gotten to know Kahn during the architect's Yale years in the 1940s and 1950s, and Scully's lectures often promoted and interpreted new projects by him long before they were published in the journals. As a result, Kahn's work was vigorously debated in the Yale studios.

Kahn also came to New Haven for public lectures, a typical one of which was published in 1965 in Volume 9/10 of *Perspecta*, the student-run Yale journal, which had begun publishing in 1952.[6] Perhaps Kahn's biggest impact on Yale architecture students in the early 1960s was through his Yale Art Gallery, completed in 1953, an epochal building that married the influences of Mies van der Rohe, Le Corbusier, and Richard Buckminster Fuller. The building exerted a powerful, positive influence on virtually all those students who spent seemingly endless days and nights in its extensively glazed, concrete-trussed, fourth-floor drafting room.

During the early 1960s the presence of brilliant visiting English architects immeasurably enriched the New Haven scene and brought to it a much-needed cosmopolitan approach that Rudolph's inherent provincialism lacked. The English offered an alternative way of looking at things. Their admiration of the uninhibited formal exuberance of American architecture, especially roadside and other commercial vernacular work, came as a surprise to the locals who were still embarrassed by the absence of high cultural aspirations in so much native building.

Moreover, the English not only seemed to admire the everyday buildings that embarrassed the Americans, they also found most American high-art efforts pretentious. According to M.J. Long—a student at Yale between 1960 and 1964—the English afforded a nexus of countervailing criticism against "the forced and rather blowsy monumentality prevalent at the school."[7] In the mid-1970s, Long recalled the English influence at Yale:

> The English used "humble" materials (brick rather than concrete) and displayed a natural reticence which sometimes emerged as anti-monumentality. They talked about Aalto as much as about Corbu. They showed that it was not necessary to resort to anemic form as an antidote to overblown form—their buildings at best had a kind of animal toughness and boniness. It was a set of images which we could use and it took hold, just before Charles Moore and Robert Venturi pointed to the possibilities in traditional American wood buildings and gave to others of us a similarly usable alternative set of images. . . . They were also interested in issues of planning and saw them in design terms. . . . And, they were never anti-intellectual; on the contrary, they were highly articulate and historically conscious.[8]

Among the visiting British critics at Yale, James Stirling exerted the most profound and lasting influence. In a break with the historical "know-nothingism" of the 1940s and 1950s, Stirling made it respectable for Yale students to consider the past. In this he was complemented by Philip Johnson, who in 1959 began a lecture at Yale by writing on the chalkboard: "You cannot not know history."

To students who were still in the thrall of antitraditionalist modernism, Stirling offered a strong dose of its opposite—a modernism that drew from both the modernist and the premodernist past. Like Rudolph, Stirling tended to see history as a justification for romantic formalism, but Stirling's grasp of the past was deeper and broader. Stirling was keenly aware of—and troubled by—the limited definition of modern architecture that had come to be accepted. In his essay, "The Functional Tradition and Expression," published in 1960 in *Perspecta* 6, Stirling not only made a plea for an expanded vocabulary of form but also exposed his own work to direct comparison with the best of the past.[9]

Stirling showed Blenheim Palace alongside unidentified medieval fortifications and walled cities, as well as passed-over nineteenth-century English brick vernacular architecture and the late work of Le Corbusier, which he suggested did not subscribe to the extreme reductionism of the cubist work of the 1920s, or similarly minimalist work by Gropius and Mies van der Rohe. This was remarkable and largely new to American architects, and perhaps also to Foster, who first got to know Stirling at Yale.

Though in one sense Stirling's argument suggested that enriched form should arise from a more careful and imaginative representation of a building's functional program, on the other hand he chose to illustrate his text with images from the past coupled with those of his own recent work. To be "modern" was no longer enough. Stirling presented Trinity College in contrast to his and his partner James Gowan's Churchill College scheme of 1958, as well as a traditional English farmhouse paired with his Woolton House of 1954, and nineteenth-century English commercial and industrial buildings seen in counterpoint with his and Gowan's Ham Common flats of 1955–58.

As a result of their publication in *Perspecta*, Stirling and Gowan's housing projects at Ham Common and Stirling and Alan Cordingley's work for Sheffield University became stylistic touchstones for Yale students, and for Rudolph as well. At a time when heroic, self-invented, and self-inventing architecture was very much the model, Stirling's bold move to show how his and Gowan's work derived from the forms of high and low buildings from the past was almost unique.

Three other Britons—Colin St. John Wilson and Alison and Peter Smithson— significantly contributed to Yale's intellectual climate, although all of them preceded Foster by a year and did not have direct contact with him at Yale. Nonetheless, their impact on the school was still apparent in 1961–62. Colin St. John Wilson— "Sandy" to students and faculty alike—offered a yet more complicated reading of the recent past than did Stirling. Wilson loved things American in a way the British frequently then did: he loved jazz, especially Miles Davis, even though most young Americans were not that interested in it, preferring folk music or rock 'n' roll. Yet despite his love of jazz—and the English version of pop art—he was appalled by pop culture as it really was in America, sharing with many American intellectuals a highbrow dislike of commercial design that Peter Blake would elaborate upon in his book, *God's Own Junkyard*, of 1964.[10]

Alison and Peter Smithson were better known for their writings and exhibitions than for their buildings, although Scully admired their school at Hunstanton and showed it in his classes. Of the Smithsons' ideas, that of "ordinariness" proved the most compelling. The idea rooted itself more deeply and lastingly into the Yale psyche than any other, resonating for years to come, perhaps as an antidote to Rudolph's heroic bluster.

Another British influence on the early 1960s Yale scene—disproportionately strong perhaps, given the brevity of the contact—was that of Peter Reyner Banham, an engineer turned architectural critic and historian, who was at Yale in 1960–61 and returned in the spring of 1962 to visit the recently completed Morse and Stiles colleges, a posthumous work of Eero Saarinen. Perhaps the most emblematic American architect of his generation, Saarinen was a graduate of the Yale architecture school and a close advisor to Whitney Griswold, the Yale president whose passionate support of modern architecture fueled the university's extensive postwar building program.

Saarinen's proto-postmodernist Morse and Stiles residential colleges "disgusted" Banham "at sight" and still appalled him four weeks later when he slammed them in a review in the *New Statesman*, stating that there were "no extenuating circumstances" to justify the design for which "the client gave the architect plenty of rope."[11] Although Banham disliked Saarinen's special kind of concrete, he really saved his venom for what he lambasted as "Gordon Craig-type scenic effects," which he felt were achieved at the price of the "medieval standards" of student accommodation. Banham had already denounced Saarinen, architect of the U.S. Embassy in Grosvenor Square, London, as one of America's "most trivial performers."[12]

For many in New Haven, Banham's hatchet job on the Yale residential colleges went too far in a too public way. Not content to take a swipe at the recently deceased Saarinen's design, he also went after the architect's wife, the art critic Aline B. Louchheim, dismissing her as the "formidable Saarinen widow," and then lamented that the dormitories employed "that creeping malady that causes an increasing number of returning Europeans to say 'Yale is a very sick place,' the malady of gratuitous affluences irresponsibly exploited."[13]

Such was the backdrop of stimulating, if sometimes overheated design and intellectual debate that greeted Foster in 1961. In Manchester, lacking a grant and forced to fund his own way through his studies, he had been compelled to live at home and to work at an array of part-time jobs, from manning the night shift in a bakery to being a bouncer in a rough cinema. New Haven, in contrast, offered the luxury of time to study and think and debate.

While the students in the architecture department were intensely focused on their work as designers—the drafting room was open to students twenty-four hours a day—the program of studies also encouraged students to pursue interests in architectural history and planning and, in fact, whatever else attracted them from among the university's broad course offerings. Moreover, in a time when there was still comparatively little cross-fertilization among cultures, Foster and the other Britons then studying in the architecture department—together with Rogers's wife Su, who was studying for a master's degree in city planning—found themselves challenged, even confounded, by the American way of doing things.

This situation was exacerbated by the fact that the English visitors were a little older than most of their American counterparts. They considered themselves to be not quite students—or at least in a different league from their Yankee student cousins. The English would-be architects did not want to be instructed, per se, preferring to discuss, debate, and deliberate at length; they put off committing their ideas to paper for as long as possible.

One day Foster and his compatriots found posted above their desks a sign that read: "Start drawing." The English response was to post another sign that read: "Start thinking." While these strikingly different approaches produced a certain degree of tension, their juxtaposition ultimately proved fertile ground for Foster's imagination. Foster has said of his time at Yale, "Looking back with the perspective of nearly forty years I can see that our practice has been inspired by those polarities of *analysis* and *action*."[14]

Though the American and English students differed in many ways, Foster got on quite well with his American classmates. In particular, he formed a close friendship with Carl Abbott, who was from the west coast of Florida. Abbott would return there after his time at Yale—and a stint in London when he worked with Foster and Rogers—to establish his own practice in Sarasota, which to this day extends the spirit of Rudolph's early architectural achievements in that city.

*Fig. 2.* Norman Foster, Richard Rogers and Carl Abbott, on their pilgrimage to see the architecture of Chicago, ca. 1961–62

While at Yale, Foster also began a life-long friendship with Richard Rogers. How amazing that friendship was between two gifted students who would later practice together before establishing separate offices. How ironic, as well, that the two architects who would subsequently dominate British architecture for decades first met as they prepared to leave their home country—at a reception for English students who had been offered Fulbright Travel Scholarships.

Both Foster and Rogers were bowled over by Yale—each in his own way. Rudolph's driven, and hard-driving, working and teaching styles were a complete surprise. He constantly pressured students to work fast and around the clock and would stage surprise late-night crits. Foster found his pressure-cooker methods exhilarating. A superb draughtsman and model-maker, Foster was used to racing the clock; having worked his way through school in Manchester he understood that time was precious. Foster recalls: "Rudolph had created a studio atmosphere of fevered activity, highly competitive and fuelled by a succession of visiting luminaries. Crits were open and accessible—often combative. It was a 'can-do' approach in which concepts could be shredded one day and reborn overnight. The only criterion was the quality of the work presented—the architecture of the drawings and models. There was no room for excuses, no substitutes of rhetoric."[15]

At Yale, Foster learned to look hard at what was around him and what was on the drawing board before him. As Rogers, who later described his time in New Haven as "wonderful heady days," would note, the Britons at Yale learned "to use our eyes, not an English tradition."[16] In the studio the importance of "using one's eyes" was stressed most of all by Rudolph, who was brilliantly and instinctively visual. In the lecture hall, this same approach was emphasized by Scully. So compelling did Foster find Scully's presentation and interpretation of Wright's uniquely American architecture that on one short, between-terms break, he, together with Carl Abbott and Richard and Su Rogers, squeezed into Abbott's Volkswagen Beetle and visited nearly every Wright building in the Midwest (fig. 2).

Foster's first studio project at Yale not surprisingly reflected Rudolph's influence (figs. 3–4). Rudolph had assigned the design of a public high school, a relatively workaday building type which—three years earlier—he had raised to the level of architectural art in Sarasota, Florida, by imaginatively translating Le

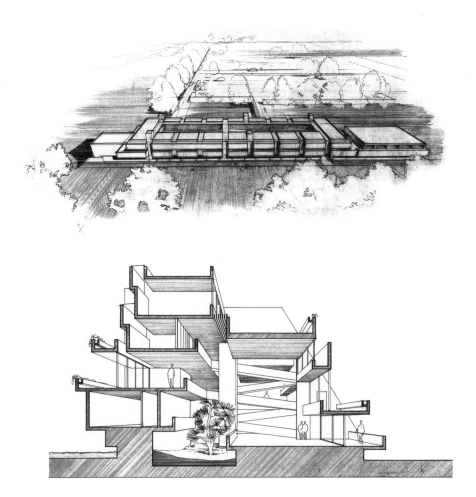

Corbusier's High Court Building at Chandigarh through the medium of American technology and the realities of American program and budgets. At the final project crit, Rudolph praised Foster for "thinking like an architect," even if the trees in his Rudolph-inspired renderings "looked like cauliflowers."[17]

Foster considers his project for an office building to be the best of his Yale work (figs. 5–7). The design problem Rudolph assigned was once again a reconsideration of one of his actual commissions—in this case his massive concrete Blue Cross Blue Shield building, completed in Boston in 1960. Foster's project consisted of a cluster of towers, which marched round the corner, "where office space was supported by a structural service core with great splayed feet," as Rogers later put it.[18] The project incorporated a structurally expressive building profile, exposed service elements, and a strong programmatic mix that represented a distinct break with the Rudolph model and strongly suggested spatial and structural lessons learned from Louis Kahn.

Foster's design also stood in sharp contrast to the prevailing open-field neutrality pioneered by Mies van der Rohe. In Foster's design the areas of office space were broken up into column-free sections spanning concrete towers that housed vertical services, surely an anticipation of his Hongkong and Shanghai Banking

*Fig. 3.* Norman Foster, Aerial perspective, American high school project, 1961

*Fig. 4.* Norman Foster, Cutaway section, American high school project, 1961

Norman Foster at Yale

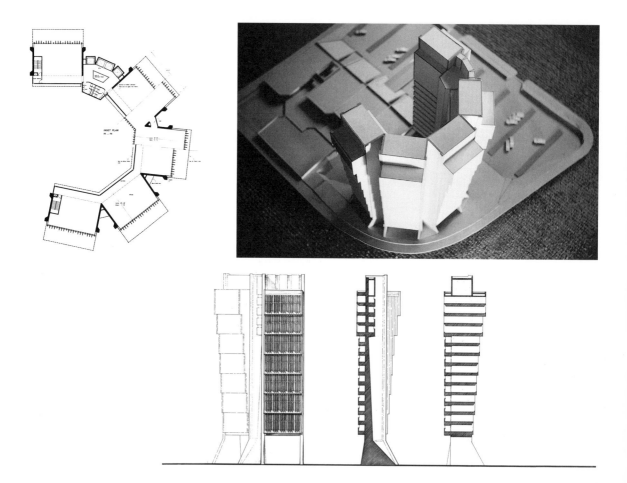

Corporation headquarters building in Hong Kong, an architectural and engineering tour de force completed in 1985.

While at Yale, Foster and Rogers collaborated on a studio design problem, the Pierson Sage Science Laboratories in the Hillhouse section of the university's campus—a complex actually entrusted to Philip Johnson, whose resulting Kline Science Center deferred to the site's older medieval-inspired buildings by Delano & Aldrich and others, while incorporating the misconceived modernist Gibbs Physics Laboratory designed by Paul Schweikher, Howe's successor as architecture department head.

In this project, Rudolph challenged the students to take into consideration not merely programmatic requirements but also what he believed to be the deplorable state of contemporary architecture as a whole. The brief he presented to the students stated: "This is an urban problem. It is also the problem of the architect, as planners and developers have failed to rebuild our cities. They are obsessed with numbers (people, money, acreage, units, cars, roads, etc.) and forget life itself and the spirit of man."[19]

According to Rogers, he and Foster worked on the project together, "to the horror of Paul Rudolph."[20] Nonetheless, their scheme was a marvel, introducing to the local scene, and perhaps to American practice as a whole, a megastructural approach that was a radical departure from the typical, isolated, building-by-building campus model. Foster and Rogers proposed a central spine of car parking, from

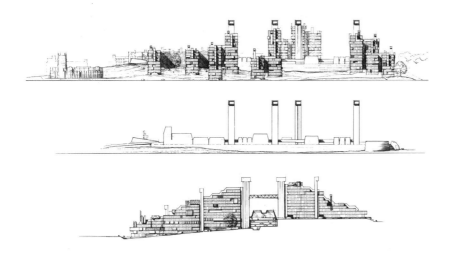

which lecture halls and other facilities projected at right angles, forming wings that stepped downhill to confront existing buildings at an appropriate scale (fig. 8).

Fig. 8. Norman Foster and Richard Rogers, Elevations and section, Scheme for Pierson Sage Science Laboratories, Yale University, New Haven, Connecticut, 1961

Though the scheme's megastructural scale and diagrammatic approach were distinctly English, or at least not American, there were aspects to the proposals that were quite familiar—especially the Kahn-inspired service towers. Philip Johnson, one of the guest jurors at the final review, adopted a typically robust approach to architectural criticism. He took a strong dislike to the buildings placed on top of the spine. After staring at the balsa wood model of the project, he proceeded to crush these blocks in his fist, saying: "Have to do something about these."[21] Whatever the project's weaknesses, however, Foster and Rogers' explosion of scale and their ability to command the entirety of the large and complex site were nothing short of astonishing.

Foster's last Yale project was for a new city (figs. 9–10). The project was realized in collaboration with Rogers and two other students but presented for jury review by Foster, who had been elected by his codesigners to act as spokesman. It was clear even then that besides talent and drive Foster possessed an attribute deemed by many to be quintessentially that of American business practice: the ability not only to work in a team but also to become its leader. The design of the new city incorporated aspects of Foster's earlier office tower project, constituting a form of self-quotation that had characterized the urban proposals of Le Corbusier and Frank Lloyd Wright.

Foster's scheme was developed under the guidance of the Russian-born, English-educated Serge Chermayeff, whom Rudolph had brought to Yale from Harvard in a deliberate if possibly misguided attempt to lodge an antiheroic, antiaesthetic point of view in the curriculum. Whatever the complex intentions behind Chermayeff's appointment as professor of architecture, his influence, particularly on Foster, was lasting and profound. Chermayeff added a distinctively European seasoning to the already rich Anglo-American soup.

Foster has argued that "my timing at Yale in 1961 was more fortunate than I could ever have foreseen because it marked the change of leadership to Serge Chermayeff. He was as European as Rudolph was American. It was not just in dress or manner, but deeply rooted differences in philosophy. For Chermayeff debate and theory took precedence over imagery—questioning was to the fore—analysis dominated action."[22]

Norman Foster at Yale

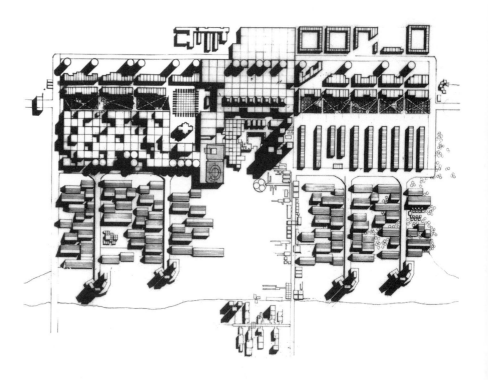

Ironically, the European influence at Yale emanated not only from Chermayeff, but also from the quintessentially American Rudolph; as Foster has noted, "In some ways I went to Yale to discover a European heritage because America had embraced those émigrés such as Gropius, who taught Rudolph at Harvard and was, I quote, 'his point of reference.'"[23]

Foster's project for a new city, executed while he was studying with Chermayeff, was decidedly European, with rationally sited *Siedlung*-like rows of houses punctuated by towers. In a way, the project directly illustrated the theoretical studies that would lead to Chermayeff's book, *Community and Privacy*, cowritten with Christopher Alexander and published in 1963.[24]

After completing his studies at Yale in 1962, Foster was invited by Chermayeff to stay in New Haven and join him as a research fellow. Tempted as he was, Foster chose instead to work as a city planner in Massachusetts before moving on to San Francisco to work with John Carl Warnecke and Anshen & Allen, who were engaged in planning a new University of California campus at Santa Cruz. Rogers was also working in California at the time, and the two young architects were excited by Ezra Ehrenkrantz's School Construction Systems Development Program.

Through journals and Scully's lectures they had already been introduced to the California Case Study houses designed by Raphael Soriano, Pierre Koenig, Craig Ellwood, Richard Neutra, and Charles and Ray Eames, which they admired. Of these, the house that the Eameses built for themselves in 1949, in Pacific Palisades, with its creative assemblage of off-the-shelf industrial components, exerted a lasting influence on Foster's work. So too did the compelling imagery of Koenig's hillside Case Study House #22 with its impossibly slender cantilevers. Foster was

also captivated by the forms of American technology: highways, Airstream trailers, and the rockets and launching pad structures of Cape Canaveral.

*Fig. 10.* Norman Foster, John Chisholm, Richard Rogers and Roy Mason, Model, Final group project at Yale, Scheme for a new city, 1962

However, it was not just specific American buildings, nor even American approaches to architecture, construction, and large-scale planning, that captured the young Britons' imaginations as they crisscrossed the country together. It was the entire sweep of the continental landscape and the national character that fired them up. As Rogers has said: "America enthralled us [with] its scale, energy, optimism and openness. We travelled by thumb, by car and by Greyhound bus, voraciously absorbing the culture, both of the massive open spaces and the tall, taut, energetic cities."[25]

For Foster, Yale had in some ways been emblematic of America: "The emphasis on tangible results in the studio summed up an American world in which everything was possible if you were willing to try hard enough. For me that was a breath of fresh air . . . America gave me a sense of confidence, freedom and self-discovery."[26]

In 1963, Foster returned to England where he joined Rogers to found the trendsetting firm Team 4. The remaining two of the "four" were the architect sisters, Wendy and Georgie Cheesman, although the latter was a member in name only; as the only qualified architect of the group, it was she who initially allowed Team 4 to meet the legal requirements of architectural practice. Soon enough, however, Foster would be on his own. After only four years together, in 1967, Team 4 split up. Foster and Wendy (by then his wife) established themselves as Foster Associates and pursued an independent direction, quite different from Rogers', although the three of them remained close.

Foster's is an architecture that, in its functional rigor, compositional clarity, and high finish, as well as its concern with means of production and far-reaching issues of urban planning and the social context of buildings, continues to reflect his experience at Yale and in America. It inspires architects everywhere to realize the expressive possibilities of advanced technology and the sheer optimism of the act and art of building. Most of all, in the generosity of his open-mindedness, Foster has demonstrated, as too few architects do, that "architects learn from architects—past and present."[27]

# 22

## Principles and Values
### 1988

To begin on a personal note: This has been a wonderful, if a little unnerving, opportunity to reflect on, and most shockingly to come to terms with, the fact that the past twenty-five years constitute virtually my entire education and practice in architecture. That indeed, all these wonderful ideas we have shared today are just about *all* I know. I can remember my first glimpse of Michael Graves—I was in third-year studio at Yale, and he was a young Princeton instructor taking Sven Silow and a group of students on the grand tour of New Haven, which, as you know, is *the* American Florence. Even then Michael was a presence—or at least his oversized Le Corbusier glasses were. He came up to my desk and started discussing the building we were in, Louis Kahn's Art Gallery, as he cast his eyes disapprovingly on the building I was drawing—a health care facility, as I recall, based on a glorious misreading of Frank Lloyd Wright's Fallingwater. Yes, I confess, I am an architect whose references are sometimes modernist and American; worse yet, I did not go to Princeton.

This has been an occasion of amazing true confessions: when Peter Eisenman confesses his desire to be in the center as he avers that stylistic movements are inevitable rather than created by architects—wow. But this is not an occasion for reminiscences, nor is it my job to offer a critique of the morning's proceedings. Rather, it is one for reflection.

Let me begin with a truism: architectural education, insofar as studio teaching is concerned, is a matter of inculcating principles—that is to say, principles of design composition. To this end, I have come to the conclusion that the teaching of architecture today is often tragically haphazard. More than ever, students drown in the modishness of magazines and faculty. In the absence of any structured pedagogy they lack organizational tools with which to tackle a project. After fifty years, ahistorical modernism has failed to develop a grammar, and classicism, though once again recognized, has not yet taken its proper place as the basis of pedagogy. Classicism is the only codified, amplified, and perennially vital system of architectural composition bringing order to the process of design, and from it grew up the only modern system of architectural education that succeeded in producing a large and diverse corps of skillful, confident, and often inspired designers: the École des Beaux-Arts. Like it or not, classicism commands our attention and offers us a basis for design. The grand tradition of classicism is a constituent fact of modern architecture, including ahistorical modernism. Without it, Le Corbusier and Mies van der Rohe would have been much diminished as architects and human beings. It is neither an accident nor a testament to declining intelligence that so many of modernism's finest achievements were those of its first generation, of Le Corbusier and Mies, who never escaped classicism's thrall even as they deliberately reduced architectural composition and proportion to a process of structural framing.

Fortunately, there is more to the teaching of architecture than principles. There are individual examples and exemplars, monuments and mentors, who may suggest a larger scheme of things even as we get caught up in transitory trends. In the post-Renaissance, modern world, individuals often stand for ideas. In architecture, this is surely so. Individuals define an understanding of architecture, and I would argue that it is impossible for architects to understand architecture without also understanding the individual points of view of the architects who create.

Given this occasion, which catches me—and I am sure so many of you—up short with a sense of stylistic transition, not to mention chronological middle age, I find myself thinking of the architecture and architectural education of the past twenty-five years in highly personal, indeed autobiographical terms. Yet I cannot believe that my experiences have not been in some way typical for each of us in our now emerged middle generation. So I hope it is not out of order to focus on the architects who led me and still lead me to question my own understanding of architecture and help to shape my work as a teacher and practitioner. In so doing, I hope to call attention to those who have shaped us all. Some of these critical figures are teachers in a formal sense, others are colleagues in the profession; some we have come to know intimately, others we may have only been privileged to know at a distance, on a lecture platform, or in the pages of a book or magazine. But each of them has helped to define our shared points of view and made our education more than the matter of a few years in a university.

From Philip Johnson we have learned that things change, that the past is a mirror of the present, and that the practice of architecture, though not a substitute for life, is a way of life.

From Paul Rudolph we have learned that a strong conviction demands continual revalidation through debate. Paul Rudolph's Yale was a world center for architectural discourse; Rudolph as an architect and teacher was the focus of the debate; the great and near-great of the time, from James Stirling and Colin St. John Wilson to Craig Ellwood and Ralph Erskine, were the visiting players; we, the students, were the fans—or better still, the privileged audience.

From Louis Kahn we learned that the common thread of architecture is order. Given the primacy of order, many of us who value Kahn's lessons have come to consider classicism as the essence of architecture.

From Robert Venturi we learned that the hierarchies of expression characteristic of traditional architecture remain valid despite the pluralistic, postindustrial world; that good architecture can be ordinary or extraordinary according to circumstances determined by physical and cultural context; that the architect's role is not to sit in judgment but to understand, and in understanding, to help elevate common things and common beliefs to the level of art. Most of all we have learned from Bob Venturi to keep our eyes open. Too bad I haven't learned from Bob to keep my mouth shut.

From Charles Moore we learned that architectural memory consists of more than the great monuments and even extends beyond buildings themselves to all the senses, and to the ordinary experiences of everyday life as they happen in a setting defined by buildings. Charles Moore has taught architecture how to relax; better still, he has taught a few architects, at least, how to smile.

From Peter Eisenman we have learned by inverse means the lesson of architecture as a rich tradition. As Eisenman continually searches for a justification outside architecture and struggles to shake things up, he has reaffirmed for many of us just how much architecture has to nourish itself from within. From Peter we have learned, most importantly, that the act of building is not a casual undertaking; not something to be taken lightly. Architecture must count for something.

From Vincent Scully we have learned that though architecture has a culture all its own, it belongs as well to a larger realm. Scully has made us all ever keen to the fact that architecture's function in the culture as a whole is largely reflexive rather than initiative. In short, that architecture is more mirror than lamp.

From James Stirling we learned that there was more to modernism than the white cardboard architecture of the 1920s or the banalities of the 1950s. We learned first of the joyous optimism of constructivism and of the industrial vernacular.

From Stanley Tigerman we learned that nothing is sacred. That the value of speaking out honestly applies as much to architects as to politicians. And that honesty must be a value for buildings—not honesty to structure or to materials, but honesty to the cultural processes, the client foibles, and the social tragedies that sometimes cause buildings to be undertaken.

From Frank Gehry we learned that when all is said and done, it is better to discover order in an intuition than to have order for its own sake.

From Rem Koolhaas we learned about the sex life of buildings, taking anthropomorphism to its logical level of post-Freudian analysis.

From Léon Krier we learned just how monumental a modest design can be.

From Michael Graves, whom we honor today, we learned about the value of a continuing commitment to education. Though the exhausting rollercoaster ride of every studio term may leave us drained of energy, the highs and lows of discourse over a student's drafting table have no substitute in the experiences of an office. Michael has shown a way to connect teaching in the studio to the development of an office, and not just an ordinary office but one where students become trusted and valued associates, working together to solidify a shared point of view. Equally, as Michael moved from cubism to classicism, we learned about change and growth, about holding on to one's ideals while reconsidering the forms they take.

This last point leads to a bit of reflection on the shared experiences of the generation that now dominates American practice. As students, we tended to see architecture in terms of pure formalism. We were in rebellion against the materialistic functionalism of the late International Style of Walter Gropius and his disciples; we were in reaction as well to what appeared to be technological determinism growing out of Mies and achieving near parody in the work of some of his disciples. By the time we came to teaching in the late 1960s, that closed world, both of Gropius and Mies, as well as of our own hyperformalism, was everywhere in disarray. Our war in Vietnam was also being waged in our classrooms. Despite all the rhetoric against the establishment, students and most architects were still unable to see a basis for design beyond functionalism or hothouse aesthetics. Besieged by war and rock 'n' roll, and in response to a heightened sense of civil liberty and social responsibility, functionalism experienced a new lease on life, in which user needs dominated virtually any consideration of tectonics. The pop sociology of street-corner surveys was confused with architectural research. Against this background, the search of the so-called New York Five for a purely aesthetic modernism was certainly notable, if somehow trivial, in the sense that the forms of pure modernism that were explored and advocated were almost completely relieved of their original cultural content, and no new content seems to have evolved to take their place.

It was not until the mid 1970s that the cultural collapse and confusion of the sixties began to be overcome. In 1973, when *Five Architects* was reviewed by the five so-called Grays, a new, more positive dialogue at last began to establish itself. The Whites, or the New York Five, represented the view that modernism needed to purify itself by a return to the forms, if not necessarily the content, of the 1920s; the Grays tried to avoid the narrow focus on a single movement, and thereby to reinvigorate architecture by engaging in a discourse across time, one that stylistically would include modernism and premodernism with the culture of the moment, however confused and vexing in its pluralism it might seem. Clearly the debate continues to affect this generation—my generation and Michael's—which, for better or worse, is now the establishment.

The debate over style and culture can be seen as ongoing, and its clearest reflection is in the pedagogical oscillations in the studios of the schools. Despite the efforts of journalists to see the debate as a succession of trends, I believe that the architectural culture of our time is much more than that. For me, it is recognition of the varieties and hierarchies of expression that are inherent in architecture but too often repressed by architects, journalists, and historians imbued with an obsessive devotion to a zeitgeist-driven view of creativity. For me, a rejection of historical determinism is essential to architecture's renewal. As I review the scene in architecture schools I see a nostalgia for the good old days of monoculture such as Gropius promoted at Harvard. As a new generation of deans and teachers emerges in the universities, I wonder whether the debate among the Whites and the Grays, the exclusivists and the inclusivists, will continue, or whether it will be swept away in a single-mindedness such as American architecture has not witnessed for a generation.

# Notes

## Chapter 1: Regionalism and the Continuity of Tradition

1. Marquis de Chastellux, quoted in William H. Pierson, Jr., *American Buildings and Their Architects: The Colonial and Neo-Classical Styles* (Garden City, NY: Doubleday, 1970), 289.
2. Lewis Mumford, "The Skyline: The American Tradition," *New Yorker* 15 (March 11, 1939): 37.
3. Lewis Mumford, *Sticks and Stones: A Study of American Architecture and Civilization* (New York: Boni and Liveright, 1924), 195–96.

## Chapter 2: What the Classical Can Do for the Modern

1. Friedrich Schiller, *On the Aesthetic Education of Man* (1795), trans. Reginald Snell (London: Routledge & Kegan Paul, 1954), 51–52.
2. Ibid., 54.
3. I wish to thank M. Lindsay Bierman for his assistance in the preparation of this text. Portions of this discussion grow out of my book *Modern Classicism* (London: Thames & Hudson; New York: Rizzoli, 1988), written with the assistance of Raymond Gastil.

## Chapter 3: Designing the American Dream

1. Frank Lloyd Wright, *An Autobiography*, 2nd rev. ed (New York: Duell, Sloan & Pearce, 1943), 228.
2. Denise Scott Brown, "Suburban Space, Scale, and Symbols," *Via* 3 (Graduate School of Fine Arts, University of Pennsylvania, 1977); see also Brown et al., *Signs of Life: Symbols in the American City* (New York: Aperture, 1976).

## Chapter 4: Housing America: 1920–1929

1. John Taylor Boyd, Jr., "Garden Apartments in Cities, part I," *Architectural Record* 48 (July 1920): 52–74; "Garden Apartments in Cities, part II," *Architectural Record* 48 (August 1920): 121–35.
2. Lewis Mumford, *Sketches from Life* (New York: Dial, 1982), 410.
3. Bruce Bliven, "Houses of Tomorrow," *New Republic* 42 (March 4, 1925): 34–37.
4. Lewis Mumford, "Mass Production and the Modern House," *Architectural Record* 67 (February 1930): 110–16.
5. Boyd, "Garden Apartments in Cities, part II."
6. A. Lawrence Kocher, "The Country House: Are We Developing an American Style?" *Architectural Record* 60 (November 1926): 385–95.
7. Edith Elmer Wood, "Recent Housing Work in Western Europe," *Architectural Record* 53 (February 1923): 173–83.
8. Frank Chouteau Brown, "Low Rental Housing: Suburban Type, Part 1," *Architectural Record* 56 (August 1924): 106–16; "Low Rental Housing: Suburban Type, Part 2," *Architectural Record* 56 (September 1924): 206–17; "Low Rental Housing: 'Community Planning' and the 'Unit' in Suburban Group Apartments," *Architectural Record* 56 (October 1924): 353–67; "Low Rental Housing: The New Immigration and European Housing,

Their Future Effect on American Conditions," *Architectural Record* 56 (December 1924): 553–65.

9. Henry-Russell Hitchcock, "Modern Architecture I: The Traditionalists and the New Tradition," *Architectural Record* 63 (April 1928): 337–49 and "Modern Architecture II: The New Pioneers," *Architectural Record* 63 (May 1928): 453–60.

10. Hitchcock, "Modern Architecture II."

11. "A Beach House for Dr. P. Lowell at Newport Beach, Calif.," *Architectural Record* 66 (September 1929): 257–61.

12. Richard J. Neutra, "Architecture Conditioned by Engineering and Industry," *Architectural Record* 66 (September 1929): 272–74.

### Chapter 6: The Suburban Alternative for the "Middle City"

1. Lewis Mumford, *The City in History* (New York: Harcourt, 1961), 490.

### Chapter 9: The Fall and Rise of New York

1. Rem Koolhaas, *Delirious New York: A Retroactive Manifesto for Manhattan* (New York: Oxford University Press, 1978), 6.

2. Ibid., 7.

3. Will Lissner, "Bienstock Sees an Upsurge in City's Economy in 80's," *New York Times* (April 5, 1976): 1, 37.

4. Koolhaas, *Delirious New York*, 7.

5. The claims were dismissed in 1989 by the United States District Court for the Southern District of New York and, after the church appealed its decision, also by the Federal Court of Appeals in 1990. The church continued fighting until March 1991, when the United States Supreme Court declined to hear an appeal. For extensive discussion of the "Battle of St. Bart's," see Robert A.M. Stern, David Fishman, and Jacob Tilove, *New York 2000* (New York: Monacelli, 2006), 506–12.

6. Ada Louise Huxtable, "Creeping Gigantism in Manhattan," *New York Times* (March 22, 1987), II: 1, 36.

7. Ibid.

8. Sylvia Deutsch, letter to the editor, *New York Times* (May 10, 1987), II: 11, 35.

9. Ibid.

10. John Dos Passos, *Manhattan Transfer* (New York: Harper & Brothers, 1925), 215.

11. Carl Van Vechten, *Parties: Scenes from Contemporary New York Life* (New York: Knopf, 1930), 138.

12. Albert Scardino, "What, New York City Worry?" *New York Times* (May 3, 1987), III: 1.

### Chapter 12: The Relevance of a Decade: 1929–1939

1. See especially his book, *Modern Architecture: The Architecture of Democracy* (New York: Braziller, 1961), 32–33.

2. Reyner Banham, *Theory and Design in the First Machine Age* (New York: Praeger, 1960), 305. Gropius was also aware of the importance of 1927 in the evolution and establishment of the International Style. In the preface (written at Dessau in July 1927) to the second edition of his book, *Internationale Architektur*, he said: "Since the appearance of the first edition [in 1925] the modern architecture of the various lands of western culture has followed the line of development indicated by this book with a surprisingly rapid tempo. Then but an idea, it is today a solid fact." Trans. Henry-Russell Hitchcock, *Architectural Record* 66 (1929): 191.

3. See John Ritter, "World Parliament. The League of Nations Competition, 1926," *Architectural Review* 136 (July 1964): 17–28. The problem of the potential for monumental expression within the International Style continued to obsess architects and writers until the early 1950s. In 1948, this important problem was discussed at two major symposia. The first, "What is Happening to Modern Architecture?", was sponsored by the Museum of Modern Art in New York. It is discussed by Vincent Scully in "Doldrums in the Suburbs," *Perspecta* 9/10 (1965): 281–90 and *Journal of the Society of Architectural Historians* 24 (March 1965): 36–47. The second symposium, "In Search of a New Monumentality," was conducted by the English periodical *Architectural Review*. See "In Search of New Monumentality," *Architectural Review* 104 (September 1948): 117–28.

4. For a discussion of the significance of Ford's decision, see William Leuchtenburg's excellent survey of the 1920s in America, *The Perils of Prosperity, 1914–32* (Chicago: University of Chicago Press, 1958), 200–01. There

is good reason to claim that Ford's Model A was the first car put into production to embody the principles and techniques of industrial design. This rules out much of Banham's elaborate treatment of automobile design at the end of his book, *Theory and Design in the First Machine Age*. Surely the Model A and not Harley Earle's La Salle car of 1934 was the first car to respond to consumer preferences in the matter of design. If we take into account the availability of the Model A—it was a cheap car introduced in a period of prosperity, while the La Salle was a high-priced car introduced in a period of economic depression—as well as the tremendous publicity that accompanied its appearance on the market, its importance and the magnitude of its influence give it a far greater historical role. See Allan Nevins and Frank Ernest Hill, *Ford: Expansion and Challenge 1915–1933* (New York: Scribner, 1957), ch. 16, "The End of Model T," especially 418–21, 431–36, and ch. 18, "Model A: A New Era"; and Charles Merz, *And Then Came Ford* (Garden City, NY: Doubleday, 1929), ch. 13, "America on Wheels," especially 271–86 and ch. 24, "The Mysterious Stranger." Sheldon and Martha Cheney have also written about the importance of Ford's transition from the Model T to the Model A in *Art and the Machine* (New York: Whittlesey House, 1936), 26–30.

5. See Norman Bel Geddes, *Miracle in the Evening*, ed. William Kelley (New York: Doubleday, 1960). According to Kelley's chronology, Bel Geddes "established the profession of industrial designer" in 1927; "that is, Norman Bel Geddes was the first designer of national reputation to surround himself with a staff of specialists and offer industrial design services" (344). The underlying commercial spirit of the Industrial Design movement in the late 1920s is suggested in Earnest Elmo Calkins' essay, "Beauty, the New Business Tool," *Atlantic Monthly* 140 (August 1927): 145–56. Calkins writes that "there is behind all these changes simply the desire to sell. Beauty is introduced into material objects to enhance them in the eyes of the purchaser. The appeal of efficiency alone is nearly ended. . . . This remarkable turn of the industrial world toward beauty in design and color is not really a new thing. It is merely the size of the movement that is startling." Sheldon and Martha Cheney see the emergence of industrial design as a result of consumer demands for "higher standards of appearance [that] resulted, in 1927, in the artist's being summoned to the factory for service in unfamiliar design fields." *Art and the Machine*, 7. They also corroborate the primacy of Geddes's position. Buckminster Fuller has a good deal to say about the "Myth of Industrial Design" in his recent "spontaneous autobiographical disclosure." *Ideas and Integrities* (Englewood Cliffs, NJ: Prentice-Hall, 1963), 76–78.

6. The year 1927 is often repeated in Fuller's *Ideas and Integrities*, in which he devotes a considerable amount of energy to criticism of the Bauhaus and the International Style. "Many people have asked if the Bauhaus ideas and techniques have had any formative influence on my work. I must answer vigorously that they have not" (9). Robert W. Marks emphasizes the importance 1927 had in Fuller's career. See *The Dymaxion World of Buckminster Fuller* (New York: Reinhold, 1960), 18, 21, 24–25, 27–28. Perhaps the most eloquent and influential exponent of Fuller's position in this matter is Reyner Banham, who concludes his book, *Theory and Design in the First Machine Age*, with a chapter on "Functionalism and Technology," in which he makes frequent reference to Fuller's achievement and includes "something like a flat rebuttal" of the International Style taken from his writings.

7. André Siegfried, *America Comes of Age*, trans. H.H. and Doris Hemming (New York: Harcourt, 1927), 347.

8. For a comprehensive view of precisionism, see *Art in America* 48 (Fall 1960): 30–61. Especially relevant to developments in the late 1920s and to their prevalence in present attitudes toward form are articles by Martin Friedman, "The Precisionist View" (31–37) and Vincent Scully, "The Precisionist Strain in American Architecture" (46–53).

9. John W. McCoubrey, *American Tradition in Painting* (New York: Braziller, 1963), 47.

10. George Howe, unpublished talk delivered before the students of the Graduate School of Design, Harvard University, ca. 1954.

11. Henry-Russell Hitchcock, Jr., "The Decline of Architecture," *Hound and Horn* 1 (1927): 28–35. See also the letter from Charles Crombie, 140–44, and Hitchcock's letter of reply, 244–45.

12. Samuel Chamberlain, "In Search of Modernism, Concerning the Dearth of Material in France for the Enquiring Reporter," *American Architect* 131 (1927): 71–74.

13. Milton B. Medary, president of the American Institute of Architects, reflected the apprehension with which the "old guard" greeted the spirit of modernism when, in commenting on "the myriad confusions and complications of twentieth century life," which tend to bewilder men with "the surface manifestations of constantly changing forms," he grudgingly acknowledged that "in literature, in religion, in sculpture and painting and music and drama, as well as in architecture, the world is in revolt." *Proceedings of the Sixtieth Annual Convention* [AIA] (1927), 5–8. George C. Nimmons, a leading architect of industrial buildings, offered the following explanation for the new modernist spirit to a reporter at the convention: "The demand on the part of the press for a new style of architecture, as they call it . . . has been very strong and the effect of that has not been so much on the architect, because he knows the causes which produce loose styles of architecture, as upon the client. The client now demands a departure from the old line of work. He wants something new." "Sixtieth Annual Convention: The American Institute of Architects, Washington, D.C.," *American Architect* 131 (June 5, 1927): 679–710.

14. The impact of this building on the profession (it was awarded the gold medal by the Architectural League of New York in 1927) and on the public was enormous. It placed its designer, Ralph Walker, at the forefront of the profession. See George H. Allen, "Dynamic Energy and Modernism," *Architectural Forum* 54 (May 1931): 609–10. The building's critical notices were enthusiastic.

15. See "The Ziegfeld Theatre, New York," *Architectural Forum* 46 (May 1927): 414–16 and plates.

16. See Lawrence Moore, "The Medical Center," *The Arts* 14 (November 1928): 284–86.

17. Thomas Tallmadge, "Louis Sullivan and the Lost Cause," in *The Story of Architecture in America* (New York: Norton, 1927), 214–33. By 1936, when Tallmadge brought out a second edition of his book, the complete resurgence of Wright's career and Sullivan's reputation is reflected in Tallmadge's new chapter title, "Louis Sullivan, Parent and Prophet."

18. For a discussion of Wright's difficulties in the late 1920s and early 1930s, see his *An Autobiography* (New York: Longman's, Green, 1932), especially 271–95. See also Finis Farr, *Frank Lloyd Wright* (New York: Scribner, 1961), especially ch. 6. In January 1927, Wright's collection of Japanese prints was sold at auction in New York. Taliesin was in the hands of a bank and, in order to protect himself from complete financial ruin, he announced the formation of Frank Lloyd Wright, Inc., which eventually led to the establishment of the Taliesin Fellowship. Wright's only executed commission for the year—and his first since 1924—was Graycliff, the Isabelle and Darwin Martin house at Derby, New York.

19. Kocher became managing editor of *Record* in August 1927 but the new format did not appear until January 1928. See Michael A. Mikkelsen, "A Word About the New Format," *Architectural Record* 63 (January 1928): 1–2. *The Architectural Forum* and *American Architect* also modernized their formats in January 1928, but neither carried their reforms over into their editorial policies with the fervor and intelligence that marked the *Record*'s efforts in the period 1927–32.

20. S. and M. Cheney, *Art and the Machine*, 8.

21. The Exposition was held at 119 West 57th Street, New York, May 16–18, 1927. See Jane Heap, "Machine-Age Exposition," in *The Little Review Anthology*, ed. Margaret Anderson (New York: Hermitage House, 1953), 341–43. See also Margaret Anderson, *My Thirty Years' War* (New York: Covici, 1930), 265, in which she states that Jane Heap made *The Little Review* the "American mouthpiece for all the new systems of art that the modern world has produced from the German expressionists and the Russian constructionists [sic] to the French *sur-réalistes*. She opened a Little

Review Gallery at 66 Fifth Avenue, where the painting, sculpture constructions, and machinery of these groups were exhibited. In 1926, she organized an International Theatre Exposition in which Russian constructionist stage-sets were shown for the first time in America. In 1927 she gave a Machine-Age show—modern art in juxtaposition with engineering and the industrial arts, the first exposition of its kind to be shown anywhere." Jane Heap wrote in the last issue of *The Little Review* that the Machine-Age Exposition was the "first exposition of its kind anywhere . . . [and the] first showing of modern architecture in America." "Lost: A Renaissance," *The Little Review* (May 1929): 5–6. The Cheneys confirm Miss Heap's claims (*Art and the Machine*, 7–8) as did Herbert Lippman, an architect who reviewed the show in *The Arts* 11 (June 1927): 324–26. Mr. Lippman wrote that the Machine-Age Exposition was "the first large aesthetically intended opportunity offered the New York public of seeing this new inspiration in process of development."

22. The press coverage was, however, nonarchitectural. On Sunday, May 22, 1927, the very day the *New York Times'* banner headline screamed "Lindbergh Does It!", amid the classified advertisements of that newspaper a small article devoted to the exposition under a photograph of a small house by André Lurçat announced that the new style of architecture was "marked by an emphasis on the undecorated facade, flat roof and horizontal window." "French Design for Small Homes," *New York Times*, sec. 12, May 22, 1927. Coverage in the *Times* for the following Sunday, May 29, 1927, was far more prominently placed on the first page of the editorial and general news section and it carried the following headline: "New Architecture Develops in Russia / Exhibits at Machine Age Show Here Indicate Trend in Building and Art / Evidence of Vast Change / Industrial Civilization the Basis of New Forms—Skyscrapers Built on Horizontal Plan." The bulk of this article was devoted to the remarks of the Russian-American painter Louis Lozowick, who delivered a talk on Russian architecture at a symposium called "Russian Night." *New York Times*, sec. 2, May 29, 1927.

23. 1927 was a significant date in the emergence of continental modernism in England as well. See, for example, *The Architectural Association Guide to Modern Architecture in London, 1927–1957* (London, 1957), whose earliest listing is Easton and Robertson's Royal Horticultural Hall, completed in that year. See also Gerald K. Geerlings, "The Royal Horticultural Hall," *Architectural Forum* 54 (May 1931): 567–78.

24. Esther McCoy, *Richard Neutra* (New York: Braziller, 1960), gives 1929 as the date of the Health House—though she is referring, no doubt, to its date of completion. Neutra, on the other hand, insists on 1927 as the significant date. See his autobiography, *Life and Shape* (New York: Appleton, Century, Crofts, 1962), especially 220–26, "Health House, Vintage 1927."

25. See "A New City," *The Architect* 9 (1928): 681–82; see also "Radburn, New Jersey, a Town of Modern Plan," *Architecture* 57 (1928): 135–36. Schemes for sorting traffic based on French and Italian precedents, fundamentally Beaux-Arts, though subjected to futurist influences, were very current in America in these years. In addition to those of Stein and Wright and of Hood, Harvey Wiley Corbett's double-decked street plan should also be mentioned. See Harvey Wiley Corbett, "The Problem of Traffic Congestion and a Solution," *Architectural Forum* 46 (March 1927): 201–08.

## Chapter 13: Television and Architecture: Notes on *Pride of Place*

1. Spiro Kostof wrote and hosted a five-part series, *America by Design*, for PBS in 1987. A companion book of the same title was published that year by Oxford University Press.

## Chapter 15: Buildings and Brands

1. Jefferson to Cabell, 28 December 1822, in *Early History of the University of Virginia as Contained in the Letters of Thomas Jefferson and Joseph C. Cabell* (Richmond, VA: J.W. Randolph, 1856), 260.
2. Lewis Mumford, "House of Glass," *The New Yorker* (August 9, 1952): 48–54

**Chapter 16: Rationalism and Romanticism in the Domestic Architecture of George Howe**

1. George Howe, Address to the American Institute of Architects, *Proceedings of the Sixty-Third Annual Convention* (Washington, DC: AIA, 1930): 25–28.
2. George Howe, "What is this modern architecture trying to express?" *American Architect* 137 (May 1930): 22–25, 106-08.
3. Henry Adams, *The Education of Henry Adams: An Autobiography* (New York: Houghton Mifflin, 1918), 65.
4. George Howe, "Architecture and 'Creative Evolution,'" *Perspecta* 2 (1953): 1.
5. George Howe, "Modern Architecture," *USA: A Quarterly Magazine of the American Scene*, no. 1 (Spring 1930): 19–23.
6. Howe, "What is this modern architecture trying to express?"
7. Paul P. Cret, "A Hillside House: The Property of George Howe, Esq., Chestnut Hill, Philadelphia," *Architectural Record* 48 (August 1920): 83–106.
8. Ibid.
9. George Howe, "Some Experiences and Observations of an Elderly Architect," *Perspecta* 2 (1953): 2–5.
10. Ibid.
11. Arthur L. Meigs, *An American Country House* (New York: Architectural Book Publishing Co., 1925), xvi.
12. Ibid.
13. "Square Shadows, Whitemarsh, Penn.," *Architectural Forum* 62 (March 1935): 193–205.
14. George Howe, in a talk at the opening of the Yale School of the Fine Arts in the autumn of 1953, summarized in his essay "Architecture and 'Creative Evolution,'" *Perspecta* 2 (1953): 1.
15. George Howe, "Training for the Practice of Architecture: A speech given before the Department in September, 1951," *Perspecta* 1 (1952): 2–7.

**Chapter 17: Robert Moses as Architect**

1. This talk was prepared with the assistance of M. Lindsay Bierman.
2. Robert Moses, "The Changing City," *Architectural Forum* 72 (March 1940): 142–56.
3. Robert Moses, "Functionalism, Sir, Is a Fake!" *New York Herald Tribune Magazine* (June 8, 1947): 5, 24.
4. Moses, "The Changing City."
5. Moses, "Functionalism, Sir, Is a Fake!"
6. Quoted in Cleveland Rogers, *Robert Moses: Builder for Democracy* (New York: Holt, 1952), 248.
7. Robert Moses, *Public Works: A Dangerous Trade* (New York: McGraw-Hill, 1970), 423.
8. Arnold Vollmer, Commentary on Robert Moses, *The Livable City* 12 (December 1988): 11.
9. Robert A. Caro, *The Power Broker* (New York: Vintage, 1975, c. 1974), 372.
10. See "For Beauty's Sake," *AIA Journal* 46 (December 1966): 52–54.
11. Gilmore D. Clarke, "Designing Small Stone Bridges," *American Architect and the Architectural Review* 121 (March 29, 1922): 249–52.
12. Gilmore D. Clarke, "New Bridges Mean Opportunity for Architects," *American Architect and Architecture* 143 (September 1933): 57–61.
13. Ibid.
14. Citation read by Robert Moses, trustee, on presentation of the Honorary Degree of Doctor of Humane Letters to Aymar Embury II, Hofstra College, February 4, 1951; quoted in Rodgers, *Robert Moses, Builder for Democracy*, 257.
15. Quoted in "Aymar Embury, Architect, Dead" *New York Times* (November 15, 1966): 47.
16. "Pattern for Parks," *Architectural Forum* 65 (December 1936): 491–510.
17. Moses, "The Changing City."
18. Marshall Berman, "Buildings are Judgement," *Ramparts* 13 (March 1975): 33–39, 50–58.
19. Aymar Embury II, "Engineering and Architecture," *Journal of the American Institute of Architects* 1 (May 1944): 223–33.
20. Moses, *Public Works*, 196.
21. Henry Saylor, "The Editor's Diary," *Architecture* 70 (November 1934): 281–82.
22. F. Scott Fitzgerald, *The Great Gatsby* (New York: Scribner, 1925; repr. 1953), 23–24.
23. Marshall Berman, *All That Is Solid Melts Into Air* (New York: Verso, 1983), 308.
24. Moses, "Functionalism, Sir, Is a Fake!"
25. Moses, *Public Works*, 421; see also Robert Moses, "Thoughts of a City Builder," *Journal of the American Institute of Architects* 26 (December 1956): 241–47.

26. Robert Moses to Colonel James A. Dawson, 30 August 1957, Robert Moses papers. Manuscripts and Archives Division, The New York Public Library. Astor, Lenox and Tilden Foundations.
27. Berman, "Buildings are Judgement."
28. Sigfried Giedion, *Space, Time and Architecture* (Cambridge: Harvard University Press, 1941; repr. 1952), 619.

**Chapter 19: Remembering Louis Kahn**

1. Robert A.M. Stern, "Yale 1950–1965," *Oppositions* 4 (October 1974): 35–62.

**Chapter 20: Charles Moore: The Architect Running in Place**

1. Charles Willard Moore and Gerald Allen, *Dimensions: Space, Shape & Scale in Architecture* (New York: Architectural Record Books, 1976), 51.
2. Charles Willard Moore, *Home Sweet Home: American Domestic Vernacular Architecture* (New York: Rizzoli, 1983), 133–34.
3. John W. Cook and Heinrich Klotz, *Conversations with Architects* (New York: Praeger, 1973), 235.
4. Ibid.
5. Ibid.
6. Charles Willard Moore, "You Have to Pay for the Public Life," *Perspecta* 9/10 (1965): 57–106.
7. Ibid.
8. Charles Moore, Gerald Allen, and Donlyn Lyndon, *The Place of Houses* (New York: Holt, Rinehart, 1974), 140.
9. Quoted in David Littlejohn, *Architect: The Life and Work of Charles W. Moore* (New York: Holt, Rinehart, 1984), 230.

**Chapter 21: Norman Foster at Yale**

1. The phrase "constituent facts" was used by Sigfried Giedion in his influential book, *Space, Time and Architecture* (Cambridge: Harvard University Press, 1941).
2. Norman Foster, "Pritzker Prize Address, 1999," in *On Foster . . . Foster On* (Munich: Prestel, 2000), 729–33. See also *The Pritzker Architecture Prize 1999: Sir Norman Foster* (Los Angeles: Jensen & Walker, 1999).
3. Paul Rudolph, "Architectural Education in the United States," Voice of America: Forum Lectures, Architecture Series, no. 9 (Washington, D.C., ca. 1961); "The Architectural Education in U.S.A.," *Zodiac* 8 (1961): 162–65.

4. David G. McCullough, "Architectural Spellbinder," *Architectural Forum* 111 (September 1959): 136–37, 191, 202.
5. Foster, "Pritzker Prize Address, 1999."
6. Louis I. Kahn, "Remarks," *Perspecta* 9/10 (1965): 303–35.
7. Letter from M.J. Long to Robert A.M. Stern, 11 February 1974.
8. Ibid.
9. James Stirling, "'The Functional Tradition' and Expression," *Perspecta* 6 (1960): 88–97.
10. Peter Blake, *God's Own Junkyard: The Planned Deterioration of America's Landscape* (New York: Holt, Rinehart, 1964).
11. Reyner Banham, "Morse and Stiles," *New Statesman* (July 13, 1962): 54–55. Reprinted in *Architectural Forum* (December 1962): 110.
12. Reyner Banham, "The History of the Immediate Future," *RIBA Journal* 68 (May 1961): 252–57.
13. Banham, "Morse and Stiles."
14. Foster, "Pritzker Prize Address, 1999."
15. Ibid.
16. Richard Rogers, "Team 4," in *Norman Foster: Team 4 and Foster Associates, Buildings and Projects*, vol. 1, *1964–1973* (London: Watermark, 1991), 14–15.
17. Ian Lambot, ed. *Norman Foster: Team 4 and Foster Associates, Buildings and Projects*, vol. 1, *1964–1973* (London: Watermark, 1991), 17.
18. Rogers, "Team 4."
19. Paul Rudolph, quoted in Bryan Appleyard, *Richard Rogers: A Biography* (London: Faber and Faber, 1986), 97.
20. Rogers, "Team 4."
21. Philip Johnson, quoted in Appleyard, *Richard Rogers*, 97.
22. Foster, "Pritzker Prize Address, 1999."
23. Ibid.
24. Serge Chermayeff and Christopher Alexander, *Community and Privacy: Toward a New Architecture of Humanism* (Garden City, NY: Doubleday, 1963).
25. Rogers, "Team 4."
26. Foster, "Pritzker Prize Address, 1999."
27. Ibid.

# Sources

---

Chapter 1: "Regionalism and the Continuity of Tradition." *Center: A Journal for Architecture in America* 3 (1987): 58–63.

Chapter 2: "What the Classical Can Do for the Modern." In *New Classicism,* edited by Andreas Papadakis and Harriet Watson, 31–32. New York: Rizzoli; London: Academy Editions, 1990.

Chapter 3: "Designing the American Dream." *Architectural Digest* 43, no. 4 (April 1986): 30–38.

Chapter 4: "1920/1929 Housing America." *Architectural Record* 179, no. 7 (July 1991): 158–61. Written with Thomas Mellins for the Centennial Issue.

Chapter 5: "Architecture and Place." Lecture. The Woman's Club, Richmond, Virginia. March 20, 1989.

Chapter 6: "The Suburban Alternative for the 'Middle City.'" *Architectural Record* 164, no. 2 (August 1978): 94–100.

Chapter 7: Acceptance Speech. Seaside Prize, Seaside, Florida, May 15, 1999.

Chapter 8: "A Conversation." Edited by Robert Ermerins. *Landscape Architecture* 77 (January/February 1987): 90–95.

Chapter 9: With Thomas Mellins. "The Fall and Rise of New York." In *New New York: Architectural Models from the Last Decade,* 8–17. Flushing, New York: Queens Museum, 1987.

Chapter 10: "The Buell Center: An Interview with Robert A.M. Stern." *Oculus* 47, no. 8 (April 1986): 6–7, 17; "The Buell Center, Part II: An Interview with Robert A.M. Stern." *Oculus* 47, no. 10 (June 1986): 12–13.

Chapter 11: Interview with Inderbir Riar, New York, New York, December 1, 2006.

Chapter 12: "Relevance of the Decade." *Journal of the Society of Architectural Historians* 24, no. 1 (March 1965): 6–10. Paper presented at the Symposium on Modern Architecture, Columbia University, New York, May 8–10, 1964.

Chapter 13: "Television and Architecture." Talk prepared, but not delivered, for 76th Annual Meeting of the Association of Collegiate Schools of Architecture, Miami, Florida, March 12, 1988.

Chapter 14: "An Architect's Impressions of France." *Architectural Digest* 44, no. 6 (June 1987): 234–47.

Chapter 15: "Buildings and Brands." Remarks delivered at the dedication of the Spangler Center, Harvard Business School, Boston, Massachusetts, January 22, 2001.

Chapter 16: "Rationalism and Romanticism in the Domestic Architecture of George Howe." Paper presented at the Annual Meeting of the Society of Architectural Historians, Baltimore, Maryland, January 28, 1963.

Chapter 17: "Robert Moses as Architect." Lecture for "Robert Moses' New York" Conference,

Graduate School of Architecture, Planning, and Preservation, Columbia University, New York, February 10–11, 1989.

Chapter 18: Contribution to Philip Johnson Festschrift, *ANY: Architecture New York*, no. 90 (1996): 60–61.

Chapter 19: Interview with Alessandra Latour in *Louis I. Kahn: L'uomo, il maestro*, by Alessandra Latour, 173–77. Rome: Kappa, 1986. Interview conducted May 13, 1982.

Chapter 20: With Raymond Gastil. "Charles Moore: The Architect Running in Place." In *Charles Moore: Buildings and Projects 1949–1986*, edited by Eugene J. Johnson, 35–38. New York: Rizzoli, 1986.

Chapter 21: "The Impact of Yale." In *On Foster . . . Foster On*, edited by David Jenkins, 344–61. Munich: Prestel, 2000. Reprinted in *Norman Foster Works 1*, edited by David Jenkins, 18–31. Munich: Prestel, 2002.

Chapter 22: "Principles and Values." Talk for symposium, "Architecture and Education: The Past Twenty-Five Years and Assumptions for the Future," sponsored by the Princeton School of Architecture to honor Michael Graves on the occasion of his twenty-fifth year teaching at the university, February 20, 1988.

# Index

Index

Index

## Illustration credits

Chapter 1: Wurts Brothers, Milstein Division of United States History, Local History & Genealogy, The New York Public Library, Astor, Lenox and Tilden Foundations (fig. 1); Santa Barbara Historical Museum (fig. 2); *The Architect* 9, no. 6 (June 1915) (fig. 3); University of Texas Buildings collection, The Alexander Architectural Archive, The University of Texas Libraries, The University of Texas at Austin (fig. 4)

Chapter 3: Robert A.M. Stern Architects (figs. 1–5)

Chapter 4: © Bettmann/Corbis (fig. 1); Richard Averill Smith, Library of Congress, Prints & Photographs Division (fig. 2); Carl Mydans, Library of Congress, Prints & Photographs Division, FSA/OWI Collection (fig. 3); Museum of the City of New York, Wurts Bros. Collection (fig. 4); © 2011 Artists Rights Society, New York / ADAGP, Paris, courtesy Fonds André Lurçat, CNAM/SIAF/Cité de l'architecture et du patrimoine/Archives d'architecture du XXe siècle (fig. 5); © 2011 Artists Rights Society, New York / ADAGP, Paris / FLC (fig. 6); Robert A.M. Stern Architects (fig. 7)

Chapter 6: Robert A.M. Stern Architects (figs. 1, 9, 12–13); Courtesy of the Rockefeller Archive Center (fig. 2); Courtesy of the Riverside Historical Museum, Riverside, IL (fig. 3); Photo by Skot Weidemann ©The Frank Lloyd Wright Fdn, AZ / Artists Rights Society, NY / Art Resource, NY (fig. 4); Engraving by W. Radcliff after a drawing by Thomas Shepherd, "Park Village East, Regent's Park," in James Elmes and Thomas H. Shepherd, *Metropolitan Improvements; or London in the Nineteenth Century* (London: Jones & Co., 1827) (fig. 5); Berry F. Berry, View of Bath Road, Bedford Park, London W4, looking east, ca. 1881–82, from a set of prints of Bedford Park commissioned by Jonathan Carr and published by Harrison & Sons of St. Martins Lane, London, 1882; Courtesy of Chiswick Library Local Collection (fig. 6); Harvard Art Museums/ Fogg Art Museum, On deposit from the Carpenter Center for the Visual Arts, Social Museum Collection, photo © President and Fellows of Harvard College (fig. 7); ©The Frank Lloyd Wright Fdn, AZ / Artists Rights Society, NY / Art Resource, NY (figs. 8, 10); A.J. Downing, *The Architecture of*

*Country Houses* (New York: D. Appleton, 1850) (fig. 11); Esther McCoy Papers, Archives of American Art, Smithsonian Institution (fig. 14)

Chapter 7: Robert A.M. Stern Architects (figs. 1, 4–6); Courtesy of the Riverside Historical Museum, Riverside, IL (fig. 2); Courtesy of the Division of Rare and Manuscript Collections, Cornell University Library (fig. 3); Smith Aerial Photos, Disney intellectual property used with permission from The Celebration Company (fig. 7); Peter Aaron/Esto, Disney intellectual property used with permission from The Celebration Company (fig. 8)

Chapter 8: Tom Lamb/The SWA Group (fig. 1); Deborah Nevins & Associates (fig. 2)

Chapter 9: Robert A.M. Stern Architects (figs. 1, 11, 12, 14–15); © Timothy Hursley (fig. 2); © Norman McGrath (figs. 3, 10); © Thorney Lieberman (figs. 4–6); © Peter Mauss/Esto (fig. 7); Jim Henderson / Wikimedia Commons / Public Domain (fig. 8); Wayne Lorentz/Artefaqs Corporation (fig. 9); Bo Parker (fig. 13)

Chapter 14: Robert A.M. Stern (figs. 1–4)

Chapter 15: Engraving by J. Serz, 1856, University of Virginia Visual History Collection. Special Collections, University of Virginia Library (fig. 1); © Peter Aaron/ Esto (figs. 2, 15, 22); Robert A.M. Stern Architects (figs. 3, 5–6, 10, 19–21); Courtesy MIT Museum (fig. 4); Harvard University Archives (fig. 7); W.P.A. Photo, Federal Writers Project, Milstein Division of United States History, Local History & Genealogy, The New York Public Library, Astor, Lenox and Tilden Foundations (fig. 8); © Cervin Robinson (fig. 9); Ezra Stoller © Esto (figs. 11–12); © Wayne Andrews/Esto (fig. 13); Kevin Roche John Dinkeloo and Associates (fig. 14); © Jeff Goldberg/Esto, Disney intellectual property used with permission from Disney Enterprises, Inc. (fig. 16); Peter Aaron/Esto, Disney intellectual property used with permission from Disney Enterprises, Inc. (fig. 17); Photograph by David Heald © The Solomon R. Guggenheim Foundation, New York (fig. 18)

Chapter 16: Philip B. Wallace, George Howe collection, Drawings and Archives, Avery Architectural and Fine Arts Library,

Columbia University (fig. 1); George
Howe collection, Drawings and Archives,
Avery Architectural and Fine Arts Library,
Columbia University (fig. 2); Mellor, Meigs
& Howe Collection, The Architectural
Archives, University of Pennsylvania,
photo by Richard T. Dooner (fig. 3);
*Architectural Forum* 62 (March 1935) (fig.
4); Mellor, Meigs & Howe Collection,
The Architectural Archives, University of
Pennsylvania, photo by Ben Schnall (fig. 5)

Chapter 17: © Peter Aaron / ESTO (fig.
1); Long Island Regional Archive, New
York State Office of Parks, Recreation and
Historic Preservation (figs. 2–3); Robert
A.M. Stern Architects (figs. 4, 14); Courtesy
of the Westchester County Archives (fig. 5);
New York City Parks Photo Archive (figs.
6, 8–10, 13, 15, 18–19); Museum of the City
of New York, Wurts Bros. Collection (fig.
7); Nathan Schwartz, Milstein Division of
United States History, Local History &
Genealogy, The New York Public Library,
Astor, Lenox and Tilden Foundations
(fig. 11); Photograph by Samuel Gottscho,
Museum of the City of New York,
Gottscho-Schleisner Collection (figs. 12, 17);
Österreichische Nationalbibliothek, Vienna
(fig. 16); Courtesy of MTA Bridges and
Tunnels Special Archive (fig. 20); Photo by
Bob Serating, Courtesy of Lincoln Center
Archives (fig. 21)

Chapter 20: Robert A.M. Stern Architects
(figs. 1, 3); © Wayne Andrews/Esto (fig. 2);
© Norman McGrath (figs. 4, 6); Moore
Ruble Yudell Architects & Planners (fig. 5)

Chapter 21: Library of Congress, Prints &
Photographs Division (fig. 1); Su Rogers,
Courtesy of Foster + Partners (fig. 2);
Norman Foster (figs. 3–10)